TOUGHEST OF THEM ALL

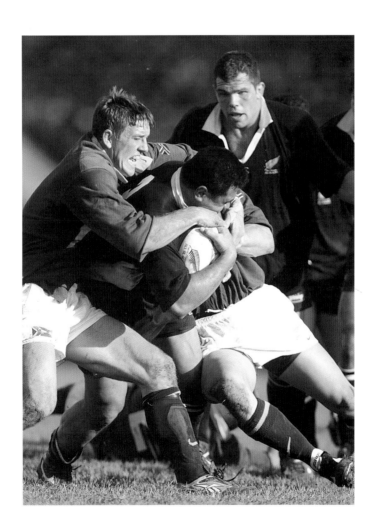

New Zealand and South Africa:
The Struggle for Rugby Supremacy

TOUGHEST OF THEM ALL

Grant Harding & David Williams

Rugby Statistics by Geoff Miller

PENGUIN BOOKS

PENGUIN BOOKS

Penguin Books (NZ) Ltd, Cnr Rosedale and Airborne Roads, Albany, Auckland 1310, New Zealand
Penguin Books Ltd, 27 Wrights Lane, London W8 5TZ, England
Penguin USA, 375 Hudson Street, New York, NY 10014, United States
Penguin Books Australia Ltd, 487 Maroondah Highway, Ringwood, Australia 3134
Penguin Books Canada Ltd, 10 Alcorn Avenue, Toronto, Ontario, Canada M4V 3B2
Penguin Books India (P) Ltd, 11, Community Centre, Panchsheel Park, New Delhi 110017, India
Penguin Books (South Africa) Pty Ltd, 5 Watkins Street, Denver Ext 4, 2094, South Africa

Penguin Books Ltd, Registered Offices: Harmondsworth, Middlesex, England

First published by Penguin Books (NZ) Ltd, 2000

Designed by Dexter Fry, Mary Egan and Amy Tansell
Typeset by Egan-Reid Ltd, Auckland

Printed in China by Midas Printing (Asia) Ltd.

CONTENTS

by Grant Harding

DAVE GILLESPIE, a good-looking truck-driver who lived opposite our house in Caroline Road, Hastings, when I was six years old, was a hero of mine. I remember him bringing a pet lamb home for us one day, which, using all our imagination, we called Curly. How we (my sister, brother and I), and I, in particular, loved that lamb.

But that wasn't the reason we liked Dave. You see, Dave was a former All Black loose forward. Not only that, but he'd toured South Africa, the hardest rugby land in the world next to ours.

In the corner of the bedroom my brother Paul and I occupied was a team photo of the 1960 All Blacks to South Africa, with a silver-fern badge attached to it. My brother also possessed a genuine All Black tie.

Dave was ultracool, although 'cool' wasn't a word we used in Hastings in 1967. His wife, Rae, was an attractive woman, and, better still, she was the daughter of double All Black Charlie Oliver. I even saw him once. Unfortunately, Dave didn't stick around our neighbourhood for long, but his time across the road certainly sharpened my interest in the great New Zealand–South Africa rivalry.

My brother and I would lie awake at night reciting the names of that 1960 All Black team, along with the many others in our repertoire. So it's strange that now the only story I can remember about Dave Gillespie's rugby experience in South Africa was one relayed to me by my mother many years later. Apparently, on the 1960 tour, women would ring the players in their rooms from hotel reception and provide them with their 'vital statistics' — now there's an ancient expression for you — in the hope that a member of the team might want to make their acquaintance.

By the time of the 1970 All Black tour to South Africa I was a rugby nut, and heightening my interest was the presence in the team of Hawke's Bay's Bill Davis, Ian MacRae, Blair Furlong and Neil Thimbleby. Kel Tremain should have been there as well. In years gone by, Furlong, a part-Maori, would not have toured.

During the tour I would often wake in the middle of the night to listen to Bob Irvine's radio commentary, and I still have scrapbooks I compiled at the time. But that tour marked the beginning of a long period of personal dissatisfaction with the New Zealand–South Africa rivalry. On that occasion I was displeased because we lost.

Three years later I remember being stunned when Prime Minister Norman Kirk called off the Springbok tour to New Zealand. Because we were a Labour family our outrage was relatively muted, and expressed itself in mumblings about keeping sport and politics separate.

Then, in 1976, I was incensed at the performance of South African referees, in particular Gert Bezuidenhout. As the matches were beamed back from that country to our television screens for the first time, the birds were chirping while I was plotting my revenge on Mr Bezuidenhout.

Along the way there was a growing realisation that all was not well in the republic. In fact it was in 1976 that Filbert Bayi didn't get to race John Walker at the Olympic Games, and I learned about the Sharpeville massacre in School Certificate history. A few All Blacks also learned the terror of tear gas as a consequence of riots in Soweto. Come 1981, however, I was still toeing the rugby line. It was a difficult line, especially for a university student.

I attended the Springboks' clashes with Manawatu and New Zealand Maori, and the second Test in Wellington. While all had merits as games of rugby, I was left wondering whether all the problems the tour had brought to the country were worth it — especially when, on the way to the Test, I saw a good friend being dragged away from a sit-in at a street corner by police. The conclusion I came to was that they weren't. The protestors' point of view — that apartheid was a disgraceful system that New Zealand should abhor and not encourage in any way — was right.

It was incongruous with my new-found beliefs, therefore, that when I heard the news in 1985 that the All Black tour to South Africa had been scuttled by legal action, I was disappointed. At the time I was on the Greek party island of Ios, along with many South Africans. They were devastated, and I felt somewhat sorry for them.

The following year, back at home, I was annoyed by the Cavaliers' tour, although mainly because I believed they were playing into the South Africans' hands. And so it proved. An aging team lost the series, with Andy Dalton's jaw being broken by a cheap shot and the final Test refereeing being roundly abused by the tourists. Nothing had changed, and my resolve against the South Africans hardened. We owed them no favours, I reasoned.

Finally, we came to the 1990s — 1992 to be precise. At last we had a rivalry that seemed able to progress into the future without being damaging to the fabric of our country. The dismantling of apartheid was starting.

I covered the 1994 tour for *Rugby News* and found the South Africans to be almost too nice. They were trying so hard to fit into a modern world that was suspicious and demanding of them. On the field there was no evidence they would be crowned world champions a year later. But they were, thanks to a victory over their old rivals, the All Blacks. Talk about personal dissatisfaction!

In 1996 I again had the privilege of covering the All Black tour to South Africa, and witnessed their first-ever series victory in that country. An enduring memory is of looking along the press bench at Loftus Versfeld in Pretoria when Zinzan Brooke dropped a goal to put New Zealand ahead 33–26, the final scoreline in the decisive Test. There, at one end, was 1981 Springbok captain Wynand Claassen, gesticulating wildly and looking absolutely shocked. His shock may in fact have been admiration for Brooke's skills, but I preferred to believe New Zealand had finally got in behind the Afrikaners' defences and dealt them a heavy blow. It was a brilliant moment.

The roar at Ellis Park a week later brought another — a roar that tore through your chest and made you quiver. The Boks were too good that day.

That tour was like an end and a beginning for me. Never again would my feelings about South Africans and their rugby be as one-dimensional. Finally, I held no grudges.

Helping maintain my equilibrium is the fact that since the introduction of neutral referees, New Zealand has won 13 Tests against South Africa, lost six and drawn one. And at the end of the century there is not a team on the planet that has beaten the All Blacks more often than they have been beaten in return.

Nevertheless, at the turn of the millennium, both the All Blacks and the Springboks know that world champions Australia stand beside them, and slightly above, as a rugby superpower. Professionalism has allowed Australia to protect its players from league poachers, and, while they have never won the Tri-Nations, they have won the World Cup more often than any other nation.

Dave Gillespie now lives in Brisbane, Australia, while Curly, my father continues to assure me, lived out his days in a paddock close to the now-closed Whakatu freezing works. As for the All Black tie, my brother wore it at rugby-club socials in England, where he now lives, until it became threadbare. And I'm quite sure that, with a little bit of effort, I could recite the names of the entire 1960 All Black squad to South Africa, even though I was born a few months after that tour had concluded.

The New Zealand–South Africa rivalry continues to be something special.

INTRODUCTION

by David Williams

THE FIRST SPRINGBOKS in my life were not rugby players or cricketers, but soldiers. Family life seemed full of veterans who had been 'up north' in World War II in the South African forces. Drawing on the nickname invented by Paul Roos back in 1906 and nurtured by the rugby glory of the 1920s and 1930s, those soldiers referred to themselves lightly but proudly as Springboks. If you go to the Commonwealth cemeteries in Egypt, as I did in 1992 for the 50th anniversary commemoration of the Battle of El Alamein, you will see that into each headstone of a fallen South African soldier is carved the head and horns of a springbok.

Later, I was delighted to discover how that war had kept alive the passionate rugby rivalry between New Zealanders and South Africans. Soldiers from both countries served in large numbers in the Western Desert in 1941–42 and then in Italy in 1943–44. Their affinity with rugby helped develop a special relationship (which excluded the Australians). Somehow, along the way, there arose the legend of The Book, an imaginary volume containing all the lore of rugby. Whenever a Kiwi met a Springbok, they greeted each other like brothers, then each asked the other if he'd read The Book — implying in the other a sad ignorance of how rugby should be played. Finally, on 10 November, 1945, all the bragging was put to the test in the Italian town of Rapallo. A team from the 6th South African Armoured Division ('Six Div' as it was known), trained by Bombardier 'Boy' Louw, took the field against a New Zealand selection and beat them 30–5. Among the 'Springbok' stars that day was Cecil Moss, who would play on the wing for South Africa four years later against the All Blacks.

But to return to the early days: even before rugby entered my consciousness, a Springbok seemed such an honourable thing to be. For me, the first personification of a Springbok rugby player was the Natal flyhalf Keith Oxlee. I cannot remember this, but my parents told me I used to run up and down the front lawn of our little railway house in the Natal midlands town of Estcourt, yelling 'Oxlee's got the ball . . . Oxlee's got the ball . . . and Oxlee scores', in uncomprehending imitation of the radio commentators. I was then just six years old, so I must have been drawing on the coverage of the 1960 home series against New Zealand. I cannot remember a time when I was not aware of something called the 'All Blacks'. When men talked about them, a note of thoughtful tension seemed to enter the conversation.

I don't remember the British Lions' and Wallabies' tours of the early 1960s, but I do retain a vivid mental image, based on a superb black-and-white photograph, of Tiny Naude shovelling the ball from the mud to win the third Test of 1965. This kick had an enormous impact — mothers picking up their children from school on the following Monday were discussing it.

Then came the first dim stirrings of political consciousness, creating an uncomfortable undertone to my enjoyment of rugby that still lingers in the late 1990s. The prime minister, Dr

Verwoerd, said Maori were not welcome in South Africa. This seemed so clearly wrong (although my uncle would argue darkly that the New Zealand whites could hardly throw stones at Verwoerd when they had treated Maori so badly, and indeed in the past had been quite prepared to tour South Africa without them. Where were their principles? he asked.).

At the age of 12 my interest in sport became a passion, especially for rugby. I went to a good rugby institution, King Edward VII School in Johannesburg, where I played hooker for Under 13A on Saturday mornings, and often went with my friends to the old Ellis Park in the afternoons. The 1967 series against the enterprising and violent French (won 2–1 by South Africa) was the first that I followed in detail. Then came the dour British Lions in 1968 (3–1) and the weaker Wallabies in 1969 (4–0). Sandwiched between these was a short but successful visit to France, with wins in both Tests. There followed the last full-length tour of Britain and Ireland by a Springbok side. It is impossible now to extract much meaning from the Test performances (defeats to England and Scotland, draws with Ireland and Wales) on a tour that was severely disrupted by protests and demonstrations, and which began pathetically with a defeat by Oxford University. But the excuses, while softening the hurt a little, were not enough to obscure the facts (a full Springbok tour without a Test win), and there were moral issues that could not be evaded.

By the time of the 1970 All Black visit, I was playing for my school 1st XV, and we followed every detail of the tour with great intensity. There was no doubt at all that the teams were contesting the world championship of rugby, although this was not discussed: we just knew it to be so. The following year I played for Transvaal Schools, an achievement that still gives me deep satisfaction, and dreamed of one day playing against the All Blacks. Given my achievements up to that point, it did not seem an impossibility.

Then rugby began to go sour for me. In 1972, during army service, I was badly concussed in a regimental match, and at university I confined myself to Friday-night faculty rugby. By the time of the 1976 All Black tour, I was torn between rejecting the entire exercise as a condonation of apartheid and watching every one of the games on TV. Much the same conflict occurred in 1981, when we followed the amazing images of the Bok tour of New Zealand. I would resolve not to get up at 4 a.m. — then would wake up anyway without the alarm clock, agonise in bed for a while, and run to the TV set just in time for the kickoff.

When the 1986 Cavaliers arrived, I was working as a freelance rugby reporter for the top radio station in Johannesburg and did as much as anyone to propagate the view that this series was the real thing. Whatever the politics, we were desperate to measure ourselves against the All Blacks.

At last we were able to do that again with the great readmission Test in 1992. The match programme that day set out to be a conscious celebration of the great history of All Black–Springbok rugby. There were details of every previous encounter between the great rivals at Ellis Park, with full team and scoring statistics. It was pointed out that the All Blacks had managed to win only the first contest, in 1928.

Leading South African rugby writers were commissioned to give historical perspectives. A. C. Parker concluded that 1970 had seen the strongest of all New Zealand touring sides. Rodney Hartman argued that the 1986 Cavaliers had 'fooled nobody' — for South African fans, the Cavaliers had been the real thing. However, the programme statistics thoughtfully omitted the Cavaliers' tour from the official records.

The All Blacks were reminded yet again that 'the greatest team to leave New Zealand' had been the 1937 Boks — and that the overall Test record showed 20 victories to South Africa and only 15 to New Zealand, with two drawn. Politicians were reminded that Springbok rugby predated the constitutional unification of South Africa in 1910. Romantic articles indulged in biographies of 'All Blacks we still remember', such as Brian Lochore, Wilson Whineray and Don Clarke. There were dramatic pictures of Bok icons like Frik du Preez, Bennie Osler, 'Boy' Morkel, Boland Coetzee, Hennie van Zyl, Wynand Claassen and Hansie Brewis.

The power of tradition and history was almost tangible at Ellis Park in 1992. It was as if we were telling ourselves: 'Yes, we have been through terrible times. But there is also honour to be salvaged from our history — and rugby expresses something of it.'

Three years later, in the World Cup final, rugby became, at least for a time, part of the fragile healing process in a country that had effectively suffered a collective nervous breakdown. No politician other than Nelson Mandela could have got away with such a cheeky gesture as when he wore the Springbok jersey; no other man would have spent 27 years in jail for his resistance to white domination and then emerged to offer such visible and enthusiastic reconciliation. And that vast crowd of white people, members of an embattled and uncertain minority which had given up its power, responded by chanting, 'Nelson! Nelson!' with instinctive understanding of Mandela's gesture — and with honest affection.

Only now, perhaps, are we able to watch the rugby without the guilt or distraction of politics. Ironically, what we see is not encouraging. Can we trust the administrators to get the law changes right, and the TV magnates to respect our traditions and rivalries? Will they devalue the currency by playing Tests as often as if they were club games? Will the doctors, lawyers and teachers desert the game as the demands of professionalism become ever more grim? Will the game be informed by the spirit of Morne du Plessis and Wilson Whineray, or by the seductively efficient gamesmanship of a Fitzpatrick or a Kronfeld?

There are men who have the power to influence both the great game of rugby and the greatest rivalry in all sport, which exists within that game — the recurring duel between the Springboks and the All Blacks. These men must tread softly, for they tread on our dreams.

1921

WHEN
GIANTS
COLLIDE

NEW ZEALAND	13	SOUTH AFRICA	5
SOUTH AFRICA	9	NEW ZEALAND	5
NEW ZEALAND	0	SOUTH AFRICA	0

CHAPTER ONE

1921
WHEN GIANTS COLLIDE

THE FIRST SPRINGBOKS IN NEW ZEALAND

by Grant Harding

COULD NEW ZEALAND'S George Aitken and South Africa's 'Boy' Morkel have known what they were starting when they led their teams out onto Carisbrook in Dunedin on August 13, 1921?

In terms of the rich history of mutual conquest that has followed, the answer is probably not. There is no doubt, however, that the captains and their teams would not have been left wondering whether this, the first Test of the first-ever series between the two nations, was something special. For in both countries this long-awaited clash was unashamedly billed as the battle for the world championship, and as far as the fans were concerned there was no need to add 'unofficial'. Both teams' supporters already regarded their side as superior to Europe's best.

New Zealand had started playing Test rugby in 1903, with the 1905–06 tour to the UK and France, under the leadership of wing forward Dave Gallaher, firmly establishing the reputation of a national side known from that time on as the 'All Blacks'. The only blight on the 'Originals'' record was their 0–3 loss to Wales, but this was not a cross New Zealanders were prepared to bear graciously, the controversial non-award of a try to All Black centre Bob Deans being related to successive generations of rugby lovers. By the time 1921 arrived, New Zealand had won 19 Tests, drawn two and lost three.

South Africa had started playing Test matches in 1891, but did not venture to the UK until the winter following the Originals' tour. It was not to be that visit that established the country's reputation, although it was on that tour that the team was dubbed the 'Springboks' on account of the players' uniform. A loss to England and a draw with Scotland meant they were thought of

RIGHT: History has been made . . . at Carisbrook in Dunedin, New Zealand and South Africa have played together for the first time ever. All Black captain George Aitken (left), referee Ted McKenzie and Springbok captain 'Boy' Morkel pose to mark the occasion.

less favourably than Gallaher's team. Their victory over Wales, however, was not lost on New Zealand rugby fans.

It was the Springboks' 1912–13 tour to the UK and Ireland, and a Grand Slam, that brought recognition of the fact that the balance of rugby power was heavily weighted to the southern hemisphere. South Africa, like New Zealand, attached great importance to its national sport, a sport that suited the rugged outdoor nature of the men who inhabited both lands.

While invitations for South Africa to tour New Zealand were turned down on grounds of timing, rugby relations had started during the Boer War. New Zealand servicemen played many games while serving with the British, and anecdotal evidence suggests Gallaher led a New Zealand XV against a South Africa XV, selected from all provinces, at Johannesburg in 1902, New Zealand winning by a handsome margin. In the same year, servicemen who settled in Natal following the war formed the Durban New Zealanders' Club, and before it was disbanded in 1907 it won the local championship three times.

The inevitability of an All Black–Springbok clash was delayed by World War I. It wasn't until the Armistice was declared in 1918 that rugby got back into full swing, when a New Zealand Army team was involved in 38 matches, with the highlight being victory in the 1919 King's Cup. During the tournament, New Zealand Army beat South African Forces 14–5 at Twickenham, after which New Zealand Army accepted an invitation to make a 15-match tour to South Africa.

The success of the tour — which saw New Zealand record 11 wins and three losses and one draw — heightened anticipation of a full encounter between the two rugby nations, although the South Africans approached the prospect with trepidation. They wondered how they would cope with a complete All Black team when their best provinces had struggled against the Army. This was an underestimation of the Army team's strength, however, as within its ranks were 15 players who had or would wear the All Black jersey, some in the 1921 series, for which South Africa toured New Zealand.

By the time of the first Test the Boks had already encountered New Zealand rugby at its best in nine tour matches, a 0–0 draw with Taranaki and a 4–6 loss to Canterbury providing the visitors with food for thought.

Interest in the first-ever Test between the two countries was intense, and many of the discussion points before, during and after were to arise repeatedly down the years whenever the All Blacks and Springboks met.

Naturally the first post-war selection of an All Black Test team raised a few eyebrows, although seven players, including legendary wing forward/loose forward 'Moke' Belliss, had appeared for the 1920 All Blacks in Australia. Captain Aitken had never played for New Zealand before and did not captain his Wellington provincial team. Front-rower Ned Hughes had not appeared since 1908, and at 40 years old remains the oldest All Black Test player of all time.

The Springboks' tour captain, Theo Pienaar, was not chosen, and was destined never to play in a Test. Non-selection of the South African captain was to be a feature of first Tests in New Zealand until 1965.

Springbok speedster 'Attie' van Heerden is obscured by flying surface water during the scoreless third Test draw at Athletic Park.

Loose forward 'Boy' Morkel led a team that had a decided weight advantage. While not big by modern standards, the South Africans were far larger than their opponents, a cause, even then, for New Zealanders to complain. But despite the size advantage there is little evidence, other than for a period in the second Test, that it caused the home side undue problems.

At that time New Zealand packed a 2–3–2 scrum, with the halfback feeding the ball and the wing forward, the eighth member of the forward pack, gathering it at the back. By contrast, the South Africans generally favoured the 3–2–3 formation.

A crowd of 25,000 — a third of the population of Dunedin at the time — packed into Carisbrook, while another 10,000 paid nothing to watch from along the neighbouring embankment and other vantage points above the ground.

When the match finally began, the importance of the occasion appeared to inhibit the players. This was highlighted by the fact that by the final whistle there had been 114 lineouts despite the fine conditions.

It wasn't until just before halftime that big winger 'Attie' van Heerden, a sprinter at the 1920 Antwerp Olympic Games, scored the first-ever try in a Test between the two countries. Fullback Gerhard Morkel added a difficult conversion.

After the break, New Zealand worked their way into the game, evening the scores in controversial fashion. A high kick by All Black first-five Ces Badeley went loose behind the South African goal-line, where referee Ted McKenzie ruled that fast-following loose forward 'Moke' Belliss had forced it first. Several observers disagreed, claiming that a South African defender had touched the ball down.

There was no doubt about the All Blacks' second score, however, just hysteria. A cross kick by Badeley was trapped by winger Jack Steel's right hand behind his back. Somehow the West Coaster threw off one defender and evaded another while still holding the ball behind him, before working it into his hands as he outpaced the cover defence on a 50-metre run. It remains one of the greatest tries in All Black history.

Gerhard Morkel's Drop Goal
SECOND TEST, AUCKLAND, 27 AUGUST, 1921

No Springbok left more of an impression on New Zealand spectators in 1921 than fullback Gerhard Morkel. His powerful tackling, prodigious punting and evasiveness earned him many plaudits.

Ability aside, Morkel's place in New Zealand–South Africa history was assured by one act of individual brilliance: the drop goal (then worth four points) he kicked at Eden Park to take South Africa to a winning 9–5 lead in the second Test. In the best traditions of rugby myth and legend, the descriptions of his feat vary wildly. All that can be ascertained is that the goal was kicked near the sideline somewhere between 30 and 50 metres out. We also know that after just a few steps infield the kick flew high and straight.

Unconfirmed reports on crowd reaction merely add to the colour of the occasion. Apparently some in the crowd were so taken with Morkel's genius they organised for a bottle of beer to be passed out to him, and he was observed to take a generous swig.

During the series the best back and forward in each Test were awarded a gold medal, and naturally Morkel was a recipient for this Test. The 32-year-old, who was a veteran of the 1912–13 Grand Slam tour, came close to an even greater achievement in the rain-affected and scoreless third Test when he struck an upright with a penalty-goal attempt, apparently leaving a 'muddy imprint'.

A try to the All Blacks' other winger, Percy Storey, completed the scoring, and New Zealand had won 13–5. But this was to be South Africa's last defeat on tour. They won the second Test, in Auckland, 9–5, and the third Test, in Wellington, was drawn 0–0 in atrocious conditions.

With their backs against the wall the Springboks took a novel approach to the selection of their second Test team. The players expressed unhappiness at their selection panel's choice of the XV at Dunedin, so it was agreed all 29 players would write down their team, for the side to be selected by popular vote. This led to six changes, including the demotion of 1.94 metre, 111-kilogram lock 'Baby' Michau. Ironically Michau had been awarded a gold medal as best forward on the field in the first Test. Perhaps the fact that the All Black selectors had made the choice raised South African suspicions.

Equally bizarre was the dumping of All Black halfback 'Ginger' Nicholls, who was awarded the gold medal for best back after the Dunedin Test. He was replaced by Teddy Roberts, who many considered should have been the original choice. The selection puzzle took another twist when Roberts was named captain for the third Test, after Aitken was dropped.

The second Test was the first to be played at Eden Park, and it attracted a crowd of 40,000, the largest of the tour. It was Gerhard Morkel who provided the decisive moment of the game. With the scores tied 5–5 midway through the second half, and the players wilting in the warm conditions, the ball came to the brilliant fullback, who slammed over a long-distance drop goal.

For the series decider in Wellington both teams made five changes, but it was the weather which proved to be the decisive factor. Steady rain fell throughout Friday night and Saturday, so that by kickoff, puddles of water lay on the muddy ground.

A crowd of 18,000 braved the conditions to watch a scoreless draw that featured a number of near misses. Jack Steel received the gold medal for best back on display, and was also awarded a cup for the outstanding New Zealand player in the three Tests.

Upon their return home the Boks were not treated kindly by their media and public. They were labelled too defensive, and no consideration was given to the injury problems they had suffered on tour. In defending them, captain Pienaar spoke wise words:

'True, we may not have done much that was sensational, but let me stress this point: there is neither time nor place for the sensational in New Zealand football,' he said. 'Go out there yourselves and fight a New Zealand team on its own soil. A team that is filled with consciousness of its own prowess and flushed with great achievements of the past. And if you do not eat humble pie on your return, well — I shall!'

The reverse was to prove a truth for New Zealand when they played in the vastly different conditions in South Africa.

A tense, somewhat inhibited series featuring selection dramas, refereeing controversy, a Springbok size advantage, crowd hysteria and heroic deeds had finished. So the template for the future battles between the rugby giants had been written. The stakes were only going to get higher.

1921

THE SOUTH AFRICAN RESPONSE

THE FIRST SPRINGBOKS IN NEW ZEALAND

by David Williams

THIS PIONEERING SERIES probably meant much less to the South African public than to the New Zealand public. Travelling sportsmen must have seemed so remote in the days before air travel and radio communication.

In the week leading up to the first Test, sports pages in Johannesburg were dominated by boxing, club golf and a mines' tennis championship. There was interest in rugby, to be sure, but the big game was an inter-provincial at the Wanderers between Transvaal and Western Transvaal.

On Saturday morning the main sports cartoon in the *Rand Daily Mail* was again devoted to boxing, but there was a preview of the rugby Test. 'The side to do duty for the Springboks will only be chosen this morning,' intoned the *Rand Daily Mail*. 'This policy has probably been adopted owing to the uncertainty of the weather conditions . . . the ground is likely to be heavy.'

Nobody seemed surprised that the touring captain, Theo Pienaar, had not been chosen for the game. The *Rand Daily Mail* noted approvingly: 'Boy Morkel will be in charge. As a tactician, no better man could have been chosen, as he is likely to get every ounce out of the pack.' The newspaper warned that the Springboks had lost some irreplaceable stars of the pre-war generation, notably Japie Krige, Jan Stegmann and Bob Loubser. There was also keen speculation on the differing scrumming techniques, with South Africa expected to use the 3–4 method and New Zealand having one man fewer in the front-row with their 2–3–2 formation.

'A fast and hard game,' reported the *Sunday Times* after New Zealand's 13–5 victory at Dunedin, 'free from roughness. The outstanding event was a magnificent try scored by Steel.' While there had been doubt over the All Blacks' first try, which 'appeared to dishearten the South African backs', it was clear that in the end 'the better team won'.

After the second Test at Auckland it was 'Honours Easy', as the *Sunday Times* headline put it. But 'the Springboks can scarcely be considered the better team . . . victory was primarily due to Gerhard Morkel's goal and his splendid kicking'. The match was characterised by 'open play and terrific pace'.

There was no sign in the Johannesburg newspapers, during the week of the third Test in Wellington, that a series decider was about to take place. On Friday the sports previews concerned amateur billiards at Crown Mines, the inter-high school athletics meeting, Cornish wrestling at Krugersdorp and the club rugby final between Diggers and Simmer & Jack.

The third Test turned out to be a 'strenuous mud scramble', reported the *Sunday Times*. 'Spray shot up after the players' footsteps and there were great splashes when the ball struck the ground.' Interestingly, the terrible conditions apparently did not prevent it being judged an

P L A Y E R   O F   T H E   D E C A D E

PHIL MOSTERT

Born: 1898, Died: 1972
Position: Prop forward, hooker
Played New Zealand: 1921, 1928 (7 Tests)

If Phil Mostert seems typical of those men who loom large in series between the All Blacks and Springboks, it is because he was one of the genuine originals who set the tone for the great rivalry. He was big, strong and fearless, playing at prop, lock or hooker with equal success. His lineout work was exceptional. One opponent said of him: 'He is the hardest thing to bring down and I do not believe he can be knocked out.' Yet, like Frik du Preez and Zinzan Brooke in more recent times, he was a forward with greater ball skills than most backs. His drop goal from a mark, fielded 45 yards out, in the second Test of 1928, remains an astonishing feat. The genius Bennie Osler thought Mostert was the best player in any position he had ever seen.

Quiet yet forceful, with a delightful sense of humour, Mostert's powerful personality made it inevitable he would captain the Springboks. He was hard and tough but never dirty. In his flair for gamesmanship he seems to have been an early Sean Fitzpatrick. One legend (denied by Mostert) was that he would use a black glove to fool the referee into thinking he had used his boot and not his hand to 'heel' the ball from the scrum.

Mostert is also an early symbol of the healing properties sport has shown in South Africa. He was born in the old Transvaal republic a year before the Anglo-Boer War started, and was interned with his mother in appalling conditions in a British concentration camp. Just a few years after the political unification of South Africa in 1910, he was playing rugby alongside the former enemies of his people.

One of only two men to play against the All Blacks in both the 1921 and 1928 series, Mostert remains a giant against whom future heroes must always be measured.

exciting game. 'A magnificent exhibition', enthused the newspaper, which was also careful to report that in Wellington 'the local opinion had it that the Springboks would have won on a dry ground'.

Of course they would have.

1928

STILL THEY STAND THEIR GROUND

SOUTH AFRICA	17	NEW ZEALAND	0
NEW ZEALAND	7	SOUTH AFRICA	6
SOUTH AFRICA	11	NEW ZEALAND	6
NEW ZEALAND	13	SOUTH AFRICA	5

CHAPTER TWO

1928

STILL THEY STAND THEIR GROUND

THE FIRST ALL BLACKS IN SOUTH AFRICA

by David Williams

IN THE FIRST Test in Durban on June 30, the All Blacks came up against two classic ingredients of Springbok victory: a brilliant flyhalf, in Bennie Osler, and an uncompromising pack, led by the formidable Phil Mostert. Forward dominance enabled the genius Osler to play a game tailored to achieve victory, taking few risks and playing to his strength as a thinking tactical kicker.

After the teams had filed onto the Kingsmead ground, the All Blacks performed the haka before Mostert led the Springboks in their own war-cry, which Osler recalled as 'a mixture of bad Zulu and gibberish. The good thing about those war cries was that it allowed you to blow off a bit of steam.'

The Springboks gradually took control, and Osler repeatedly drove back the New Zealanders with his kicking. He opened the scoring with a drop goal after his scrumhalf, Pierre de Villiers, had managed to slip past the All Blacks' tackling 'rover', and it was 4–0 at halftime. But centre Bernard Duffy had been concussed in a tackle, and South Africa would have to play the entire second half with 14 men.

Bennie Osler added another drop goal and two penalty goals, and also broke clear to within 10 yards of the try-line to make a scoring pass to Jack Slater. The Springboks came close to scoring several more tries, with All Black fullback Lindsay tackling heroically. Twice, Bennie Osler's brother, Stanley, nearly touched down; Mostert almost got over; and winger Boet Prinsloo, in what would be his only Test, dropped the ball after crossing the line. The final score was 17–0, the heaviest defeat for New Zealand since 1893.

As Bennie Osler said afterwards: 'I might have scored the points but Phil Mostert and the forwards did the work.' The *Rand Daily Mail* remarked on 'the brilliant work of the South African forwards, who maintained a stranglehold that was never released at any moment of the game'. Osler knew, too, that his complete understanding with the versatile scrumhalf Pierre de Villiers

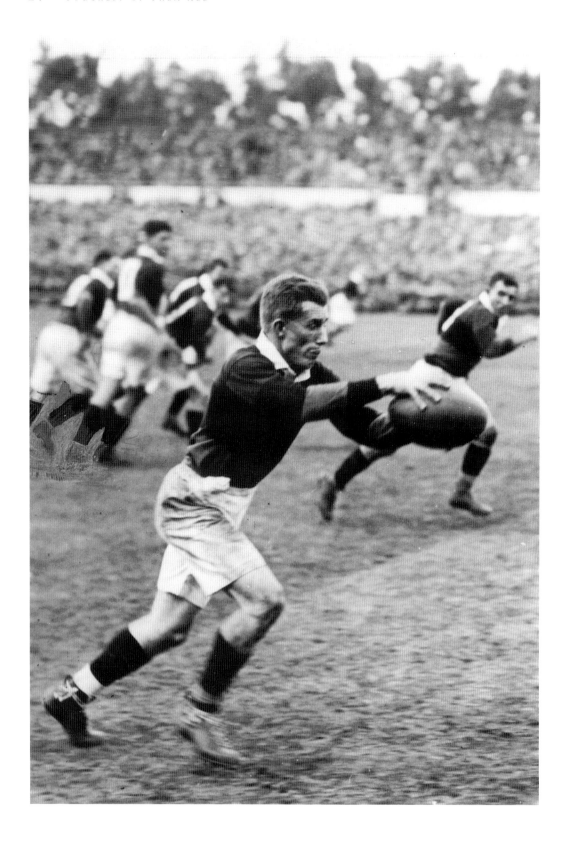

DEFINING MOMENT

Bennie Osler Takes the High Ground
FIRST TEST, DURBAN, 30 JUNE, 1928

The Springboks were reduced to 14 men for the second half of the first Test. The All Blacks must have been optimistic about getting the upper hand. But not long after halftime, Bennie Osler dropped a second goal (8–0) and was then late-tackled on the New Zealand 10-yard line after a kick ahead. Referee Boet Neser (an international cricketer who was to blow all four Tests) awarded the penalty where the ball landed, not where the offence had taken place. The crowd and some of the players were bewildered. It was the first time this new penalty law had been enforced, and as a result the shaken Osler was able to convert an easy kick (11–0). It was as if Osler was making a point: the Springboks refused to be handicapped by the loss of a man.

For the rest of the second half the All Blacks suffered 'an utter and complete eclipse', as F. M. Howard put it in the **Rand Daily Mail**. *'New Zealand never looked like scoring and only crossed the halfway line for a few brief moments at long intervals.' This was despite New Zealand's domination of the lineouts by two to one, and a 15–6 penalty count in their favour. Their backs had almost as many opportunities as came to the Springboks. Perhaps if Mark Nicholls had been playing, instead of acting as one of the touch judges, the visitors would have done better.*

But the All Blacks failed to sustain a challenge in the scrums, where the Springboks packed down in the 3–4–1 formation, switching to 3–3–2 when they wanted to wheel (which was often). As a result of constantly going backwards in the set scrums, even after flanker Nick Pretorius had been pulled out of the Bok scrum to cover for the concussed Bernard Duffy, the All Blacks could not get going in the loose.

Osler's drop goal and late-tackle penalty confirmed the strategic imperative of the series: the All Blacks would have to limit Osler's effectiveness if they wanted to beat the Springboks.

had been another key factor. 'No line could have been better served,' wrote the *Sunday Times*.

The Springbok selectors proceeded to make a decision outrageous even by modern South African standards. They replaced De Villiers with the Transvaal scrumhalf, Dauncey Devine, for the second Test, at Ellis Park on July 21. The Springboks were further weakened by the loss of

LEFT: One of the greatest Bok flyhalfs, Bennie Osler, displays his impeccable skills and perfect balance.

Springbok lock Phil Nel scores the first try of the third Test.

the injured Stanley Osler. But there was some compensation, in hindsight, in the selection of Gerry Brand on the wing.

From the start, just as the South African forwards had dominated the Durban Test, so the All Black pack took charge at Ellis Park. They had successfully adapted their scrumming, with their rover coming up to join the front-row at the last minute to secure the loosehead. The excited crowd nevertheless saw the Springboks lead for most of the game, Mostert kicking an amazing drop goal from a mark and Lindsay and Osler trading penalties (6–3). Finally, late in the game, Strang put over an excellent drop goal (7–6) to level the series. Although both sets of backs were said to be weak and uninspired (Osler battled to strike a rhythm with Devine), the Springbok forwards also lacked fire and were pinned down for much of the game. It seemed justice had been done when Gerry Brand's long-range drop attempt struck an upright to deny the Springboks a last-minute victory.

'It was a very hard game,' admitted Mostert. While there was general agreement that the All Blacks had thoroughly deserved to win, according to the *Rand Daily Mail* it had been 'one of the

1928 All Black captain Maurice Brownlie leads his team out.

poorest international matches, lamentably devoid of good rugby'. It was pointed out that 27 points had gone to the boot in the first two Tests for 'just once over the try-line'.

Politically, in a country where memories of the Boer War were still fresh, the second Test proved a powerful unifying influence for whites. Prime Minister Barry Hertzog attended the match, and on the Saturday evening the Administrator of the Transvaal, the Hon. Jan Hofmeyr, told a special banquet at the Carlton Hotel that it had been 'one of the greatest days Johannesburg has seen . . . a representative gathering of the South African people . . . almost all parts of the Union were represented in that vast concourse. Afrikaans seemed as much spoken as English.'

Despite this nationalistic surge, the All Blacks were still expected to win the third Test in Port Elizabeth on August 18, so emphatic had been their victory in Johannesburg. In fact, the home selectors had come to their senses. They brought back Pierre de Villiers and picked prop 'Boy' Louw for his first Test (which was also the first in which the Springboks wore white shorts). Louw did fine work in resisting the physicality of the All Black forwards. Another new cap, Manus de Jongh, scored a try after suffering a broken nose. The halftime score was 8–6 to the Springboks, and in the second half Bennie Osler delivered what was arguably the most balanced performance of his career. He kicked mercilessly for touch but took every reasonable chance to use his backs. South Africa won 11–6 because they took their chances better, and 15 of 17 points in the match came from five tries. The match was acclaimed as the best and most open of the three internationals so far.

For the fourth and final Test at Newlands, on September 1 — the 'Umbrella Test' — the All Blacks brought back Mark Nicholls at centre. (He had been restored to favour before the third Test but had been suffering from a boil on the neck.) Nicholls showed he might have won the series for New Zealand if only he had been picked in Durban. His forwards developed a solid platform, the slushy conditions suiting the New Zealand players. Two penalty goals and a drop goal by Nicholls, kicking an appallingly soggy and shapeless ball, made the difference between two sides which otherwise scored a try each. This decisive 13–5 victory for the All Blacks made it 2–all in a memorable series, and, all square in what was already rugby's greatest rivalry.

PLAYER OF THE DECADE

MARK NICHOLLS

BORN: 1901, DIED: 1972

POSITION: SECOND FIVE-EIGHTH, CENTRE THREE-QUARTER

PLAYED SOUTH AFRICA: 1921, 1928 (4 TESTS)

The fact that Mark Nicholls was the only All Black to appear in the first two series against South Africa is not what makes his role in the rivalry's history significant. Responsibility for that lies in the unusual circumstances that led to him making his only Test appearance of the 1928 tour to South Africa in Cape Town, in the fourth and series-deciding match. That appearance proved to be as successful as it was controversial.

Despite being the tour vice-captain, Nicholls — a brilliant five-eighth whose deeds with the 'Invincibles' in Europe in 1924–25 had sealed his reputation as a master tactician — had so far been ignored by the selectors. But chosen at last, and playing at second-five, the Wellingtonian's boot made the difference in difficult conditions as New Zealand claimed a 13–5 victory to inflict South Africa's first defeat at Newlands since 1891 and to square the series. After kicking two penalty goals, he added a drop goal — then worth four points — five minutes from fulltime.

His performance threw his earlier omission into stark relief, and the comments were many.

To this day his being left out of the first three Tests' teams remains a mystery. There was talk of a rift between the tour captain, Maurice Brownlie, and Nicholls. Also, shortly before his death in 1990, team-mate Alan Robilliard said it was felt, perhaps wrongly in hindsight, that Nicholls' game was not robust enough to take on the Springboks.

Incredibly, Nicholls wrote a book about the tour, **With the All Blacks in Springbokland,** *and failed to mention his omission, and it is said that throughout his life he held true to the story that it was form which decided his fate. But many refuse to believe that. The theorists maintain Nicholls, a forthright and sometimes difficult character, had fallen out with the taciturn Brownlie and other members of the touring party.*

As a 20-year-old Nicholls made his All Black debut in the first Test of the 1921 series, alongside his brother, halfback 'Ginger' Nicholls. He played the first two Tests at second-five and the third at centre, contributing three conversions in the low-scoring series.

1928

THE NEW ZEALAND RESPONSE

THE FIRST ALL BLACKS IN SOUTH AFRICA

by Grant Harding

CONSIDERING THE FACT that it took 68 years to better the achievement of the 1928 All Blacks in drawing a series in South Africa, it is strange Maurice Brownlie's team is not talked of in the same breath as many other great All Black touring sides. Perhaps because of its historical proximity to the 'Invincibles', that remarkable team that took the 'Originals' template and embellished it with a galaxy of characters who walked onwards to rugby's hall of fame, it will never receive quite the recognition it deserves.

Brownlie's team didn't have a Bert Cooke or a George Nepia to capture the imagination, and there were good reasons for that. The tiny second-five Cooke, who was the Invincibles' leading

All Black halfback Bill Dalley skips past his opposite Pierre de Villiers in the fourth Test.

try-scorer and regarded by all who saw him play as a genius, was unavailable for business reasons. As for Nepia, who as a 19-year-old had played in all the Invincibles' 30 games in the UK, Ireland and France, and many other fine Maori players, the reasons were more complicated.

During the Springboks' tour in 1921, controversy followed the match against New Zealand Maori in Napier when a newspaper report bound for South Africa was leaked to the *Napier Daily Telegraph*. Reporter Charles Blackett, who travelled with the tourists, wrote: 'Most unfortunate match ever played. Bad enough having play team officially designated NZ Natives, but spectacle thousands Europeans frantically cheering on band of coloured men to defeat members of own race was too much for Springboks who frankly disgusted.'

The racism inherent in the cable naturally caused an outcry in New Zealand. But the unfortunate outcome for the future of the rivalry between the two countries was that the New Zealand Rugby Football Union chose not to confront the issue in 1928, choosing an all-Pakeha touring side. What was consequently an understrength team then had to battle the effects of altitude and travel as well as fierce and talented opposition. Under these circumstances, a drawn series proved to be a great achievement. But for New Zealand, as it had been for South Africa in 1921, the result was satisfactory, nothing more.

Debutant P.K. Morkel clears for touch during the fourth Test. The Springboks lost and Morkel never played for South Africa again.

1937

THE STALEMATE IS BROKEN

NEW ZEALAND	13	SOUTH AFRICA	7
SOUTH AFRICA	13	NEW ZEALAND	6
SOUTH AFRICA	17	NEW ZEALAND	6

CHAPTER THREE

1937
THE STALEMATE IS BROKEN

THE SECOND SPRINGBOKS IN NEW ZEALAND

by Grant Harding

IF THE DECISIVE Test of the 1937 series had been played under today's scoring system, South Africa would have beaten New Zealand 27–6. That would have provided a record-winning margin for South Africa in Tests between the two countries, which shows how dominant Philip Nel's side was.

Not that any of the 58,000 people who filed, dejected, from Eden Park and every vantage point surrounding, on September 25, 1937, thought they had witnessed anything other than a thrashing of their All Black side. The scoreline may 'only' have been 17–6 — the All Blacks having been beaten 17–0 in South Africa in 1928 — but the Springboks had scored five tries to nil. For the first time a Test series between New Zealand and South Africa had a winner, the Springboks having also won the second Test in Christchurch.

Footage of the Test confirms the visitors' dominance, and shows a team playing 15-man rugby. Their back play is breathtaking. However, the highlights do not pinpoint the reason why the All Blacks could not compete. For that one must turn to the history books and statistics. The Springboks' success in the third Test was based on their scrummaging superiority. Before the game they had received a cable from Paul Roos, the first-ever Springbok tour captain to the UK and France, in 1906–07, urging them to 'Scrum, South Africa, Scrum, Scrum, Scrum.' And that's just what they did, with a helping hand from the laws of the day, which allowed captain Nel to opt for scrums rather than lineouts.

New Zealand's scrum, still struggling to come to terms with the enforced change from 2–3–2 to 3–4–1, was destroyed by a heavier, more focused, more technically efficient unit. South Africa scrummed, scrummed, scrummed, and, without ball and no forwards to support them in defence, New Zealand's backs capitulated.

Praise was unanimous for a team which had won 16 of its 17 matches, scoring 87 tries, 55 by the three-quarters. And that was after the tourists had won 10 of 11 matches in Australia, including both Tests.

The All Black haka fails to move either the Springboks or referee Joe King.

Given the Springboks' superiority in the scrum, the All Blacks' victory in the first Test with a pack reduced to seven men after an injury to winger Don Cobden belongs unquestionably to the believe-it-or-not category. Perhaps the answer to the 13-7 win lies in the Springboks' flawed selection and a degree of overconfidence after five quality victories over New Zealand provincial sides. Indeed, legend has it that Danie Craven turned to Philip Nel in the dressing room and predicted defeat because of the relaxed air of the players.

Nel and experienced prop 'Boy' Louw were left out of the team, while a third veteran of the 1928 series against New Zealand, fullback Gerry Brand, was injured. Strangely, Craven captained the team from first-five, allowing the fourth 1928 veteran in the 29-man squad, Pierre de Villiers, to play at halfback. Incredibly, these decisions were made by a five-man panel of players, including the 34-year-old Nel, Louw and Craven.

New Zealand fielded an uncapped backline behind an experienced forward pack featuring just one new cap. Played at Athletic Park, the unexpected win was achieved through a magnificent forward effort and first-five Dave Trevathan's kicking, which contributed 10 points, including four from a drop goal.

ABOVE: Do it with meaning . . . is this foul play, or just a dribbling rush being ended by Springbok bravery?

BELOW: Untouchable . . . Danie Craven lets fly. While he didn't invent the dive pass, the Springbok vice-captain made it famous.

Springbok flyhalf Tony Harris and his fellow backs ran rings around their All Black counterparts in the final Test at Eden Park to secure a series victory for the first-ever time.

PLAYER OF THE DECADE

JACK SULLIVAN

BORN: 1915, DIED: 1990

POSITION: CENTRE THREE-QUARTER, WINGER

PLAYED SOUTH AFRICA: 1937 (3 TESTS)

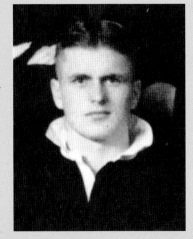

Jack Sullivan's life was inextricably linked with South African rugby over six decades. His Test career began against the 1937 Springboks. He appeared in all three Tests, the first two at centre and the last, in a selection faux pas, on the wing. After setting up New Zealand's only try in the first Test, he scored two tries — New Zealand's only points in a 6–13 loss — in the second Test at Lancaster Park.

The **Dominion** *of Monday, September 6, 1937, stated: 'His second try was one of the most sensational seen in big football for many years. After breaking through the opposition backs in his own territory, he chased the ball and in an exciting neck-and-neck race with Williams, the flying South African three-quarter, got over by inches.'*

Unfortunately World War II denied Sullivan the opportunity to tour South Africa in 1940. He rose to the rank of corporal in the 22nd Battalion, suffering a serious injury in 1942 that ended his rugby career. However, he had had the satisfaction of leading the Second New Zealand Division team to victory over a South African Division

side in a famous game in the Western Desert (at Baggush, Egypt) the previous year. After the victory, Sullivan and General Bernard Freyberg had celebrated with a bottle of beer, said to be the only one in the whole desert.

Sullivan went on to become an All Black selector for the white-hot 1956 home series against South Africa, and to coach the 1960 All Blacks in the republic. As NZRFU chairman between 1969 and 1977, he alone bore the brunt of media inquiries and the slings and arrows of an aggressive, growing anti-apartheid movement as the All Blacks toured South Africa twice and a Springbok tour to New Zealand was cancelled. His refusal to take part in public discussion on sporting contact with South Africa was made famous by his frequent 'no comment' pronouncements. While his family were subjected to unwanted phone calls, he would not take an unlisted number.

Sullivan attended South African rugby's centennial celebrations in 1989, the year before he died.

New Zealand made just two changes for the second Test at Lancaster Park, King Country's Bill Phillips replacing Cobden, and Jack Rankin replacing Ron Ward as flanker, Ward having spent most of the first Test on the wing in place of Cobden (although both new players were to be dumped for the third Test).

The Springboks made the necessary changes — Brand at fullback, Freddie Turner back on the left wing, Craven at halfback, the clever Tony Harris at first-five, Nel in as lock and captain, and Louw in as prop.

Despite a huge weight advantage and immediate scrum superiority, the Boks found themselves 6-0 down at halftime, thanks to two Jack Sullivan tries, the second an absolute classic from an intercept and kick-and-chase foot race with South Africa's fastest man, D. O. Williams.

It was then that the decision to coax Natal farmer Nel out of semi-retirement to lead the team paid dividends. Recalling his halftime message many years later, Nel said, 'I called the boys together and said it was today or never. Just concentrate on possession, is what I instructed them. Concentrate on getting the ball.'

Farmer Philip Nel was lured out of virtual retirement to lead the 1937 Springboks.

DEFINING MOMENT

Gerry Brand Turns the Series
SECOND TEST, CHRISTCHURCH, 4 SEPTEMBER, 1937

Gerry Brand had played two Tests against the 1928 All Blacks as winger, but in the intervening years he had become a fullback of international renown. After injury ruled him out of the first Test in the 1937 series, he returned in Christchurch to make his mark with a crucial penalty goal. Reports vary on the exact length of the kick, and the time it was taken, but all are unanimous on its impact.

One Test down, and trailing 6–5 well into the second half, the Boks were desperate. Then a penalty was awarded just inside New Zealand's half.

'A 55 yards kick,' according to A. C. Parker in his **The Springboks 1891–1970**. *'Brand, as he lined up after placing the ball, as usual, in a sloping position, knew it was the most crucial kick he had ever attempted. The cross-field breeze would not assist him, but neither would it hinder him. He moved in and swung his left boot. The ball travelled beautifully straight and true to raise the touch judges' flags, and to the jubilant Springboks, who had nosed into an 8–6 lead, that kick of Gerry's will remain "a thing of beauty, a joy forever".'*

Another try and Brand's second conversion completed a series-equalising victory, from whence South Africa went on to win the series.

Brand, captain Philip Nel and Louis Babrow were named among the **Rugby Almanack's** *'Five Players of 1937'. 'Gerhardt Hamilton Brand will be remembered by us as the greatest fullback of his time', it said.*

With such a practical, simple philosophy the Boks returned to the battle. It was brilliance, however, which started their march to victory early in the second half. Left-winger Turner got outside his marker, Johnny Dick, — who was dropped for the next Test — then chopped inside the remaining defence to run in a try under the posts. With Brand's conversion the Boks were in the game.

With the series in the balance, a number of unsavoury incidents followed, with players on both sides suffering injuries. The outcome remained uncertain until Brand kicked a magnificent penalty goal from near halfway, sending the South Africans into a frenzied high that pushed them onwards to another try by flanker Ebbo Bastard.

After the Eden Park rout had completed the series victory the Springboks were widely acclaimed as 'the greatest team to leave New Zealand'. Underlining the side's incomparable

PLAYER OF THE DECADE

DANIE CRAVEN

BORN: 1910, DIED: 1993

POSITION: SCRUMHALF, FLYHALF

PLAYED NEW ZEALAND: 1937 (3 TESTS)

Danie Craven played 16 Tests (four as captain) in seven years against Australia, New Zealand and the British Lions. In 38 matches in the Springbok jersey, he played in five different positions: scrumhalf, centre, flyhalf, fullback and No. 8.

Craven's devotion to the Springbok cause was ruthless, romantic, intense and unquenchable. His whole life would be dominated by it. After war service he graduated inexorably to coaching and management, directly influencing the great Bok teams of the early 1950s. In 1956 he was elected president of the South African Rugby Board and kept that position virtually until his death in 1993.

What made Craven so powerful was that he could not be scandalised. For once, here was a man who did not seem to have his price. He was not interested in money, smart clothes or cars, wining and dining, or any kind of office beyond rugby. Politically, Craven often seemed surprisingly naive for a man of such obvious intelligence and worldly experience. He operated with a peculiar blend of cunning and guilelessness. But as a motivator of men and a shrewd analyst of their personalities, he was an acknowledged master. One of his theories was that great rugby players have something of the artist in them, and that temperamental genius cannot be coached. Another was that sporting greatness runs in the genes. And he assiduously cultivated the superstition (some say he invented it) that every Springbok team should contain at least one Jewish player.

When the Springboks won the World Cup in 1995, there were many rugby men who wished, as they might of their own father, that Danie Craven had been there to see it.

ability is the fact that the touring teams of 1956, 1965, 1981 and 1994 were unable to repeat its success.

On the way home Nel announced his retirement by throwing his size-13 boots overboard, after which he drank a toast with his team-mates to a job well done. It was to be 12 years before the All Blacks and Springboks met again, a 1940 tour to South Africa falling victim to World War II.

1937

THE SOUTH AFRICAN RESPONSE

THE SECOND SPRINGBOKS IN NEW ZEALAND

by David Williams

A PLEASING IRONY of the 1937 tour was that the Springboks expected an easy win in the first Test. The Johannesburg *Star* wrote confidently that the Boks were 'superior to the All Blacks in every department . . . collectively, they play the type of game which looks certain to quell the New Zealanders'. It was pointed out that none of the New Zealand backs had international experience.

Yet the All Blacks won, despite having only seven forwards on the field for two-thirds of the game. The Boks were repeatedly penalised for going foot-up, a pattern against which 'the visitors registered mute despair'. Generally the Bok forwards, said beforehand to be blessed with 'an embarrassment of riches', were outplayed. Tony Harris had been dropped for Craven at flyhalf, on the erroneous grounds that Harris would have not have coped on a wet, slippery ground.

By the time of the second Test it was clear Harris should not only be picked, but that his should be the first name on the team sheet, with Craven back to his best position at scrumhalf. Leadership was restored with the return of Nel, although there was concern that, like 'Boy' Louw, he might be too slow. In fact the Bok forwards were 10 pounds per man heavier, which increased the advantage already gained through New Zealand's technical deficiencies in the scrum. 'There was awe in their eyes,' recalled Craven, 'because they knew that we could push anything aside.' And there was the return of the genius Gerry Brand. Those three men — Harris, Nel and Brand — made all the difference in the remaining two Tests.

The tension that built before the deciding third Test seems to have been unbearable, even by modern standards. Danie Craven was to say 50 years later that he was still burnt out by it. The explanation of the Springbok superiority, meanwhile, was neatly summarised by Johannesburg journalist H. B. Keartland: 'New Zealand have never made a thorough study of the 3–4–1 scrum and its possibilities as a means of aggression.'

1949

WHITEWASH

SOUTH AFRICA	15	NEW ZEALAND	11
SOUTH AFRICA	12	NEW ZEALAND	6
SOUTH AFRICA	9	NEW ZEALAND	3
SOUTH AFRICA	11	NEW ZEALAND	8

CHAPTER FOUR

1949

WHITEWASH

THE SECOND ALL BLACKS IN SOUTH AFRICA

by David Williams

'AFTER 11 YEARS the struggle for world rugby football supremacy resumes.' That was how the *Rand Daily Mail* introduced its preview of the first Test of the 1949 series. Men had been starved of international rugby by the war, and the series was eagerly, almost desperately, awaited.

It was difficult to pick a favourite for the first Test. South Africa had not fielded a team since 1938, and every Springbok was making his debut. New Zealand was slightly better off as it had played against Australia in 1946 and 1947.

Goalkicking was expected to be decisive in the series. In the six weeks before the first Test, at Newlands on July 16, more than 75 per cent of the points scored by provinces against the tourists had come from penalty kicks at goal. Although the All Blacks had scored 20 tries in 11 games to their opponents' three, they had clearly betrayed a degree of indiscipline that the Springboks might exploit.

And so it proved. The Springboks won 15–11: five penalty goals were better than two tries (one converted), a penalty goal and a drop goal. Newspapers muttered that the victory had been fortuitous and that the All Blacks 'simply did not deserve to lose'. It was acknowledged that the five goals by prop forward Okey Geffin represented a personal triumph, but otherwise there had been 'little flavour' in the win. Debates about the value of a try in relation to a penalty goal invariably concluded with a call for the try to count more. To make matters worse, said the South African critics, the Bok backs (including the talented Hansie Brewis at flyhalf) had been deeply unimpressive, and the forwards had lost the lineouts.

Some words of common sense came from Danie Craven, manager of the Springboks. He disagreed that the win was lucky. He pointed out that his men had done well to come back from 8–0 down, and reminded everyone that the Boks had never played together before. As for his team's failure to score a try, Craven complimented the defensive work of the All Blacks. It was

The All Blacks practised on the long boat trip to South Africa, but it proved far from ideal with several players arriving overweight.

left to the New Zealand writer Claude King to point out that before Geffin had been called up by captain Felix du Plessis to go for posts, fullback Jack van der Schyff had already missed three times. In other words, the margin could have been greater.

The fact is that several penalties against the All Blacks in that first Test were for obstruction, a far greater offence against the spirit of the game than winning by kicking goals. The referee, Eddie Hofmeyr, later gave a detailed and convincing justification for each of the penalties Geffin had converted.

Ten All Blacks were dropped for the second Test, at Ellis Park on August 13, while South Africa made four changes — not enough, in the view of most commentators. Selection issues were overshadowed by the growing view that there was too much dirty play on the tour.

In the event, the match was clean and the more settled Springboks were much better value. Their backline was strengthened by the inclusion of Fonnie du Toit at scrumhalf and Ryk van Schoor at centre, the forwards by Chris Koch and Salty du Rand. All four replacements would go on to be major influences in Springbok rugby in the 1950s. Hennie Muller, whose disruptive speed from No. 8 had been more influential in the first Test than the critics had realised, was even more predatory at Ellis Park.

With the score at 3–3, the Springboks proved they could score good tries. Brewis received the ball from a scrum near the touchline, deep in the All Black half, and shaped to drop for goal. The dummy bought him a second's grace and he evaded the charging defenders by slipping down the blindside. Deep inside the New Zealand 25-yard area, he feinted again, aiming to kick for the corner flag. Again the All Blacks bought the dummy. Brewis moved closer to the line, dodged yet another desperate defender and went over to score. The 70,000 spectators, said rugby journalist Chris Greyvenstein, 'went raving mad'.

A second superb Springbok try followed good driving and dribbling work by the forwards, with new caps Koch and Du Rand prominent. The All Blacks were in disarray when the ball came to Brewis and he linked to the ever-present Muller, who had made the extra man. The All Black centres now had to mark three men, and Tjol Lategan nipped through for the score. Brewis and Kearney exchanged drop goals, a last New Zealand attack was snuffed out by Muller and Van der Schyff, and the final score was 12–6.

The home critics were much happier. South Africa had been the better side, they agreed, and were more than worth the margin of victory. Now it was off to Natal for the third Test, with New Zealand two down and two to play. It was the first time in three decades of rivalry that either country had been in this miserable position. Newspapers delighted in reminding everyone that in the Durban Test 21 years before, New Zealand had been thrashed 17–0. All Black manager Jim Parker put on a brave face and said his players were 'returning to form'. Less publicly, the All Blacks had identified a chronic problem in the way they were heeling the ball from the scrums, and much work was done on this at secret practices. Local experts like Jack Gage, a 1933 Springbok, expected New Zealand to gamble everything on an attacking policy 'to enable them to play their natural game'.

That is what the All Blacks tried to do, launching many sweeping backline movements. They were rewarded with a try by Maurice Goddard after a fumble by van der Schyff, but the defence of the Springbok centres, Tjol Lategan and Ryk van Schoor, proved deadly. So again did the boot of Geffin: three goaled penalties were enough to give the match to South Africa by nine points to three. But the home critics were even more unimpressed than they had been after the first Test.

Bok captain Felix du Plessis was more realistic. He paid tribute to the tackling by Lategan and Van Schoor, and declared, 'people who blame us for not scoring a try just don't realise what good defenders New Zealand are'. But few people in either country were disposed to listen to him. The victory was seen as hollow, with Geffin as much a villain as a hero, while the view from New Zealand was that the South African loose forwards were playing unfairly as 'spoilers'. In particular, there was a call for the No. 8 to be removed completely because he was such a destructive force. This was in fact less a comment on the laws of the game than a compliment to the speed and skill of Muller, although it seems not even South Africans appreciated his full value at the time.

PLAYER OF THE DECADE

OKEY GEFFIN

BORN: 1921
POSITION: PROP FORWARD
PLAYED NEW ZEALAND: 1949 (4 TESTS)

Hennie Muller may have been the strategic cause of the whitewash of Fred Allen's 1949 All Blacks, but the series will always be associated with the deadly boot of prop forward Okey Geffin. As a prisoner-of-war in Poland, Geffin had practised goalkicking endlessly, but his rugby education had started before the war at Johannesburg's Pirates club, where he had been coached by the 1937 Springbok Freddie Turner.

Geffin was known to his fellow POWs as Ox because of his great strength. After the war his nickname somehow became Okey (which is also a South African slang equivalent of 'bloke' or 'lad'). He enjoyed pointing out that, being Jewish, his father had refused to give him Christian names when registering his birth. It was only as an adult that Geffin had the names Aaron Okey officially inserted on his birth certificate.

It seems strange now that Geffin's feats in 1949 were almost resented by the home critics. After the third victory of the series, achieved once again by Geffin's goalkicking, there was talk in the Durban papers of a 'Test flop', and the manner of victory was described resentfully as 'more of a loss than a gain in prestige'. Geffin himself succumbed to the propaganda, shaking his head sadly as he came off the field and saying: 'Another win by penalty goals!' Later generations have been more forgiving.

Geffin scored 32 points in the 1949 series.

Du Plessis' reward for winning the series was to be dropped. The captaincy went to Basil Kenyon, who had done so well in leading Border province to its famous 9–0 win over the All Blacks.

Port Elizabeth was a sad story of missed chances for the demoralised All Blacks. There were good scores by Peter Johnstone and Elvidge for New Zealand, and several thrilling runs by both sides that almost resulted in tries. In the first half Muller was diving for the line when he was tackled in mid-air by Peter Henderson. Muller was concussed and had to be told where to run for the rest of the game. Fonnie du Toit scored a try for South Africa, Geffin added the conversion and a penalty goal, and Brewis contributed a huge drop goal. The final score (11–8) sealed a

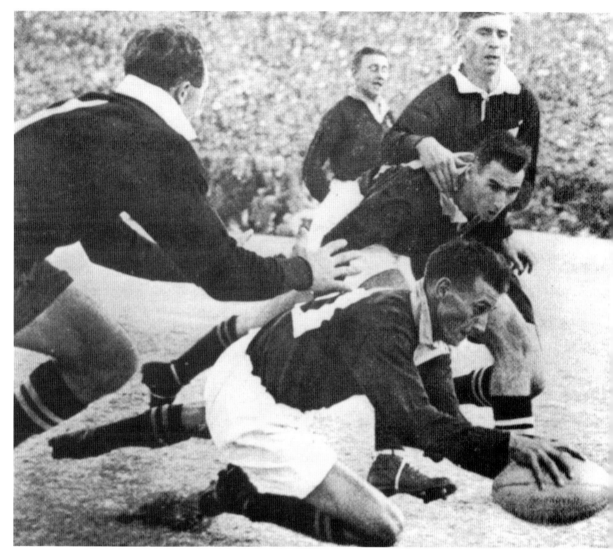

While the Springboks achieved a whitewash in the 1949 series only once did they score more tries than New Zealand. That was in the second Test where Springbok flyhalf Hansie Brewis scored one of two brilliant tries.

whitewash but New Zealand had had its chances, not least through its domination of forward play. Afterwards Bob Scott cried in the dressing room because he felt his place-kicking had cost his team the game.

In hindsight, it is clear the entirely uncapped South African side of 1949 provided the foundation of a great attacking era in Springbok rugby. The All Blacks were probably better than was appreciated at the time, but the might of their opposition disguised the fact.

1949

THE NEW ZEALAND RESPONSE

THE SECOND ALL BLACKS IN SOUTH AFRICA

by Grant Harding

IT WASN'T UNTIL 1998 that baby-boomer New Zealand rugby followers could understand what 1949 had been like. As the All Blacks crashed to five consecutive defeats, finally there was comprehension of the nightmare Fred Allen's tourists to South Africa had endured. Making matters worse in 1949 was that another New Zealand team lost the Bledisloe Cup to Australia in a two-Test series.

Analysis of the situation reveals the contributing factors in this worst of all years for New Zealand rugby.

Fred Allen's pain at a second consecutive Test loss is well hidden, but the All Black captain refused to select himself for the final two Tests of the series and announced his retirement on the voyage home by throwing his boots overboard. Arm-in-arm is Springbok captain Felix du Plessis, who was dropped for the fourth Test, after winning the first three.

PLAYER OF THE DECADE

KEVIN SKINNER

BORN: 1927

POSITION: PROP FORWARD

PLAYED SOUTH AFRICA: 1949, 1956 (6 TESTS)

Notoriety has attached itself to Kevin Skinner's role in the 1956 series against South Africa. What is often forgotten, however, is that he would not have participated in that series had it not been for his experiences as an All Black on the 1949 tour to the republic.

On that tour the 20-year-old Otago prop made a powerful impression, earning selection for all four Tests ahead of vice-captain Ray Dalton. The All Blacks might have suffered a humiliating white-wash, but in unison with Johnny Simpson and Has Catley, Skinner formed a front-row that equalled the previously acknowledged scrummaging masters.

Skinner retired from international rugby in 1954, recognised as an all-time great for his combination of strength and mobility. But in 1956 circumstances conspired to earn him a call-up against his old rivals. He had moved to Waiuku, in south Auckland, to start farming. Playing for the local rugby club and at provincial level for Counties, he was already swept up in the fever of the Springboks' tour when the selectors came looking for him after Mark Irwin was injured in the first-Test win. Then, when Frank McAtamney was destroyed in the second-Test loss, Skinner was recalled.

'The Springbok front-rowers were built up as larger than life,' he said. 'These were the same guys that I had opposed in 1949. They were big and strong, but no better than us.'

Despite returning to the international

arena at his lightest playing weight — of 89 kg — Skinner set about demonstrating the strength he'd shown in becoming the 1947 New Zealand heavyweight boxing champion. His performance proved to be the stuff of myth and legend, especially since the All Blacks won the Test and went on to win a series against the Springboks for the first time.

According to the man himself, the legend was born of two incidents. His 1949 adversary and friend Chris Koch, who visited Skinner's mother while in Dunedin, was warned, then hit, for lineout indiscretions. Koch was not sighted on New Zealand's side again. Then, at halftime, Skinner switched to the loosehead side of the scrum at the request of Ian Clarke. Up against Jaap Bekker, 'who liked to throw his weight about and work on you', he quickly became annoyed with negative tactics. 'So I hit him,' Skinner said. 'It led to a scuffle which was soon sorted out and that was that.'

The All Black selectors' desperate decision to recall Skinner had paid dividends. Despite a South African plot to take revenge on Skinner in the fourth Test, there was not another incident until a cheap shot on 'Tiny' White late in the game.

'They were tough men,' Skinner said. 'They would have ridden us if they could have, but once they knew that there was no nonsense they got on and played rugby.

'Helping beat them at home in 1956 was a way of squaring my account with them.'

DEFINING MOMENT

Hennie Muller Proves His Fitness
SPRINGBOK TRIALS, JOHANNESBURG, 1949

There was little home jubilation at the 1949 series victory. It was pointed out that South Africa had goaled 10 penalties to New Zealand's two, and, that if the scores had been reckoned on tries alone, New Zealand would have won three of the four Tests. This was a facile analysis because it ignored three key factors, all integral to the spirit of the game: the influence of a good defence; the need to enforce the laws by awarding penalties; and the failure of New Zealand to convert its kicks. In any case, the South African backs had often been enterprising, and Brewis, at flyhalf, had shown rare creativity after the first Test.

In any event, an even greater factor was undoubtedly Hennie Muller's rampaging offensive defence, combining the speed of an Olympic sprinter with the bulk of a lock forward and the courage and stamina of a Gurkha. Add his innate rugby intelligence and his flyhalf's ball skills, and one can see that Muller was way ahead of his time. His contribution in disrupting the New Zealand pattern was both creative and underestimated. Many South Africans have since argued he is the greatest Springbok of all time.

In the light of this, the decisive moment in 1949 arguably occurred before the series had even begun. Muller had to test the recovery of his badly injured knee, first in a club game and then in the national trials. After making a powerful tackle in the trial on Transvaal team-mate Jimmy Kotze, Muller knew he was fit, and so did the selectors. Geffin won the series, perhaps, but Muller made it possible.

First of all, the 49ers were coached by 67-year-old Alex McDonald, who had coached the All Blacks against the 1921 Springboks. This was a ludicrous situation given Otago master coach Vic Cavanagh was at his peak, and McDonald was simply not robust enough for such an arduous journey. By halfway through the tour Allen was running practice.

Then there was the travel. A 26-day trip on a boat poorly equipped for fitness activities but well equipped for social activities ended with several forwards grossly overweight.

Internal train travel was horrendous, and never more so than when the tourists were involved in a head-on collision that killed one railway employee.

Despite the series whitewash, the All Blacks scored more tries than South Africa in three of the four Tests (yet managed just two penalty goals to the Springboks' 10 during the series). It was a statistic that drew suspicion from New Zealand audiences linked only by newspapers and radio to their team. While brilliant fullback Bob Scott's goalkicking form was unusually poor, many a small boy was to be brought up on the stories of Okey Geffin, the goalkicker who converted goals their grandmother could have thrown over.

It's true New Zealand lacked a quality halfback, part-Maori Vince Bevan being ineligible to tour, as were the great centre Johnny 'J. B.' Smith and talented five-eighth Ben Couch. Interestingly, the first anti-racism anti-tour march was led in Wellington in 1949 by Brigadier General Sir Howard Kippenberger.

Allen probably made a mistake by standing down from the third and fourth Tests. By the tour's end he was so shattered by the experience that he announced his retirement by throwing his boots into the Indian Ocean.

In a 1990 rugby documentary on his career, Allen said of the tour, 'The refereeing wasn't, probably, as fair and just as we'd have liked it to have been. And they haven't improved really.'

That's our story, and we're sticking to it.

All Black captain Ron Elvidge finds Bill Meates with a pass during the third Test.

1956

THE BOKBUSTERS

NEW ZEALAND	10	SOUTH AFRICA	6
SOUTH AFRICA	8	NEW ZEALAND	3
NEW ZEALAND	17	SOUTH AFRICA	10
NEW ZEALAND	11	SOUTH AFRICA	5

1956
THE BOKBUSTERS

THE THIRD SPRINGBOKS IN NEW ZEALAND

by Grant Harding

WHEN I MET Bill Gray in 1990 I was shocked to hear him say: 'I really didn't enjoy my games playing for the All Blacks because the pressure was so intense, so severe.' It wasn't what you expected to hear from an All Black. But four of Gray's six Tests at second-five were in the most infamous series in New Zealand rugby history, against the Springboks in 1956.

Dramatic film of the series gives a clearer understanding of where Gray was coming from. During the most brutal Test — the second, at Athletic Park — there is the sight of him obviously 'out of his mind' after being kicked in the head. He is thrashing his arms about in what appears to be an attempt to shake normality back into his body. Later, as he dives on the ball, a Springbok, leading with his leg, drives the full weight of his thigh into Gray to bring him to the ground.

Other lowlights show Tiny White overdoing a scragging of a Springbok player, then slipping off him to the ground, where he is promptly stomped on.

Today the offending players would either have been sent off, or seriously dealt with by the judiciary. But this was 1956, and rugby's version of war. The Springboks hadn't been beaten in a series since 1896, and, more importantly, from a New Zealand perspective the All Blacks had failed miserably against them in the last two series. By 1956, New Zealand, a far less sophisticated country than it is today, was united in its desire to beat the Boks, and at all costs.

Through the summer of 1955 players trained more assiduously than they had ever previously contemplated. A fever had taken grip of the nation, and it would not be cured until the Boks had been busted.

The South African team included just two players who had appeared in the 1949 series — lock Salty du Rand and prop Chris Koch. Du Rand had been favoured to captain the team until a scuffle with fellow tourist Jan Pickard following a trial match. After that uncapped fullback 'Basie' Viviers was named captain.

Salty du Rand secures the ball during the Wellington Test.

Danie Craven, who had become South African Rugby Board president in 1956, was the coach. At the start of the tour Craven said he knew New Zealand was after the Boks' 'blood', but that the tourists were here 'not to win at all costs, but to play the right kind of rugby'. Perhaps the sarcastic phrase 'famous last words' was coined for 'Mr Rugby'.

Journalist Terry McLean, who wrote *Battle for the Rugby Crown* after following the tour, contends Craven received the shock of his life when Waikato, who had been training since December 1955, beat South Africa 14–10 in the opening match on June 9. Test losses were one thing; provincial losses were quite another.

It was first blood to New Zealand, and each member of the Waikato team was carried from the field shoulder high. At the after-match function, Waikato coach Dick Everest received the prized Springbok head from Viviers.

After that initial disappointment the tourists played a further eight matches without defeat before the first Test, at Carisbrook in Dunedin. For the third successive tour, the tour captain was omitted for the first Test, and Du Rand duly got the honour of leading the team.

The New Zealand team featured great names like prop Ian Clarke, lock Tiny White and winger Ron Jarden, but the captain was Canterbury halfback Pat Vincent, who was one of three All Blacks making their Test debut.

In a match blighted by injuries, the All Blacks sneaked home 10–6, two tries to one. The All Blacks' tries came in a 10-minute period before halftime. White scored off a ruck close to the line, and Jarden pulled off an astonishing intercept. As the Boks broke towards halfway with an overlap, the Wellington speedster ran with his back to them, then, at the moment the errant pass was made, he chopped back, took the ball and raced 40 metres for the try.

Injuries effectively meant only 14 All Blacks played just 12 Springboks in the second half, but the Boks continued to attack, and at the final whistle it was agreed the All Blacks had been fortunate to win.

Craven's displeasure at the result was further heightened by a loss to Canterbury a week later. Gripes about New Zealand referees were taken to New Zealand Rugby Football Union officials. Referees' attitudes to the ruck was the major cause of dissent. As the tour progressed the All Blacks devised a strategy based on the up-and-under kick followed by pressure on the ball through vigorous rucking.

With the All Blacks one up in the series, the Boks were left in no doubt that every possible measure had to be taken to make sure they won the second Test. 'There was a fervour amounting to almost a hatred within the Springboks,' Terry McLean said. 'They were going to win whatever.'

Tiny White remembers the All Blacks coming across the Springbok bus at a training venue they were sharing for the day. As he walked past he noted that not one of the players in the bus turned their eyes towards him or his team-mates, and concluded that 'their indoctrination was probably 50 times worse than ours'.

All Black winger Ron Jarden (at left) appears to be stuck to the spot, as three Springbok invaders zone in on the ball in this action from the second Test.

Despite the All Blacks having won the first Test, the New Zealand selectors surprisingly made five changes, including the introduction of three new caps. South Africa made six changes, including bringing in 'Basie' Viviers as fullback and captain, and 1949 veteran Chris Koch as prop.

On a cold, windy day New Zealand failed to make use of the elements in the first half, and only led 3–0 come the break. With just two minutes of the second half gone, South Africa hit the front when flanker Daan Retief scored from a blindside move and Viviers converted from wide out. With the visitors' forward pack dominant, New Zealand were pinned in their own half, and despite poor goalkicking by South Africa there was never any doubt who would win. Du Rand eventually sealed the victory with a try 10 minutes from time.

After the second Test, concerns about New Zealand's scrummaging reached national-crisis proportions. In the opening minutes of the game a succession of scrums had been packed down, and in one dramatic moment the Boks had asserted their superiority by crashing over the top of the New Zealand front-row.

Public and media pressure demanded answers for the third Test in a fortnight's time. NZRFU councillor Tom Pearce, who had played prop for Auckland against the 1937 Springboks and was considered unlucky not to have appeared in the Test series, called a special meeting of the New Zealand Rugby Football Union council, from which it is believed the selectors received their instructions. Action needed to be decisive, and when the All Black team was announced there were seven changes.

Among them was 1949 veteran Kevin Skinner, who had retired from international rugby at the conclusion of the 1953–54 tour to the UK and France, then had his interest renewed by the Boks' tour. Bob Duff took over the captaincy from the discarded Vincent.

Springbok props Jaap Bekker and Chris Koch had bullied Mark Irwin and Frank McAtamney in the first two Tests, but had no chance of doing the same to Skinner. His sorting-out of both props became legendary, but Skinner's explanation of it rested on the simple philosophy that the Afrikaner would play rugby if he realised he wasn't going to get away with any nonsense. That he took such action in front of referee Bill Fright is an insight into the rugby of the day.

In any event, Skinner's contribution to the 17–10 third Test victory was just one of many mighty efforts. Don Clarke's debut started with two massive penalty goals to take New Zealand 6–0 ahead after nine minutes. Jarden soared to gather in a kick ahead by centre Ross Brown and score a crucial try two minutes from fulltime. And White finished off a burst by Peter Jones and winger Morrie Dixon, who had scored the first try, to complete a victory that ensured the series would not be lost.

Once again it had been a titanic struggle, the Boks clawing their way back to within one point midway through the second half after trailing 11–0 at halftime.

RIGHT: Bill Fright plays ringmaster as Springbok prop Jaap Bekker and All Black prop Kevin Skinner shape up during the third Test.

61,240 patrons witnessed Peter Jones deliver on the prayers of New Zealanders from Cape Reinga to Bluff at Eden Park on 1 September 1956. Finally the Boks would be beaten, and for all-time Jones would be a legend.

Injury to first-five Robin Archer saw him replaced by Brown for the final Test at Eden Park, with Pat Walsh, fullback in the first two Tests, coming in at centre. The Boks made six changes, four in the backs and two in the forwards.

A record crowd of 61,240 crammed into Eden Park to watch New Zealand claim a historic victory thanks to a brilliant try by Peter Jones five minutes into the second spell. That, plus a Clarke penalty goal in each half, was enough, the Boks collecting just a late consolation try.

Typically, Craven added theatre to the occasion by symbolically handing the crown of world rugby supremacy to New Zealand with these words: 'For a long time you people have fought to get what you have. You will find what we have found — that to be there is one thing, to stay there is another,' adding, 'It's all yours New Zealand.' The Springboks had finally submitted.

But they had not accepted defeat easily. Late in the match White had been brutally kicked in the back by Bekker. For a moment it had appeared the crowd would spill onto the ground, before order was finally restored. White, who retired following the last Test, later remembered the series as being unequalled for intensity. 'It was as if the world would come to an end if we didn't win against the Boks. And I can still recall some team talks which left me somewhat gasping for breath. For the All Blacks, therefore, the result brought relief more than exultation.

PLAYER OF THE DECADE

PETER JONES
BORN: 1932, DIED: 1994
POSITION: NO. 8, FLANKER
PLAYED SOUTH AFRICA: 1956, 1960 (3 TESTS)

Fine All Black that he was, the name of Peter Jones will always be linked with 1956 and the try that finally allowed New Zealand to enjoy its first series win over South Africa.

Jones missed selection for the first two Tests because of his questionable fitness. Unusually large for a loose forward of his era — he weighed in at 111kg — he made a slow start to the season, and was in Dunedin and Wellington only as a non-playing reserve.

With the series in the balance, Jones was selected for the third Test at Christchurch, and his most telling contribution in that victory was a trademark bullocking run that led to the All Blacks' third and final try by lock 'Tiny' White. But it was the final Test at Eden Park that bestowed immortality upon him, when he scored a try that made a nation roar from Cape Reinga to Bluff.

It started from a lineout just inside the Springbok territory early in the second half, and was described by good friend and broadcasting legend Winston McCarthy as follows:'[Ron] Hemi comes through with the ball at his toe ... going on it he knocks it out of Dryburgh's hands. Jones is coming down. He takes it and he's running for the goal-line. This is a try for New Zealand. It's a try for New Zealand. Peter Jones has scored. I'll tell you about it when the crowd stops roaring. Listen to them. Listen to them. The crowd is going absolutely crazy.'

Jones had plucked the ball from the air just as Springbok fullback and captain

Basie Viviers had grasped for it, then used his exceptional pace to keep the cover at bay on a 40-metre run. When he dived under the posts the enormity of the moment immediately hit him, forcing his arm into the air in an appeal to the referee not to make a mistake. He did not, and New Zealand, with Don Clarke's conversion, went out to an 8–0 lead that eventually became an 11–5 win.

After the match Jones embellished his feat by unwittingly challenging the conservative broadcasting standards of the day. 'Well, ladies and gentlemen, I hope I never have to play in a tougher game than what I did today,' he said. 'I'm absolutely buggered.' His statement drew great laughter from the still-assembled crowd of 61,240. Exhausted, Jones was in bed by 10 p.m.

In 1960, Jones' tour of South Africa turned into a disaster when, after playing flanker in the 0–13 first Test loss, he tore a groin muscle playing against the Junior Springboks. He took part in just two of the remaining 14 matches.

'Many times I had thought back to Eden Park in 1956,' he was to recall, 'and that long second which remained forever frozen in my mind — [Basie] Viviers reaching up for the ball and me reaching out and bringing it down just a finger touch before him, perfectly. I felt that I'd been meant to achieve something great one day. And I had felt — I knew, I swear it — that I would never be great after 1956.'

The anger evident in 'Tiny' Hill's (middle) facial expression tells the story of the violent kick which sickened Eden Park patrons and left All Black lock 'Tiny' White fearing for his mobility.

Never again would the pursuit of victory have the full force of nationalism behind it. Risking limb in the quest for glory was part and parcel of a physical contact sport, but risking life was not. White's injury was a final reminder that this series, while a glorious victory for New Zealand, had come at a price which could never again be paid. No country could afford to come to a standstill over, nor expend so much nervous energy on, what in the end was just a game.

I'm certain the late Bill Gray would concur.

DEFINING MOMENT

All Black Selection for the Third Test
THIRD TEST, CHRISTCHURCH, 18 AUGUST, 1956

The All Black selectors got it right before the third Test. In came powerfully built Waikato fullback and kicking sensation Don Clarke, to make his Test debut alongside his lighter brother, prop Ian. In, too, came a new inside-back combination in the shape of Waikato's Ponty Reid and Southland's Robin Archer, who had appeared in the first Test. Other first-Test casualties Tiny Hill and Ron Hemi were restored to the forward pack, while Peter Jones and Kevin Skinner were now considered fit enough to resume their international careers. Clarke, Jones and, in particular, Skinner, were major contributors to a first-ever series victory over the Springboks, and the three are regarded as all-time greats.

The magnificent 24 who won the war, such was the intensity of the contest, against the 1956 Springboks.

1956

THE SOUTH AFRICAN RESPONSE

THE THIRD SPRINGBOKS IN NEW ZEALAND

by David Williams

THE 1956 SPRINGBOKS were left in no doubt about the importance of their visit. The All Blacks had been humiliated in 1949 and had been planning revenge for seven years. New Zealanders welcomed the visitors with the fervour and respect reserved for special sacrificial offerings. 'You cannot believe the welcome we got,' recalled centre Wilf Rosenberg. 'There were huge crowds everywhere we went, everyone knew who you were. I've never seen such hero worship. We never had to pay for anything and a lot of us came back with a lot of money in our pockets.'

It was ironic that the Springbok team for this most ruthless of series had been picked with the specific intention of playing clean, open rugby. 'We left the toughies behind,' complained Rosenberg. 'There were several northern players who would soon have sorted out the All Black pack — renowned hard men like Gert Dannhauser, Stoffel Bosch and Piet Malan. But Danie Craven was the coach and he let it be known to the selectors that he didn't want to play it that way.' Men like Chris Koch, Jaap Bekker, Johan Claassen and Daan Retief were known in South Africa as tough but clean players. Certainly none of them was regarded as dirty in the often violent underworld of club and provincial rugby in those pre-TV days.

Craven's idealism in this respect was hardly balanced by his over-innovative approach to training in the fortnight before the tour. In the firm belief that the Springboks needed to get used to wet, heavy grounds, Craven insisted they train, literally, with lead in their boots. 'But he trained us too hard,' said Rosenberg. 'As a result, and nobody outside knew this, we went into the tour carrying serious injuries to no less than five key players.'

Rosenberg remained convinced in 1999 that the whole of the New Zealand rugby establishment had conspired against the 1956 Springboks from the start of the tour. 'Our first game was against Waikato, the Ranfurly Shield champions — no easing in, that's for sure. And they roughed us up and the referee saw nothing. It was like that right through the tour.'

Even so, the Springboks did not feel wronged until the third Test. Touring journalist Reg Sweet of Durban, who rivalled Chris Greyvenstein and A. C. Parker as the fairest and greatest South African rugby writer of that generation, pointed out that the Bok tactics had been faulty in the first Test. He thought they could only win the series with ball in hand, yet they had persisted with short-range tactical kicking. In the second Test the Boks were better balanced and they managed to expose the All Black vulnerability in the front-row, taking four tightheads.

Kevin Skinner remains a demon in South African rugby mythology. But enduring resentment

PLAYER OF THE DECADE

CHRIS KOCH

BORN: 1927, DIED: 1986
POSITION: PROP FORWARD
PLAYED NEW ZEALAND: 1949, 1956, 1960 (7 TESTS)

Chris Koch remains the only man to have played for the Springboks in three different decades. He is also one of only four men (Frik du Preez, Lofty Nel and Jan Ellis are the others) who has played for the Boks in three full series against the All Blacks. Tall for a prop at 6ft 2in (1.87m), and with the strength of the farmer he was, Koch was also a sprinter of the highest class and a skilful ball-player. Experts believed both he and legendary No. 8 Hennie Muller could have played at international level as three-quarters.

In Danie Craven's mind, Koch was the ideal forward for the 1956 tour of New Zealand, when he was probably at his peak.

Sadly, his all-round abilities were wasted as New Zealand chose to make ball skills and even honest strength superfluous by turning the forward battle into one of crude punching attrition. New Zealanders did not see his full quality, but Koch would probably rival Phil Mostert and Du Preez as the closest South African equivalent to Zinzan Brooke. He was probably seen at his best on the 1951–52 tour of Britain and in the 1955 home series against the British Lions. Koch briefly held the record for the most Tests played by a Springbok (22), and when he retired in 1960 he had scored more tries (five) than any other front-row Bok.

over his selection and prize-fighting performance in the crucial third Test has obscured the deep divisions in the Springbok team. When these were raised in New Zealand newspapers, Craven responded angrily with talk of the 'filthy press'. It was alleged that three Springboks — Paul Johnstone, Ian Kirkpatrick and Jan Pickard — had been dropped for disciplinary reasons. Clearly the considerable smoke was coming from a real fire. Craven confirmed nearly 40 years later that 'Basie' Viviers had been a compromise choice as captain after Pickard and Salty du Rand had had a dressing-room punch-up before the tour. Viviers had not even been in the original team.

Reg Sweet noted New Zealand had brought back the 'experienced and skilled' Skinner for the third Test. He argued after the All Blacks' 17–10 win that 'there must be no recriminations . . . there was little play which could be classed as dangerous'. Craven himself said the match 'had gone to the better side'. Terry McLean said the Boks had 'allowed themselves to be intimidated', although the All Black backs had shown an 'astonishing lack of skill'.

But there seems to have been much 1950s euphemism about these reports. Several players were in danger of being sent off, and Skinner and Bekker in particular were warned by referee Bill Fright. Wilf Rosenberg remembers bitterly how he watched one of Don Clarke's kicks go wide of the uprights, only to be signalled good by Fright. (In those days the touch judges did not go behind the posts for attempts at goal.) Rosenberg says he turned to Fright and protested: 'That wasn't over, ref!' And Fright replied: 'Shut your fucking mouth, sonny!' It was that sort of series.

For his part, Danie Craven denied he had said the 1956 side was 'the worst team ever to leave South Africa'. But he admitted it was 'the least serious-minded'.

Springbok flanker Daan Retief scores the try which proved the matchwinner in the brutal second Test at Athletic Park.

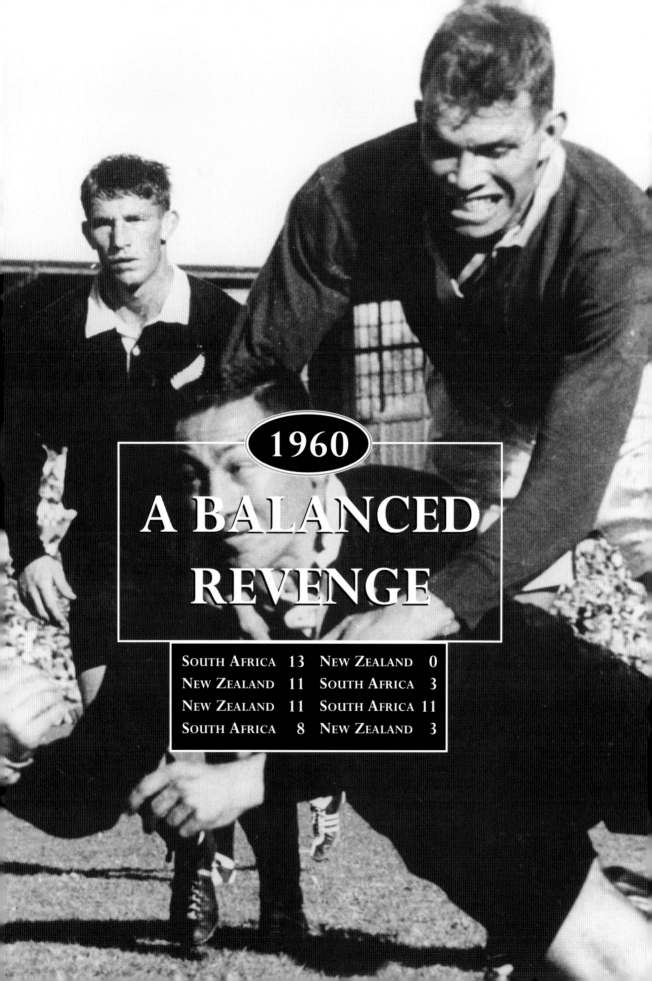

1960

A BALANCED
REVENGE

SOUTH AFRICA	13	NEW ZEALAND	0
NEW ZEALAND	11	SOUTH AFRICA	3
NEW ZEALAND	11	SOUTH AFRICA	11
SOUTH AFRICA	8	NEW ZEALAND	3

CHAPTER SIX

1960
A BALANCED REVENGE

THE THIRD ALL BLACKS IN SOUTH AFRICA

by David Williams

THE 1960 ALL BLACKS nearly didn't tour because of distress in New Zealand at South Africa's continued refusal to accept Maori players in the touring side. Forty years later, it seems astonishing not only that South Africans should have applied such an insulting policy, but that New Zealand was still prepared to go along with it.

There were three survivors from 1956 in the Bok team for the first Test at Ellis Park on June 25: fullback and now captain Roy Dryburgh, lock Johan Claassen and prop Chris Koch. The All Blacks had only fullback Don Clarke from 1956, but they came with the foundation of their great sides of the 1960s, men like Kel Tremain and Colin Meads. In Wilson Whineray they had a captain with that rare quality of being able to earn unquestioned respect from both sides.

True to history, the visiting All Blacks went into the first Test as favourites, yet were beaten by a convincing margin (13–0). *Sunday Times* writer Eric Litchfield described the game as 'the Springboks' finest hour for 11 years'. This judgment breezily overlooked the outstanding performances against British and Australian teams in the early 1950s, thus unconsciously confirming that Springbok rugby prefers to define itself by its contests against New Zealand.

Ellis Park was crammed with a crowd primed by the press to remember the violent defeats of 1956. After 10 minutes, the spectators went silent as Don Clarke attempted a penalty goal from two yards inside his own half. It fell short and, according to the *Sunday Times*, 'there was a gasping sigh like a sudden breeze as 75,000 ceased to hold their breath'. Two minutes later Clarke tried again from the same distance, but sliced the kick. Manager Hennie Muller spent the match on the touchline, crouching tensely like an alert member of the St John's Ambulance.

Twenty minutes after kickoff, winger Mike Antelme made an electrifying break, having come in from the blindside to take the ball just outside Keith Oxlee in the flyhalf position. It was a rehearsed move. The scrum had been just inside the All Black half, and Antelme took Dick Lockyear's pass at full speed, knifing through the orthodox New Zealand backline defence.

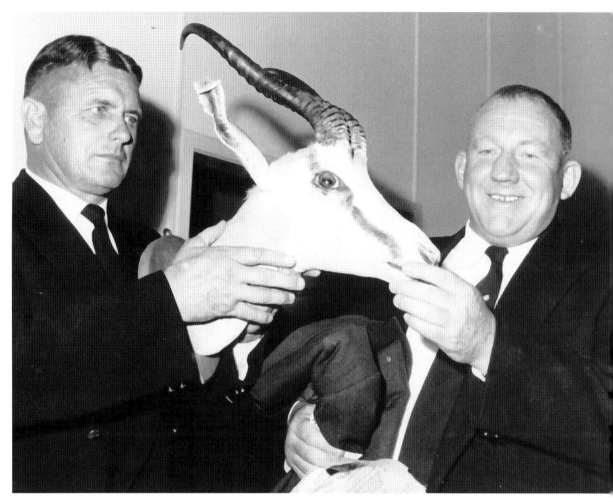

All Black coach Jack Sullivan (left) and manager Tom Pearce have the Springbok head, but their 1960 team failed, as previous tourists had, to win a series in South Africa.

Antelme passed to Ian Kirkpatrick, who drew Clarke and then put Hennie van Zyl away for a try. Dryburgh converted, and the emphatic brilliance of the score seemed to demoralise the All Blacks.

Whineray was apparently so rattled he pulled No. 8 Dick Conway (the man who had had a finger amputated to ensure his availability for the tour) out of the scrum to beef up the backline defence. It was an elementary and grave error: the Springbok pack took command and the All Blacks lost any chance of getting back into the game.

The feeling afterwards was that the Boks were worth far more than Van Zyl's two tries, brilliant as they were. His second try also began with a break by Antelme, but this time Van Zyl had more work to do. Forty yards out when he got the ball, he first shook off the challenge of his opposite number, Russell Watt, then used his awkward, stilted running style to battle through

Clarke, Conway and Kevin Briscoe to score in the corner. Lockyear converted again, and added another three points with a difficult penalty goal (13–0).

In essence, the talented All Blacks had not found an answer to the neat kicking up the sidelines by Oxlee and Lockyear. The tourists seemed sluggish throughout, and some of their forwards appeared to lack commitment: in the second half, it was common to see three or four of them standing off from rucks and mauls. Exceptions were Peter Jones, Colin Meads and Kel Tremain. The key breakdown point for the All Blacks was Lineen at centre, who suffered all afternoon from the Boks' speed on defence and fierce tackling.

There were tears and relieved embraces in the old Ellis Park 'glasshouse' from where the VIPs watched the game. Danie Craven flung his arms round 'Basie' Viviers, the 1956 losing captain in New Zealand. Muller noted his team's superiority had been founded on excellent lineout work, which outweighed the several tightheads conceded. It was the first time on tour, he said, that the All Blacks had met a balanced side. The post-match spirit seemed good, with no complaints from the All Blacks about referee Bertie Strasheim.

Craven said the Boks had played to 'a plan which the All Blacks could not fathom', but he refused to elaborate. Tour manager Tom Pearce said the Boks' play had reminded him of Phil

An extraordinary touch-finder coming up against the Springboks at Newlands. From behind his goal-line Don Clarke found touch on the South African 10-yard mark.

Springbok flanker Martin Pelser, described by Colin Meads as 'one of the hardest, most skilful players in any position I have played against' and a 'bloody pain in the neck', pressurises All Black halfback Kevin Briscoe. Kel Tremain and Lofty Nel watch on.

Nel's 1937 side. New Zealand journalist Noel Holmes said there was not the slightest argument that the better team won. 'What is more,' he wrote, 'you beat us at our own game — the game of tactical kicking and being first to the loose ball . . . I hang my head in shame for having suggested that your forwards might be too slow, even unfit.'

One possible effect of winning as underdog is to bathe in complacency. That may have been one factor in the 11–3 Springbok defeat at Newlands in the second Test. It was also suggested that the altitude in Johannesburg had made the All Blacks sluggish. Whatever the reason, two things were beyond dispute at Newlands: the All Blacks forwards were dominant, and Don Clarke gave the best all-round kicking performance in Test rugby since the days of Bennie Osler. This enabled the All Blacks to turn the tables, driving back their opponents with accurate kicking and then pressing home the territorial advantage, just as Oxlee and Lockyear had done in Johannesburg.

Clarke's amazing performance at Newlands included repeated 60-yard touch-finders, a penalty goal, a left-footed drop goal and a conversion. It may not have been coincidence that Clarke had also succeeded with all three kinds of goal-kick the previous week against Western Province at the same ground. He was settled, confident, bang on form. As if to symbolise the resurgence in All Black forward play, their try was scored by the impressive Meads, who was playing at No. 8. The Springboks had no answer beyond a clever try by Oxlee.

Dismayed at the drastic change in fortune after Ellis Park, the South African selectors dropped three veterans. Chris Koch and Bertus van der Merwe, who had first been together in the Bok front-row in the 1955 series against the British Lions, were finally retired. This meant that ironman Piet 'Spiere' ('Muscles') du Toit was joined in the front-row by Abie Malan at hooker and Fanie Kuhn at prop. Roy Dryburgh was controversially dropped as fullback in favour of the virtually unknown Lionel Wilson, with 24-year-old Avril Malan taking over the captaincy. Lofty Nel at No. 8 was replaced by the faster Doug Hopwood.

In retrospect, it seems the selectors got to the heart of the matter. They knew they had brilliant backs, but Whineray's poor tactics in the first Test had enabled the Boks to mask a lack of energy and pace in their forwards. All the changes proved justified, notably the inclusion of the immensely talented Wilson and Hopwood.

In fact, the side for the third and fourth Tests can be adjudged one of the great Bok selections, with genuine flair in almost every position and a strong emphasis on youth. Only one man, Du Toit, had played for South Africa before 1960, against the French (in 1958). This new generation would go on to achieve a Grand Slam in Britain and beat the 1962 British Lions and the 1963 Wallabies. There were superb loose forwards in Hopwood, Hugo van Zyl and the intensely shy, one-eyed Martin Pelser. In Mike Antelme and Hennie van Zyl, the Boks had two wings who were very fast and difficult to stop. They also had the rare luxury of two slick and settled combinations in the backs: John Gainsford and Ian Kirkpatrick at centre, and Oxlee and Lockyear the halves. Wilson astounded the critics with his courage and composure at fullback and went on to play 27 Tests. But the All Blacks probably had greatest respect for Pelser, described by Meads in 1974 as 'one of the hardest, most skilful players in any position I have ever played against . . . I'd have loved to have him on my side.'

It was appropriate, with both sides containing an unusual proportion of present and future legends, that the third Test, in Bloemfontein, should turn out to be one of the most exciting between the great rivals.

The early exchanges were dominated by New Zealand, but, with the tourists feeling the dry heat of Bloemfontein, the Springboks began to get back into the game. In the twentieth minute Lockyear converted a difficult kick after Tremain had been caught well offside on the New Zealand 10-yard line (3–0). There was no further score before halftime.

Just after the interval New Zealand made it onto the board. This time Lockyear was penalised for putting the ball under his hooker's feet, and Clarke landed a difficult kick (3–3). Two minutes later, South Africa were given a penalty for that familiar All Black offence, obstruction: again

DEFINING MOMENT

Don Clarke Touches Perfection
THIRD TEST, BLOEMFONTEIN, 13 AUGUST, 1960

Don Clarke's kick to level the scores in the dying moments of the third Test, in Bloemfontein, was described by coach Jack Sullivan as the greatest of his career. Clarke had not had a good game overall, especially when compared with his performance at Newlands. If he missed this conversion, the Test would surely be lost and the series out of reach. The pressure was increased by the knowledge that only minutes, possibly seconds, remained in the game. Yet he lined up the ball calmly from an acute angle, neither rushing nor delaying, and it flew high and true to make it 11–11.

Clarke deservedly remains a legend in South Africa because of his all-round performance in the 1960 series. His presence blunted the man-for-man superiority of the Springbok backs. That touchline conversion seemed to sum up his role: if he was on form, as at Newlands, the All Blacks were able to dominate. Where conditions did not suit him, as at Port Elizabeth, they were eclipsed with relative ease.

Lockyear goaled (6–3). Now the Springboks appeared to be getting well on top. Pelser was harassing Briscoe round the scrums and his team-mates were outplaying New Zealand in the loose.

The pressure produced results. Clarke, on his own 10-yard line, had a kick charged down by Pelser. Kirkpatrick picked up the loose ball, cut inside and sent Oxlee over for a try between the posts (11–3). Two minutes later Clarke failed to cut the deficit with a 45-yard penalty attempt and was then caught in possession inside his 25-yard area by Gainsford. With 15 minutes to go New Zealand seemed beaten: their backs had not threatened and their forwards seemed worn down.

With only five minutes to go, Clarke at last found his form and goaled a tremendous penalty kick from five yards inside his own half (11–6).

With a minute to go, Briscoe threw out a bad pass from a scrum on the South African 10-yard line, but the Bok backs were slow to come up. Lineen was able to pick up and pass to Laidlaw, who made 20 yards, drew Wilson and then kicked ahead over the try-line. McMullen got to the ball in the corner in front of the covering Hopwood, and the score was 11–9. Clarke converted coolly from the touchline (11–11). There was only time left for Clarke to place a final signature on a game where he had not always been assured: he fielded a high kick from Wilson and put it safely into touch. The series was still level; now with one Test to play.

'It was a fascinating although not inspiring game,' wrote the New Zealander Noel Holmes, who believed the Springboks had deserved better than a draw. 'The Springbok forwards were machine-like, particularly in the lineouts. The backline tackled solidly and conscientiously, hard up on the line of advantage . . . New Zealand now have a fortnight to consider new tactics — for it seems pretty clear they cannot confidently expect to beat the Springboks at their own game.'

The Springbok selectors made only one change for the fourth Test: Stompie van der Merwe came in at lock for the injured Johan Claassen. They wanted to pick Jannie Engelbrecht on the wing, but he went down with tonsilitis, so Antelme was retained. Conditions were difficult with Port Elizabeth's traditional swirling, battering wind ensuring caution on both sides.

The All Blacks started well and believed they had scored when McMullen, running hard for the line, was tripped by Oxlee's outstretched hand. He fell short, but reached out and placed the ball behind the line. Referee Ralph Burmeister ruled instead that he had played the ball from the ground after the tackle and awarded a penalty to South Africa. (One newspaper noted that black spectators booed whenever a penalty was given to the Springboks.)

New Zealand never recovered from this setback, although they opened the scoring with a Clarke penalty in the 13th minute. Their halfbacks were again harassed efficiently by Pelser and Hugo van Zyl, while the Boks' forwards played superbly as a unit. Again the All Black forwards were less committed, with only Tremain and Meads leaving an impression.

With so much at stake, tempers frayed on both sides. Briscoe and Pelser, who had been niggling each other throughout the series, were lucky not to be sent off. A. C. Parker wrote in the *Cape Times* that the referee was unsighted when Briscoe kicked Pelser, who retaliated with a knockout punch. This violence seems to have been considered as unremarkable, perhaps in view of what had happened in 1956, although later Watt was spoken to for trying to kick Hennie van Zyl.

The All Blacks failed to take advantage of the wind in the first half and were then visibly wearied by it in the second, with Clarke in particular being neutralised. Pelser scored a try from a scrum near the All Black line, Lockyear converted to add to his penalty goal to make it 8–3, and that was the final score. 'The pressure was there all the time,' wrote Noel Holmes of Pelser's try, 'unrelenting and remorseless, and it was just a question of time where the breach would be made'. Terry McLean described the South Africans as 'livelier, more spirited and more efficient'.

Close as the series was, the impression was that South Africa had marginally the better team and played substantially better. They had been unlucky to be held to a draw in the third Test and had thoroughly deserved their victories in the first and fourth. Only in the second match had the All Blacks been able to take and keep control. The Bok combinations were more settled, with a marked superiority at halfback, where Oxlee and Lockyear played together throughout but Briscoe had to work with three different flyhalves (Adrian Clarke, Steve Nesbit and Tony Davies). When the All Black pack did manage to dominate, their backs were seldom able to translate this into points.

1960

THE NEW ZEALAND RESPONSE

THE THIRD ALL BLACKS IN SOUTH AFRICA

by Grant Harding

THE ONLY REAL blight on Wilson Whineray's magnificent record as All Black captain was the series loss to South Africa in 1960. While many factors were involved, the margin of defeat was so slim that the non-award of a try to All Black centre Frank McMullen in the first half of the fourth Test has to be seen as crucial.

Having seen the footage, I can say that if referee Ralph Burmeister had been applying for a driver's license at that time he would have been referred to an optician. There is no doubt McMullen scored. There is no doubt that to say Burmeister erred is too kind. Playing with the benefit of a strong wind, New Zealand needed points in the series decider, and his decision robbed them.

Never mind the fact that New Zealand might not have deserved victory. When has 'deserved' had anything to do with success at Test level? The All Blacks have won many Tests they haven't deserved to win by gaining the crucial scores. This time they were denied that.

Beyond this incident the 1960 series will be remembered for Don Clarke's prodigious kicking, the continuing decline of New Zealand's back play, and the growing anti-tour movement.

Undoubtedly one of the highlights of the tour was Clarke's last-gasp conversion of a McMullen try to draw the third Test, a moment shared with his brother Ian who, as touch judge, signalled the goal.

But reliance on Clarke's boot had led to a 10-man style of rugby — the All Blacks scored just two tries in the series — which played into South Africa's hands. Indeed, during the late 1950s and much of the early 1960s, New Zealand failed to use their backline well, preferring to kick into touch on the full from all parts of the field as was allowed under the rules of the day. Consequently the names of backs from touring teams such as the 1959 British Lions are remembered more fondly than our own.

While there had previously been unease about the non-selection of Maori on All Black tours to South Africa, by 1960 anti-racist sentiment was a growing force. Under a 'No Maori, No Tour' banner, the Citizens' All Black Tour Committee tried to have the tour called off. A petition presented to the New Zealand government calling for it to be abandoned was signed by 162,000 New Zealanders and South Africans. News of the Sharpeville massacre, in which peaceful protestors were shot by South African police on 21 March 1960, simply made the protestors more determined, and would eventually shift the focus from 'No Maori, No Tour' to the apartheid system of South Africa's Nationalist government, which had taken power in 1948, and to whether or not New Zealand should tour at all.

1965

THE SPRINGBOKS' DARKEST HOUR

NEW ZEALAND	6	SOUTH AFRICA	3
NEW ZEALAND	13	SOUTH AFRICA	0
SOUTH AFRICA	19	NEW ZEALAND	16
NEW ZEALAND	20	SOUTH AFRICA	3

1965

THE SPRINGBOKS' DARKEST HOUR

THE FOURTH SPRINGBOKS IN NEW ZEALAND

by Grant Harding

AS A NEW ZEALANDER, it can be peculiar watching South Africa play other rugby nations. Often the Springboks don't appear to be the same passionate, intense, never-say-die bastards we've come to take for granted. At times they even play poorly. By contrast, even moderately talented Springbok XVs have somehow managed to overcome, or stay within reach of, their black-shirted opposition.

That's how it was in 1965 when South African rugby was at a particularly low ebb. On arrival in New Zealand the Springboks were already halfway to hell, having lost their previous five Tests. Naturally expectations were for a comfortable All Black victory, and Wellington's emphatic 23–6 win to take the prized Springbok head in just the second tour match had rugby followers dreaming of complete revenge for 1949.

That the revenge never proved to be quite as sweet as anticipated is still unfathomable to the likes of the then All Black captain Wilson Whineray. In what was his last series, Whineray triumphed over the Boks 3–1, but it has never been enough. He has remained perplexed as to why New Zealand threw away a 16–5 halftime lead in Christchurch in the third Test. Of course, there were practical reasons such as poor tackling, brilliant Springbok back play, and a slackening of the All Black forward effort after they found themselves in such command at halftime. (Remember tries were worth just three points then.)

Nevertheless, it was typical of New Zealand–South Africa clashes down the years. Rarely has one side been completely shut out of a series. Even in 1996, when New Zealand clearly had a more settled selection and more talented players, the first-ever winning of a series in South Africa came down to a do-or-die situation on the All Black goal-line at Loftus Versfeld in Pretoria. Often superior talent has not equalled success in the history of this rivalry. The battle has always been as much mental as it has been about physical strength and skills.

In 1965, it was perhaps natural justice that the Boks avoided a whitewash, as all evidence points to them being hard done by in the first Test at Athletic Park in Wellington, a match played on a soft surface in a typically stiff wind.

A dubious try scored by All Black flanker Kel Tremain was all that separated the two teams, in a 6–3 result. Given first use of the wind, New Zealand had scored only one try — admittedly a well-worked one to the team's sole new cap, winger Bill Birtwistle — as halftime approached. Then, dashing down the blindside, fullback Mick Williment was tackled and appeared to lose the ball forward. Not so, said referee Pat Murphy, who raised his arm after Tremain had gathered the ball and dived over.

In the second half the All Black forwards took masterly control, Ken Gray and Colin Meads dominating the lineouts, from which drives led to scrums, from which the blindside was continually probed by Chris Laidlaw — in other words, the perfect tactics for playing into the wind.

New Zealand's forward dominance had been asserted, and but for 40 minutes in Christchurch that was to be the story of the series. And what a magnificent pack the All Blacks fielded. Whineray, Bruce McLeod and Gray in the front-row, the Meads brothers — Colin and

All Black centre Ron Rangi scores in the second Test at Carisbrook.

Stan — in the second-row, and a back-row of Tremain, Dick Conway and Brian Lochore. Substitute Waka Nathan or Ian Kirkpatrick for Conway, and there would be few who would argue this wasn't the pack of the 1960s. Yet Conway, like Whineray, Colin Meads and Tremain a veteran of the 1960 South African campaign, was an excellent contributor to the series, his first since the visit to the republic.

The All Black forwards' *pièce de résistance* was the second Test at Carisbrook in Dunedin, in which they took the Boks apart 13–0. It was the first time the home team had won the second Test of a series against the old foe. So the Boks approached the third Test on a seven-Test losing streak. Just a few days before the match, South African Rugby Board president Danie Craven arrived in the country. But at halftime, with New Zealand leading 16–5, it didn't appear his presence was proving inspirational.

Rather than growing dispirited at the events of the first half, the Springboks' captain, Dawie de Villiers, had spotted a weakness in the opposition. He believed the All Blacks were showing no interest in defence. Brilliant centre John Gainsford, making a record 29th appearance for South Africa, had carved through once already, and De Villiers pleaded with his forwards for the ball.

In a huddle not far away Whineray delivered his message. That complacency had set in is evident from the fact that, in the years since, nobody has been able to remember what he said.

The Springbok tries that followed were a treat: Brynard flying in at the corner almost too quick to stop on the soft ground (8–16); Brynard again cutting back across the defence, then springing into the air like a gazelle to score by the posts (13–16); then Gainsford on one of those unusual mesmerising runs when the defence fails to recognise the line is coming up (16–16).

With 17 minutes to play it was all square, and so it remained until two minutes from time when Colin Meads, playing a record-breaking 32nd Test for New Zealand, was ruled offside. An unlikely hero, lock Tiny Naude, then stepped up.

Naude's earlier conversions of the tries by Gainsford and Brynard had been from in front of the posts. This attempt was from close to the left-hand touchline, approximately 35 metres from the target, with mud oozing out from the sides of his boots. It wasn't a pretty kick, but somehow it flew far enough to raise the flags and secure an unlikely victory. All Black dreams of a series shutout had evaporated with their concentration, but spectators at the ground were so taken with the Boks' comeback that they gave them warm support.

The jubilant Boks, who had made five changes for the match — including the reintroduction of 1960 No. 8 Doug Hopwood, one of six Bok veterans of that series to play in 1965, and a player believed to have been rejected as tour captain by the Afrikaner element — now had a chance of redemption.

As the fourth Test approached, critics were split on the possible outcomes. Would the Springbok backs once again cut loose? Or would the All Black forwards reassert their dominance? That Eden Park was firm and dry heightened local anxiety.

With their confidence boosted, the Boks fielded an unchanged team, while the All Blacks

Gifted runner John Gainsford mesmerises the All Black defence on the way to his second try in the Springboks' remarkable third Test victory at Lancaster Park.

made four alterations to their backline. Injuries to Williment and winger Malcolm Dick opened the door for Fergie McCormick to make his Test debut and North Otago's Ian Smith (who had played in the first two Tests) to return. Poverty Bay's Johnny Collins, who had played in the first Test, took the place of Moreton, and Mac Herewini came in for Peter Murdoch.

At 3–3 early in the second half, South Africa started to behave in a most un-South African manner. Twice when running out from their own half they lost the ball, and twice the All Blacks scored. On the first occasion Brynard spilled a pass from De Villiers, allowing Birtwistle to glide down the right-hand touchline, stop when challenged and step inside two tackles to score. Then first-five Jannie Barnard — a success in the third Test — failed to find Mannetjies Roux with a pass, and Smith scored.

To make matters worse Barnard once again erred in chipping a kick downfield from a defensive situation. Lochore swooped, beat three tackles and linked with Ron Rangi who put Smith across in the left-hand corner.

Herewini added to the whirlwind scoring with a drop goal to take New Zealand 15–3 ahead with still nearly a quarter of the match remaining. Had South Africa panicked after conceding the first try? Or was their backline more confident of its abilities than it should have been? Whatever the answer, it was rugby suicide, New Zealand profiting from opposition mistakes and sealing a series victory. Prop Ken Gray finished it in style when, on fulltime, he took a menacing stroll round behind the posts, from where McCormick finally got on the board.

In Whineray's 32nd and final Test, and his 30th as captain, the All Blacks had inflicted the most comprehensive defeat South Africa had suffered against any nation. It remained the All Blacks' highest winning margin against the Springboks until the 55–35 thumping at Eden Park in 1997, and the highest score until the third Test of 1981. The All Blacks thoroughly deserved their series victory, having outscored the Boks 13 tries to four.

A particularly wet winter and an arduous travel schedule had not helped the visitors' cause. However, Colin Meads probably summed up the difference between the two sides when he described the South Africans' forward play as 'loose and shiftless'. Coach Hennie Muller, the

Great All Black captain Wilson Whineray has played his final Test, and conquered his final challenge . . . a series victory over South Africa.

PLAYER OF THE DECADE

COLIN MEADS
BORN: 1936
POSITION: LOCK FORWARD, FLANKER, NO. 8
PLAYED SOUTH AFRICA: 1960, 1965, 1970 (10 TESTS)

Durability alone makes Colin Meads a special figure in the New Zealand–South Africa rivalry. His participation in three series over 10 years was an outstanding feat.

But it was the bizarre happenings of the 1970 tour to South Africa which carved his name indelibly into All Black–Springbok folklore.

Having started the tour in form which moved journalist Terry McLean to declare 'he had never played better and seldom so well', the 34 year old veteran was tipped to inspire the All Blacks to a first-ever series victory in South Africa. Then tragedy struck when he suffered a broken arm as a result of foul play in an ill-tempered midweek match against Eastern Transvaal. It was an injury that should have ended his tour, but after missing two Tests the All Blacks' vice-captain convinced the authorities he could play with a leather casing protecting his arm. Few New Zealanders questioned the sanity of the decision such was the mana of the man. Meads duly played the last two Tests, although he subsequently maintained he only played the third at the request of his three fellow selectors. 'The arm was not right and I knew it,' he said. Predictably he was unable to influence the final outcome.

In the 1960 series in South Africa, Meads had appeared at lock (twice), No. 8 and flanker. In the second Test victory, at Newlands in Cape Town, playing at No. 8, he scored a crucial try with his trademark one-handed finish. After that tour McLean wrote, 'Colin Earl Meads by general consent became the greatest forward in the team.'

Meads enjoyed further success in the 1965 series victory at home, in which he locked the All Black scrum in all four Tests with his brother Stan. In the final Test at Eden Park, the attitude that made him an All Black great showed itself near halftime when his brother lay on the ground in agony. The exchange between them went like this:

Colin: 'How are you?'

Stan: 'No bloody good.'

Colin: 'Well, you'd better get yourself right. In one minute's time you and I have got to lock a New Zealand scrum together and we're not going backward.'

Colin Meads knew what it took to battle the Boks.

A strident supporter of sporting contact with South Africa, Meads coached the New Zealand Cavaliers in 1986, and was All Black manager during the series in New Zealand in 1994 and the World Cup the following year. That tournament ended a 39-year association begun when, as a 20-year-old, he scored a try for Wanganui–King Country against the 1956 tourists.

DEFINING MOMENT

Second Half Scoring Blitz
FOURTH TEST, AUCKLAND, 18 SEPTEMBER, 1965

The All Blacks' three tries within five minutes in the third quarter of the fourth Test put the series beyond doubt. But this was a series the All Blacks were destined to win from the start. They were simply the better team.

great destructive force of the 1949 series, lamented the lack of commitment shown by some of his players throughout the tour. According to journalist Terry McLean, one of their problems was that they did not lack commitment when it came to New Zealand women, amongst whom they were popular.

As the 56,480-strong Eden Park crowd sang 'Now is the Hour' to send off the popular tourists, whose visit had excited none of the unhealthy intensity of 1956, there was an air of uncertainty with regard to the future. Just two days after the South Africans' Christchurch triumph, news had come through that their prime minister, Dr Verwoerd, had made a speech indicating Maori would once again not be welcome in their country in 1967. With the tide turning against such sentiment — there had been occasional demonstrations in 1965 — the 1967 tour was in jeopardy.

1965

THE SOUTH AFRICAN RESPONSE

THE FOURTH SPRINGBOKS IN NEW ZEALAND

by David Williams

There are three periods of extended misery in Springbok rugby history: 1964–65, 1972–74 and 1996–97. In the first of these, defeats in the first two Tests on tour against New Zealand created an appalling record of seven losses in a row. South African press lamented the weakness of the Springbok forwards, their reluctance to back up, their inept rucking and their poor lineout work. In the second Test the lack of defence round the scrum led directly to two All Black tries.

The puzzle in 1964–65 was that the tourists had excellent backs in men like John Gainsford and Jannie Engelbrecht, and could draw on some considerable forwards: Rhodesian prop Andy McDonald, who had fought a lion with his bare hands and won; Natal hooker Don Walton; and legends past and future such as Frik du Preez, Tiny Naude, Jan Ellis, Doug Hopwood, Tom Bedford and Lofty Nel. Players of their calibre would have excelled in any era, so clearly there was something wrong with the South African spirit, although it also has to be remembered they were up against one of the great All Black packs.

It may have been relevant that, in the country as a whole, relations between English- and Afrikaans-speakers had been somewhat strained since the achievement of a republic in 1961. The National Party's rigid separation not only of black and white, but also of schools for the two predominant white cultural groups, had had its effect.

For the first time in Springbok history, the fate of a series was less important than victory in a particular match, so anxious was everyone to break the losing run. In the Springbok camp before the third Test, nothing was as it seemed. Hopwood, the Cape English-speaker who many believed should have been captain in the first place, was restored as No. 8 and unofficial pack leader. The controversial Transvaal Afrikaner Jannie Barnard, capable of brilliance but inconsistent, replaced Natal's pedigreed veteran flyhalf, Keith Oxlee. When Naude kicked the penalty goal for a 19–16 win, the relief was out of proportion to the achievement, indicating how severely a leading rugby nation had lost its confidence.

Ironically, the lack of Springbok leadership manifested itself in the build-up to that great penalty goal under pressure. When the kick was awarded, winger Gert Brynard was keen to take advantage of the turned backs of the retreating All Blacks by running in for a cheeky try. But Naude insisted the responsibility in the clinging mud would be his. There is no mention in any account of a decision by captain Dawie de Villiers.

TOP RIGHT INSET: Springbok lock Tiny Naude lets fly with his famous kick . . .
RIGHT: And it's over, the third Test is won, the series can be saved, Naude (right foreground) is a hero.

I am convinced the statements about Maori by Prime Minister Verwoerd, in what became known as his Loskop Dam speech, shamed both the country's rugby fans and the players who were on tour in New Zealand. They were creatures of their time and little was said, but to this day the sour aftertaste informs perceptions of the 1965 tour, which has become a backwater in the history of South African rugby. It was probably the only series this century in which the Springboks lacked passion as well as the necessary skills, and were, therefore, lacking in honour.

PLAYER OF THE DECADE

FRIK DU PREEZ

BORN: 1935

POSITION: LOCK FORWARD

PLAYED NEW ZEALAND: 1965, 1970 (8 TESTS)

It is tempting to choose Dawie de Villiers as the key Springbok player of the 1960s. He captained his country in 22 Tests, with series victories over the All Blacks, the British Lions, Australia and France. He went on to personify an Afrikaner ideal: Springbok captain, ordained minister, cabinet minister.

But the people's hero of the 1960s was the Northern Transvaal lock and flanker Frik du Preez. He was years ahead of his time in his capacity to influence all-round play. He scored numerous spectacular tries and a few startling drop goals, and in a Bok jersey was successful with 22 kicks at goal. His sheer athleticism meant that, in the days before lifting was tolerated in the lineout, he frequently rose to take the ball unchallenged.

Danie Craven called Du Preez a genius,

a once-in-a-lifetime phenomenon. If he was flawed by laziness in training, he was also legendary for his mimicry of the radio commentators and his ability to lift the morale of his team-mates. Despite being dropped from the national side several times, he would for many years hold the record for the most Springbok Test caps (38).

Frik du Preez was renowned for his loyalty. Once, when a few Pretoria companions were singing the praises of Piet Uys, the Northerns scrumhalf, and running down Dawie de Villiers of Western Province, Frik stood up for his national captain over his provincial team-mate. 'Piet is my friend but I have the greatest respect for Dawie. I don't drink with people who talk behind other men's backs,' he said, and left the clubhouse.

1970

DEFINED BY A TACKLE

SOUTH AFRICA	17	NEW ZEALAND	6
NEW ZEALAND	9	SOUTH AFRICA	8
SOUTH AFRICA	14	NEW ZEALAND	3
SOUTH AFRICA	20	NEW ZEALAND	17

CHAPTER EIGHT

1970

DEFINED BY A TACKLE

THE FOURTH ALL BLACKS IN SOUTH AFRICA

FEW TEST MATCHES in the 80 years of rugby between Springboks and All Blacks can have been more eagerly awaited than the first game in the 1970 series. If there was ever a time when everyone knew the unofficial world championship was at stake, this was it.

by David Williams

The All Blacks came to South Africa on a winning streak unprecedented in international rugby, stretching to 17 Tests, while the Boks had lost 10 of their 24 Tests since the beginning of 1965. The tourists' performances in the provincial games increased the awe in which they were held. In the five weeks before the first Test the All Blacks won all 10 of their matches, scoring 56 tries to their opponents' six. True, some of the opposition was provided by minor rural provinces, but the victims included the powerful Transvaal and, on the last Saturday before the first Test, a tough Free State side.

Perhaps for the first time since 1921, the home side in a Springbok–All Black clash was the clear underdog. Very few local journalists were predicting a home win, but the more thoughtful among them had cautiously drawn some comfort from the match against Free State. It was pointed out that, although the All Blacks had won 30–12, they had not been impressive. It was speculated that the All Blacks had become stale by playing their stars into the ground. Why, for instance, had the tour management found it necessary to play Fergie McCormick in seven of the first nine games? And Colin Meads in five of the first six, even against weaker sides? As if to support this judgment, Meads had sustained a broken arm in a Wednesday match against lowly Eastern Transvaal (the worst injuries often happen in the less important games) and would be out of the first two Tests at least.

For reasons of respect and honour, any Springbok would have preferred to play against the legendary Meads, but his absence undeniably represented a chink in that formidable black armour. And for those who looked beyond the impressive tour statistics, another chink seemed to have appeared against Free State. The young 1.88-metre-tall centre Joggie Jansen, unknown

Just three minutes into the first Test at Loftus Versfeld in Pretoria, Springbok flanker Piet Greyling toes ahead, and seconds later his captain Dawie de Villiers (at left) scored a try which started the All Blacks on the downward spiral to defeat for the first time since 1965.

outside Bloemfontein until the Springbok trials the previous week, had shocked the composed New Zealand backline with his crash-tackling. Jansen's running with the ball was no less impressive: in one charge he took on three men in succession, blasting through the tackles of Grahame Thorne, Earle Kirton and Wayne Cottrell. The *Rand Daily Mail* compared Jansen to one of the great Springbok centres, John Gainsford: rare praise indeed, in South Africa, for an uncapped player.

So it was no surprise Jansen was one of four new caps in the Springbok team for the first Test, at Loftus Versfeld in Pretoria on July 25. The others were Ian McCallum, the green young fullback from the University of Cape Town and Western Province; Piston van Wyk, the successor to Gys Pitzer in the no. 2 jersey for both Northern Transvaal and South Africa, and the Northerns lock Johan Spies, who had played his way in at the expense of the out-of-form Gawie Carelse. Dawie de Villiers was the captain, playing in his 21st Test; while the coach, Johan Claassen, had locked the Springbok pack in New Zealand in 1956.

The last All Black practice contained no kicking, only handling and running drills. This emphasis was gloomily reported as an omen that the Boks would be run off their feet. And as if to ensure the All Blacks would get enough ball to do exactly that, New Zealand journalists who attended the Springbok practice session were reported to be 'disappointed' with the size and calibre of the South African front-row.

On the morning of the match, the *Rand Daily Mail* headline announced sombrely: 'All Blacks have the edge.' Pessimism abounded in the newspaper predictions. 'There is a shakiness about the Springbok midfield,' wrote Neville Leck, 'with Mannetjies Roux off form and Jansen new.' Piet Visagie at flyhalf was also out of form, argued the experts. The Boks could be suspect at loose forward, while the All Black forward play on tour indicated the South African tight five would lack technique.

A resentful note was struck by Paul Irwin, the most robust and aggressive of South African columnists. He alleged Lochore's All Blacks had a 'deliberate policy of giving away penalties in order to save certain tries against them . . . I say they are out-and-out wreckers.' Nearly 30 years later we might say that nothing has changed, but Irwin did always set out to be provocative. He had also pointed out that the Springboks were flouting International Rugby Board regulations by gathering more than 48 hours before a Test. The final Springbok 'trial' on the Tuesday, he said, had been little more than an excuse for a practice. Irwin was one of the very few journalists to predict a South African victory at Loftus Versfeld.

If Newlands is the shrine of South African rugby, Loftus is the citadel, favourite stadium of the city that was, in 1970, at the heart of Afrikaner military and administrative power. On that still, dry highveld Saturday afternoon, none of the 53,000 spectators could have expected the All Blacks to be 9–0 down after 12 minutes. But that is what happened, and the consensus remains that the whole 1970 series was decided in that brief period. Napoleon wrote that, in war, 'the moral is to the physical as three is to one'. And four distinct moments marked South Africa's snatching of the moral ascendancy.

In the fourth minute, while the sides were still trying to settle, flanker Piet Greyling unexpectedly kicked through a ball won from a scrum near the All Blacks' 25-yard line. The ball skidded over the try-line, and the darting Dawie de Villiers won the race for the touchdown. Loftus Versfeld's parched atmosphere suddenly moaned and sang. We had not been expecting this! And so soon!

The seventh minute saw the key blow for South Africa. New Zealand flyhalf Wayne Cottrell received the ball from a set scrum and moved to the blindside. As Cottrell shifted weight to pass, Joggie Jansen's shoulder hurtled into his stomach in a textbook tackle that was ruthless but fair. Suddenly Cottrell was on his back, knees up, head on the grass and eyes closed, gasping with surprise and windedness. He stayed there for some minutes, receiving first aid. The Loftus murmur that had followed De Villiers' try swelled to a roar: these All Blacks were not as tough as we had thought!

Just minutes later, as if the rugby gods had decided such a tackle deserved to be rewarded with points, Visagie put over a drop goal from an unpromising position while on the run after a lineout, and Ian McCallum put over an astonishing kick from beyond the halfway line after Laidlaw had been penalised for offside. With McCallum converting another penalty for offside, the halftime score was 12–0, and there was now no question that these All Blacks could be beaten. Although the Boks only added another five points in the second half, to win 17–6, the victory was emphatic.

PLAYER OF THE DECADE

BRYAN WILLIAMS

BORN: 1950

POSITION: WINGER, CENTRE THREE-QUARTER

PLAYED SOUTH AFRICA: 1970, 1976 (8 TESTS)

Not even the series defeat in South Africa in 1970 could dim the brilliance of Bryan Williams. One of the first four Polynesian players to tour the republic, the 19-year-old was credited with the greatest post-World War II tour performance by an All Black.

The young Samoan ended the tour having notched up 14 tries in 13 appearances — a fabulous effort, but not the whole story of his genius. His ability to sidestep effortlessly off both feet had to be seen to be believed, and some of the tries he scored were masterpieces.

A big man — he stood 1.78m and weighed 89 kg — Williams devastated his opponents. Fellow All Black Fergie McCormick wrote of him on the tour: 'He's a bloody six million dollar man.'

In the first Test loss, Williams scored the All Blacks' only try. It was a typical 40-metre effort, past and through the defence, after a Sid Going blindside break. In the final Test he scored another try, finishing it by evading three players in the in-goal area to touch down under the bar.

His greatest try was against Eastern Province. When a pass went behind him, he stopped and back-heeled the ball in soccer fashion between two opposition players, picked it up and beat three other defenders before racing away to score under the bar. His form was so good that NZBC commentator Doc Williams said, 'They'll never stop him', when he still had three men to beat!

It was one of the many selection vagaries of the 1970 tour that Williams was chosen as centre for the third Test. The match proved to be notable for just one fact: the All Blacks'

only points came from a Williams' penalty goal.

During the tour Williams became the focus of coloured and black South African supporters' affections, and he believed he had knocked a chink in their country's armour regarding apartheid.

'I felt I had illustrated to white South Africans how I, a Samoan, could compete on their level and excel. I hope I also illustrated that good manners and acceptable social behaviour were possible from someone they had previously regarded as a second-class citizen. When I returned I was branded naive by some of those who opposed all contact with South Africa, but I didn't see it that way. I felt I had made a significant contribution.'

It wasn't as if he had been closeted from the apartheid system. A cousin thought it prudent not to kiss him when he arrived in South Africa; some coloured guests of his were treated shabbily by a hotel's management; a riot broke out in Kimberley between whites and coloureds after he was lifted shoulder high by the latter at the conclusion of a game; and when he toured again in 1976 he was affected by tear gas used to disperse a downtown riot.

Williams never reached his 1970 form again, but was equal top try-scorer on the 1976 tour and contributed 43 points with his boot. Because the established goalkickers did not perform, he reluctantly took several kicks during the Test series. In the third Test, at Newlands, he landed a 55-metre penalty goal, the ball still climbing as it went between the uprights.

It had all been set up in that first quarter of an hour. The Bok tight forwards were uncompromising and the loose forwards fast and shrewd. Above all, there was enormous assurance at halfback. De Villiers and Visagie, like McCallum behind them, would go on to torment the All Blacks right through the series. At Loftus, Visagie's tactical kicking repeatedly placed Fergie McCormick out of position, while McCallum's positional sense proved immaculate.

Inevitably, as in the postmortems after any contest between these rugby giants, there were harsh words. Former Bok centre Wilf Rosenberg described the All Blacks as 'a team of crumblers' who had turned to 'jittery jelly-beans' after Jansen's tackle on Cottrell. Rosenberg thought they had been overtrained to the point of exhaustion. The injured Meads, having sat in frustration in the crowd, complained that there had been 'nobody to tidy up'. Chris Laidlaw was blamed for allowing the first try by De Villiers and for conceding a penalty for being offside, but it was also recognised he had been concussed as early as the fourth minute. The New Zealand journalist Peter Devlin described it as 'a great Springbok performance' and acknowledged the All Blacks never recovered from that 'crippling' first 12 minutes.

Former Springbok Ben Myburgh went to the heart of the matter when he wondered why Lochore hadn't even attempted to pressurise McCallum with high kicks, and asked what had become of New Zealand's driving forward play. Indeed, while Lochore's performance as a player was praised, it seemed that his captain's tactical sense had been shattered. It was Lochore's aimless lobbed pass, following a tap penalty by replacement scrumhalf Sid Going, that resulted in an interception and a soft try by winger Syd Nomis, sealing South Africa's win.

Before the second Test at Newlands, the Springboks riled journalists by choosing to train behind the walls of Pollsmoor Prison in Cape Town. The Boks were less confident than their fans about a second victory in the series. Perhaps coach Johan Claassen, a naturally conservative man, sensed everything could not go South Africa's way again. But his secretive approach indicated a lack of assurance that was ominous.

The All Blacks had to win at Newlands to retain a realistic chance of a series victory, and they did so with ruthless intent, helped by the kind of luck that had gone South Africa's way at Loftus. They gained more possession from the loose and the set pieces, having gained in options through astutely moving Brian Lochore to no. 3 in the lineout. But it was a game where robustness tipped over into dirty play. According to Chris Greyvenstein, the 'rucks were so fierce that it sickened many in the crowd'.

New Zealand were worth more than their 6–0 lead at halftime, after tries by Laidlaw and flanker Ian Kirkpatrick. But in the second half the Boks got back into the match with Joggie Jansen's try, scored under great pressure after taking a clever reverse pass from Visagie (6–5). Then, 25 minutes into the second half, another All Black offside infringement was punished by McCallum (8–6). Could the Springboks hang on to make safe the series?

Controversial veteran Mannetjies Roux made the crucial mistake. The whole of Newlands groaned when he tackled Bill Davis from a blatantly offside position, almost in front of the posts

Powerful and fast Springbok winger Gert Muller heads upfield with Grahame Thorne in pursuit during the third Test at Port Elizabeth. Muller's three tries in the final two Tests were a decisive component of the Test series result.

and deep in South African territory. McCormick had been kicking like a novice but he goaled the penalty and New Zealand led 9–8 with minutes to go. 'Now followed the most uncompromising three minutes of a Test that I have ever witnessed,' wrote Fred Labuschagne in the *Sunday Times*. 'A series of three rucks showed just what the combination of weight, determination, patriotism and studs can do to the human body.' The All Blacks kept possession and won the game. Brian Lochore, who had brought off a match-saving cover tackle on McCallum near the end, described it as the hardest Test he had ever played.

But the scoreline flattered the Springboks. New Zealand had come close to scoring at least four more tries. De Villiers had been dominated by Laidlaw, who this time had had all the luck when he got a good bounce after a Springbok lineout tap, to go over in the corner for New Zealand's first try. Mannetjies Roux was made the scapegoat for conceding the final penalty and it was assumed he would be dropped.

The match had been tense and violent. Piston van Wyk came out from a ruck bleeding from mouth and nose, and had to be replaced by Robbie Barnard. But the South African anger was reserved for Fergie McCormick. He committed a 'blatant and extremely dangerous stiff-arm tackle' on Syd Nomis, who 'hit the deck like a man struck by a bazooka shell', according to the *Sunday Times*. Nomis needed three minutes of first aid and eventually carried on without one tooth and with two others loosened. He had been following up his own kick after making an interception, and there was no excuse for McCormick's foul. The incident led to much media comment, including the suggestion that touch judges should be empowered to alert the referee to dirty play. (Administrators took heed a quarter of a century later.)

With the series all square, the build-up to the third Test in Port Elizabeth on August 29 was intense. Another All Black win was widely predicted, although there was much muttering in the pubs about the selection of Colin Meads. The South African Board ruled he could play with a 'protector' on his broken arm, but there was no question that the hard cast might be dangerous to other players. Bryan Williams, who had been really dangerous on the wing for New Zealand, was moved to centre, which probably weakened the All Blacks' attacking potential.

No doubt spurred by the return of Meads (for his 50th Test), the South African selectors decided the Springbok pack needed toughening. They controversially recalled two hardened veterans: the huge Northerns prop Mof Myburgh (aged 34), who had been in and out of the Bok team since 1962; and No. 8 Lofty Nel (35), who had seen action against the 1960 and 1965 All Blacks but had played only nine Tests since. This smacked of Afrikaner conservatism at its worst. The Bok pack might be tougher but it would also be slower and heavier, less likely to counter the handling, driving game that was still expected from the All Blacks. Calls to drop Roux were ignored, and the Boks fielded an unchanged backline.

Preparations were tense and draining. But while the South Africans had time to relax at home and take stock, the All Blacks had to keep travelling. From the second Test at Newlands they went to George, then back to Cape Town, then further up the coast to East London and Durban, back to Cape Town, and finally up the Garden Route to Port Elizabeth. They had now been on the road in South Africa for over two months and must have been getting tired.

Port Elizabeth had recently experienced some of the worst floods in South African history and perhaps the evidence of physical damage and the mood in the city unsettled the players on both sides. In any case, Boet Erasmus is always a difficult ground. Being set in a natural gorge, it is laid out from east to west rather than north to south. It is seldom full and it lacks atmosphere even when internationals are played there. Wind and rain seem to make Boet Erasmus even more depressing.

Whatever the reasons, it was agreed both sides were well below form for the third Test. But the Springboks were better able to rise from the trough and they delivered a surprisingly convincing victory, winning 14–3. Western Province winger Gert Muller had been relatively quiet in the first two games, but now his talent forced its way through. He scored two thrilling tries: the first when Dawie de Villiers fed him on the blindside, the second after the much-criticised Mannetjies Roux had kicked the ball out of Bryan Williams' hands.

Although the All Blacks could still square the series in Johannesburg on September 12, the wear and tear of a long tour was showing. Northern Transvaal were barely dispatched (19–15)

A meeting of greats . . . Colin Meads charges upfield clutching the ball under his broken arm, while Frik du Preez moves in for the tackle.

the previous Saturday, in a fixture that in those days was known as the 'fifth Test' for touring sides. Chris Laidlaw needed an appendix operation, and his understudy, Sid Going, was sporting a knee injury. Coach Ivan Vodanovich confessed he was shaken by the tremendous depth of South African rugby. The All Blacks were no longer sure of their best team and they made no fewer than eight changes and one positional switch (Williams moving back to the wing) for the game at Ellis Park. They used 27 of their 30-strong tour party in the series, whereas the Boks picked only 17 men.

The All Blacks came agonisingly close to winning that final Test. They gave the Bok pack a battering, but in the end went down 20–17. They were beaten to some extent by fatigue and injury (Going was troubled by his knee and Lochore played much of the second half with broken ribs), but mainly by a familiar selection of Springbok match-winners. As Peter Devlin put it: 'The Springboks just kept playing the kind of rugby New Zealanders could not match.'

The series is won . . . Springbok captain Dawie de Villiers is carried shoulder high from Ellis Park in Johannesburg after his team won the fourth and final Test 20–17.

Ian McCallum's positional sense was again superb and he kicked four penalties, one of them a monster from 65 yards. McCallum had also told flyhalf Piet Visagie before the match that the new All Black flyhalf, Blair Furlong, was a reluctant defender. In the fifth minute, after a Springbok wheel near the New Zealand 25-yard line, Visagie took the inside gap past Furlong and the dozing All Black loose forwards. He was tackled on the try-line but forced his way over to score. After 45 minutes the Boks were leading 17–3, a huge margin in those days.

The All Blacks fought their way back to 17–14. But after another Joggie Jansen crash-tackle, Roux snatched the loose ball and put Gert Muller away for the Boks' second try. That took the score to 20–14 — the first time New Zealand had ever conceded 20 points in a Test. Gerald Kember made it 20–17 with another penalty, but there were no more scores thereafter. The Springboks were visibly relieved when the final whistle blew. Now they could justifiably claim to be the world champions.

DEFINING MOMENT

Joggie Jansen Tackles into History
FIRST TEST, PRETORIA, 25 JULY, 1970

Those who saw Joggie Jansen's tackle on Wayne Cottrell at Loftus Versfeld still talk about it. So do those who may have been a thousand miles away listening to the match on the radio, but who have gradually come round to the view that they did, in fact, see that tackle. Men still approach Jansen at rugby dinners to discuss it. Perhaps, like all legends, it has grown in the telling. But the fact is that it was recognised at the time as having had a dramatic impact on an entire series, primarily because it had given the Springboks a great surge of self-confidence. The late Chris Greyvenstein, greatest of South African rugby writers and always measured in his judgments, believed Cottrell was never the same afterwards. And nor were the All Blacks in that series.

But was Jansen's tackling really that impressive when compared to the frequent big hits of the 1990s? The answer must be yes, because he was so destructive. He seems to have had the ability and the presence to disrupt an entire opposition backline, not merely block a particular movement. His tackles were also genuinely offensive, in that the ball often went loose, to be snatched up by him or one of his team-mates.

Springbok lock Frik Du Preez (No. 4) delivers a knockout tackle on All Black halfback Chris Laidlaw in the early stages of the first Test at Loftus Versfeld. Does Dawie de Villers' (extreme right) expression symbolise the completion of a pre-match plot?

1970

THE NEW ZEALAND RESPONSE

THE FOURTH ALL BLACKS IN SOUTH AFRICA

by Grant Harding

ALL GREAT ERAS must inevitably be defined by an end. On 25 July 1970, a great All Black era of 52 matches without defeat since 1965, including 17 internationals, ended with an emphatic loss at Loftus Versfeld. There could be no complaints.

Grainy as the black-and-white footage of the day was, there was no mistaking the superhuman effort of the Springboks. Tackles were fierce — none more so than Joggie Jansen's fair challenge on Wayne Cottrell, and Frik du Preez's unfair closed fist effort to disorient Chris Laidlaw. Forwards hit rucks as one. Goals were landed. Try-scoring chances were taken. The All Blacks, having lorded it over 10 provincial opponents prior to the Test, simply could not adjust their game to the ferocity of the Springbok challenge.

It was the end of an era, but the foundations of success had begun to crumble long before.

The tour had been scheduled for 1967, but New Zealand would no longer tolerate a visit to the republic without multi-racial representation. With no backdown forthcoming from South Africa the tour was cancelled, and All Black coach Fred 'The Needle' Allen saw his chance of revenge for 1949 fade. Instead he took his team to the UK and France, where it finished a 17-match tour unbeaten, thrilling crowds with 15-man rugby. Sensing political skullduggery at the New Zealand Rugby Football Union headquarters, Allen jumped, thinking he would be pushed following the 1968 season. It was a judgment made on a sixth sense, that he wasn't 'flavour of the month'. Whether that was so or not, it surely would have been difficult for the NZRFU to dump an unbeaten coach.

That was strike one, for Fred Allen was this era's coach.

Then, at the end of 1969, the powerhouse of the All Black scrum, prop Ken Gray, announced his retirement. Privately he was against the following year's tour to South Africa, even though the Pretoria government had relented on the issue of a multi-racial team. He reasoned that if South Africa beat New Zealand, they would use that to endorse their apartheid system. Strike two.

With the fourth tour underway, the All Blacks most experienced player, Colin Meads, making his second tour of South Africa, was playing extraordinary rugby. Despite his 34 years, he was in form equal to, if not better than, his previous best. That was until a midweek game against Eastern Transvaal at a place called Springs. Well, Springs took the spring out of Meads' step — or, more precisely, an opposition boot did. In what was surely a cynical foul, Meads' arm was broken by a kick. From then on, therefore, the All Blacks would also be without Meads. And they were already without Kel Tremain, too, who had been dropped in 1969 and promptly ended his lengthy All Black career.

Two more All Black greats, experienced in the ways of the Springboks, absentees as the series began. Strike three? Perhaps not. We'll call it foul ball. Because from that moment on the All Blacks were on the edge of failure, and they found the methods to achieve that failure.

Certainly their provincial record was awe-inspiring, leading to milestones such as the most tries by a touring team and individual (Grahame Thorne) in South Africa. But the All Blacks found the fast-and-loose style of rugby they played could not be translated to the Test matches. There were grumblings about referees not playing advantage, late tackling, offside play and the like. Justified or not, the All Blacks' inability to adjust to their opponents and the referees meant a talented team failed just as their predecessors had. Furthermore, it is apparent coach Ivan Vodanovich's training methods left much to be desired, though he was obviously a popular man, and tactical appreciation was non-existent. Endless fitness exercises had prop Brian Muller quipping that 'he would need to play more matches to become sufficiently fit for the training runs'.

All Black halfback Chris Laidlaw remembers asking Earle Kirton if he'd been given instructions before the second Test at Newlands. The answer was, as he suspected, in the negative, so the two theorised that kicks in behind the opposition would nullify the Springboks' offside play in midfield. That theory played a part in the only victory of the series.

Yet after that victory, Vodanovich and his selection committee made four changes for the third Test. Included in the reshuffle was the foolish recall of Meads, wearing an arm protector, and the moving of Bryan Williams to centre, when a natural centre, Thorne, was available. Three long-serving All Blacks — centre Bill Davis, prop Brian Muller and hooker Bruce McLeod — were dumped. The pattern was the same after each Test — four changes had been made after the first, and an incredible eight followed the disastrous third.

The All Blacks failed to fire a shot in the third Test, and the woes of Fergie McCormick, who was receiving hate mail for perceived foul play on Syd Nomis in the second Test, were heightened by Williams taking over the goalkicking. Admittedly McCormick suffered when hit in a fierce Piet Greyling tackle early in the match, but his kicking form was lamentable anyway.

Although the All Blacks lost the final Test by just three points, the weaknesses which had plagued them — defensive lapses and mistakes behind the advantage line — were once again highlighted. Error-free rugby had disappeared under the weight of easy provincial victories — and, according to Laidlaw, under the weight of extracurricular activities. In his early autobiography, *Mud In Your Eye*, he asserted that the team had split into two camps: 'the triers by day and the triers by night'.

Yet this All Black team still came close. In the end, however, the brilliance of some of the younger players — Williams, Thorne, Going, who many believe should have been preferred to Laidlaw for the first three Tests, and Kirkpatrick — was not enough to overcome all the obstacles. Many mighty contributors to the All Black cause were at the end of their careers, and unfortunately some of them played like it. One who didn't, Thorne, also ended his All Black career, moving to South Africa to marry a woman he met on the tour. They later divorced.

The only happy endings from this tour were for the Springboks. New Zealanders were left to contemplate the names and deeds of, in no particular order, Hannes Marais, Mof Myburgh, Lofty Nel, Jan Ellis, Piet Greyling, Frik du Preez, Johan Spies, Piston van Wyk, Dawie de Villiers, Piet Visagie, Gert Muller, Joggie Jansen, Syd Nomis, Mannetjies Roux and Ian McCallum. Even today, the nine-year-old boy in me gets a shiver down his spine when thinking of those players. On four Saturdays in July, August and September of 1970 they made their mark.

In 1973 many of them would have toured New Zealand, but Labour prime minister Norm Kirk decided it was in the best interests of his country that the tour be called off. A police report had predicted violence on a scale never seen in New Zealand, and he was not prepared to take the consequences.

Bryan Williams continued to evade players in the in-goal area before scoring in the fourth Test.

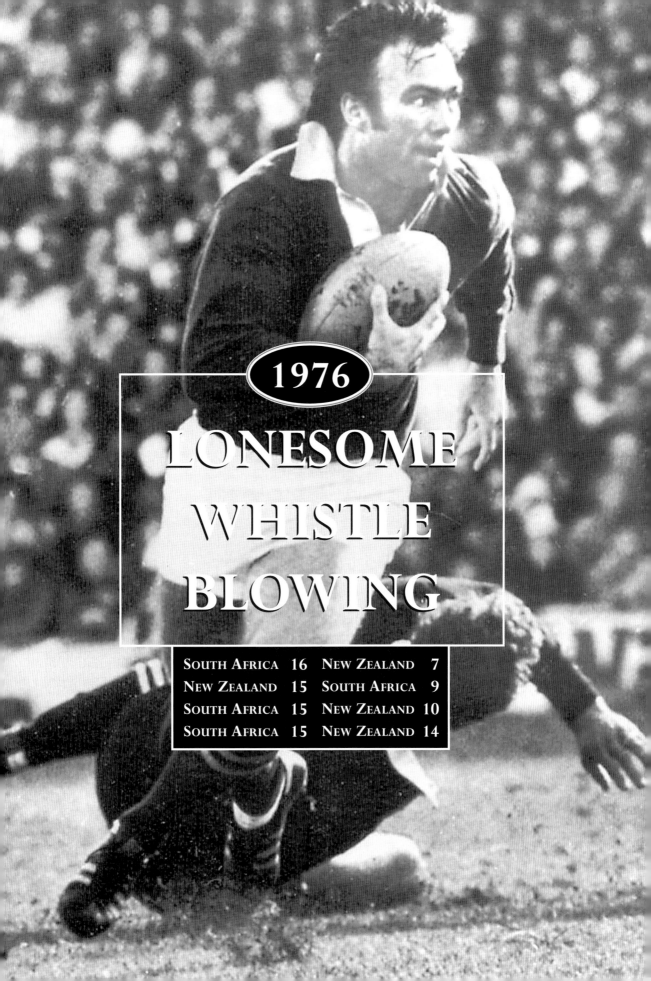

1976

LONESOME WHISTLE BLOWING

SOUTH AFRICA	16	NEW ZEALAND	7
NEW ZEALAND	15	SOUTH AFRICA	9
SOUTH AFRICA	15	NEW ZEALAND	10
SOUTH AFRICA	15	NEW ZEALAND	14

CHAPTER NINE

1976
LONESOME WHISTLE BLOWING

THE FIFTH ALL BLACKS IN SOUTH AFRICA

by David Williams

SPRINGBOK RUGBY BADLY needed a good series against Andy Leslie's 1976 All Blacks. Isolation had begun to bite and there had been limited success since 1971, when Hannes Marais had led the Boks on an unbeaten tour of Australia. In 1972 England had shocked a smug South African rugby establishment with an 18–9 win in a one-off Test at Ellis Park. There was no international rugby for the Springboks in 1973, and the following year saw the ultimate humiliation: a virtual whitewash in four Tests against a great British Lions side led by Willie-John McBride. It was no consolation that an earlier Lions side, containing many of the same brilliant players, had beaten New Zealand at home in 1971, or that the Boks had beaten the French in two Tests in 1975. What was needed to restore Springbok (and white South African) pride and confidence was a win against the All Blacks.

Like Brian Lochore's 1970 side, the tourists dominated the provincial fixtures, but Leslie's men did not invite comparable awe. A week before the first Test, Western Province beat them 12–11 in a tense fixture that confirmed No. 8 Morne du Plessis as the right man to captain the Springboks (as his father Felix had done in 1949).

As the teams prepared for the first Test, in Durban, it was announced that Egypt had become the 29th country to boycott the Olympic Games in Montreal — a direct protest against the All Black tour. A month earlier, the huge black township of Soweto, outside Johannesburg, saw the shooting of hundreds of schoolchildren as police panicked in dealing with protests against Afrikaans as a medium of instruction. John Vorster's government cracked down, and whites escaped by watching rugby. (As it happened, the 1976 series was the first to be broadcast in South Africa on TV.)

On the Tuesday before the Test, the All Blacks beat the Gazelles, a junior Springbok selection, with a last-minute try. (Future Springbok coach Nick Mallett was the Gazelles No. 8.) There were reports in the press of a tourist conspiracy to 'get Bosch' by fair means or foul. Gerald

Springbok flyhalf Gerald Bosch proved the difference in the series, but he was given more than his share of chances.

PLAYER OF THE DECADE

MORNE DU PLESSIS

BORN: 1949
POSITION: NO. 8
PLAYED NEW ZEALAND: 1976 (4 TESTS)

Morne du Plessis was one of those select few Springboks who overcame provincial prejudices and selectorial doubts over his ability to achieve national household-name status. Nearly 20 years after he last played in 1980, a newspaper poster can refer simply to 'Morne' and everyone will know who the story is about.

The son of 1949 captain Felix du Plessis, Morne began his career as Springbok No. 8 at the age of 22, in three Tests on the great 1971 whitewash tour of Australia. He missed the home disaster against England in 1972, then made the side for the first Test against the 1974 British Lions. The Boks lost 12–3 and the selectors panicked, first moving Du Plessis to the flank, then dropping him completely. He reclaimed his place and was made captain against the French in 1975.

It was against the All Blacks in 1976 that Morne established himself not only as a great player but also a great captain. Although he was relatively quiet in the first two Tests, his physical courage and superb defensive work in the third gained him the respect nationally that until then had been extended mainly by Western Province alone.

By 1980 he was a national institution, and he played an inspirational role that year in the series defeat of Bill Beaumont's British Lions, followed by a crushing 37–15 victory over France.

The South African rugby community was deeply shocked when Morne announced his retirement in January 1981. It had been taken for granted that he would lead the Springboks to New Zealand. Surely this would be the pinnacle of his career. Danie Craven made a personal appeal to him to change his mind, without success. Morne had lost the passion, and that was that.

Morne continues to command enormous respect. He served with distinction as manager of the 1995 World Cup side, but perhaps his most important contribution to rugby following his retirement was the founding of the Chris Burger Fund for disabled players, named after one of his Western Province colleagues who died after being injured in a game.

Tough, honest, uncompromising, patriotic but critical, the perfect gentleman: Morne du Plessis seems to embody all that is great in the Springbok tradition.

Bosch of Transvaal was enjoying cult status at the time. He was the third modern South African flyhalf to be an unusually talented all-round goalkicker, following in the footsteps of Keith Oxlee and Piet Visagie. Absurdly, there were even debates about whether his round-the-corner place-kicking style, then fairly novel, actually put him offside before he kicked the ball.

But there was nothing frivolous about a Test against the All Blacks. Joggie Jansen, whose tackle on Wayne Cottrell had inspired the Boks in 1970, was picked as a reserve. When asked to smile for the camera during a photo session, he refused: 'You don't smile when you may be playing the All Blacks.'

Du Plessis was superb in a match that the All Blacks dominated for the first half but could not finally control. Bosch was unexpectedly subdued — he had taken the field with flu — and, contrary to expectations, the Boks ran the ball and created two great tries by Gerrie Germishuys and Edrich Krantz. It was fullback Ian Robertson, rather than Bosch, who scored a drop goal from 40 metres, although the All Blacks were convinced the ball had gone under the crossbar. In the end the Springboks' 16–7 win was convincing and deserved.

In the second Test at Bloemfontein, 'South Africa's problems started in the front-row and ended at fullback', according to one scathing newspaper summary. Encouraged by their try-scoring in Durban, the Boks tried to run the ball whenever they could. These were strange tactics, given their most creative back, Peter Whipp, had been inexplicably dropped, along with the impressive Edrich Krantz.

Paul Bayvel had a poor match at scrumhalf, not least because his opposite number, Sid Going, and the All Black loose trio of Kevin Eveleigh (playing in place of Ken Stewart), Ian Kirkpatrick and Andy Leslie were outstanding. Going had a great all-round game, with sensible tactical kicking and two penalties and a conversion. Added to Doug Bruce's drop goal and a try by Joe Morgan, this was more than enough to hand South Africa a 15–9 defeat. But towards the end it took Peter Whiting's outstanding cover tackle to save a seemingly certain try by flanker Boland Coetzee.

Morne du Plessis admitted that the All Blacks had deserved to win. True to form in All Black–Springbok history, the touring side had won the second Test after losing the first. Until the 1990s, the only years in which this did not happen (out of 11 tours) were 1949 and 1965.

The Springbok selectors decided their pack needed beefing up for the third Test at Newlands, which was done to great effect. They also implicitly acknowledged their error in dropping Whipp by bringing him back at centre, although they waited another Test before admitting Ian Robertson was a better choice at fullback than the erratic Dawie Snyman.

South Africans could not understand the New Zealand selections for the Newlands game. Eveleigh had been a key factor in their second-Test victory, and Doug Bruce had been coolly impressive at flyhalf, yet both were dropped. It was also puzzling that the fearsome prop Bill Bush, who had earned great respect in the provincial games, could still not make the Test side. Batty was picked again on the wing, even though his knee had broken down in Bloemfontein, causing him to miss the second half.

The South African pack changes proved decisive. New prop Johan Strauss in particular dislocated the All Black scrum with his utter domination of Perry Harris, although he was accused of boring in illegally. With the forwards dominant, Bayvel came back to form with

Is that a smirk on Johan Oosthuizen's face? The Springbok midfielder is about to profit from a calamitous All Black backline error and set up victory in the third Test at Cape Town.

excellent tactical kicking, and it was Sid Going's turn to have a stuttery game. Perhaps the poor quality of Going's service explained why Duncan Robertson seemed obsessed with kicking everything that came his way. With Gerald Bosch opposite him, it was unlikely the All Blacks could win a kicking duel.

Again, true to history, with the series at stake, the third Test was a grim affair. Du Plessis, who again had an outstanding and inspirational game, was kicked in the mouth, while Whiting was dangerously raked, it being said afterwards he could easily have lost an ear. The All Blacks became angry with the interpretations of referee Gert Bezuidenhout, who had also whistled the second Test. Their frustration boiled over when, with the All Blacks leading 7–6, he disallowed an attempt at goal by Sid Going after the ball had fallen over three times and more than 60 seconds had elapsed.

Whipp's return at centre gave the Bok backline much more cohesion, which further frustrated the All Blacks. The score reflected the tight contest. There was one try each and both were opportunistic: Oosthuizen intercepted after a fumble by Kit Fawcett, and Bruce Robertson followed his own kick ahead when Germishuys threw the ball away after getting into trouble on his own line. Bosch and Williams got two penalty goals apiece, and in the end a 40-metre drop goal by Snyman three minutes from time was decisive. But Bosch had missed another six attempts at goal.

For the fourth Test, at Ellis Park, the tour selectors at last seemed to get it right. They picked Bill Bush and brought back Eveleigh and Doug Bruce. But Batty was selected again on the wing (and once more he would break down, this time midway through the second half).

Bezuidenhout was in charge for his third successive Test of the tour. Even the home critics believed he should have awarded a penalty try when Bruce Robertson, set to score by touching down a loose ball in the Springbok goal area, was openly obstructed by Johan Oosthuizen. The law says that, in such a case, the referee must be sure that a try 'would' have been scored, and Bezuidenhout was apparently uncertain that Robertson would have beaten Whipp and Chris Pope to the ball. At that point a penalty try would have put the All Blacks into a 17–12 lead; as it was, Bryan Williams converted the ordinary penalty. New Zealand's 14–12 lead was then overtaken when Bosch goaled his last penalty for a 15–14 win. The All Blacks' bitterness over Bezuidenhout's refusal to award a penalty try was exacerbated by the knowledge that they had scored two tries to one.

Danie Craven was in no doubt: he said publicly that the All Blacks should have won at Ellis Park, and there was a widespread feeling that a drawn series would have been a fair conclusion. At the post-match function Andy Leslie called for neutral referees in Test rugby, but the South African media were not slow to point out that, before the tour, the All Blacks had rejected an offer of neutral officials.

'Generally speaking,' wrote Chris Greyvenstein, 'it was an All Black team that could not bear comparison with any of their predecessors.' That seems harsh, given Leslie's side had needed only another two points in Johannesburg to draw the series.

DEFINING MOMENT

The Bok Selectors Get it Right
THIRD TEST, CAPE TOWN, 4 SEPTEMBER, 1976

The announcement of the Springbok team for the third Test suggested the selectors had finally put in place not only the eight best forwards in South Africa at the time, but also (it does not always follow) the best possible combination. And so it proved at the scrums, rucks, mauls and lineouts in the final two Tests.

Powerful Free Stater Rampie Stander was the only front-row survivor from Bloemfontein, as the selectors dropped Western Province partners Derek van den Berg and Robert Cockrell. In came the veteran Northern Transvaal hooker, Piston van Wyk, who had played against the 1970 All Blacks, and Transvaal strongman Johan Strauss for his first cap. There had been much clamour for the inclusion of Transvaal lock Kevin de Klerk, and now he was brought in to replace the injured John Williams. De Klerk and Moaner van Heerden proved a robustly aggressive lock partnership that did much to ensure Springbok forward dominance. The power of the front five was bolstered by a flank who could have played lock, Klippies Kritzinger, and the restless, creative energy of Boland Coetzee and Morne du Plessis.

This pack played together only twice as a unit, but it was one of the Springboks' greatest. On the day the team was announced, many South African fans at last had the sense that the best available team was representing them (although there was still a question mark, removed for the fourth Test, about Snyman instead of Robertson at fullback).

Perhaps the Springboks were superior man for man, but they did not play to their potential. The culture of Springbok rugby at the time, after the shattering defeats of 1974, was defensive and insecure. Bosch's boot was expected to be decisive, and he did score 33 of the side's 55 points in the series, but the Bok tactics were distorted as a result. They either ran the ball recklessly or withdrew into their shells. The service from the talented Bayvel was erratic, and the sharp three-quarters beyond Bosch were often neglected. It was the Springbok pack, led outstandingly by Du Plessis, that ensured victory in the end.

The overall impression is that the 1976 All Blacks, like their 1970 predecessors, were undermined by poor selection decisions and lightweight coaching.

Despite the excitement of narrow points margins in the Tests, the 1976 tour is somehow not one that lingers in the collective memory of South African rugby.

1976
THE NEW ZEALAND RESPONSE

THE FIFTH ALL BLACKS IN SOUTH AFRICA

by Grant Harding

WHAT POSSESSED THE New Zealand Rugby Football Union to accept South African referees for the 1976 Test series when, before the tour, neutral referees had been offered by the South African Rugby Board? That the answer to this has never been given is understandable, since there can be no sane one.

Just as there was no sanity in the refereeing of Gert Bezuidenhout. His final crucial call of the series, at Ellis Park in Johannesburg, would have been laughable if it hadn't made us cry. There he was giving his first lineout penalty of the day — possibly a correct call — for Gerald Bosch to kick a final penalty goal for South Africa to win the fourth Test 15–14 and wrap up the series 3–1. Why laughable? Because throughout the series he was caught on camera watching South African lineout exponents being lifted — illegal at that time — sky high by supporting players. Nary a peep was heard from his whistle.

Such decisions simply added to New Zealanders' feelings of frustration at being cheated. As a 15 year old schoolboy who idolised the All Blacks, John Walker and Muhammad Ali — a curious mix given the year's events — I simply grew to hate Bezuidenhout as I watched the matches beamed in live from South Africa for the first time.

How could he rule out Sid Going's penalty-goal attempt in the third Test because the ball fell over? The law clearly stated that for any kick that took over 40 seconds, time was added on.

How could he allow the scrum-collapse fiasco in the third Test to continue on and on?

How could he give a drop goal to Dawie Snyman in the latter stages of the third Test when the attempt clearly missed? (Maybe it didn't, but by then we were paranoid.)

How could he deny Bruce Robertson what were, quite clearly, two penalty tries in the fourth Test?

How could he allow a chicken-hearted thug like Moaner van Heerden to wreak such havoc, with Morne du Plessis not far behind?

There were other causes for complaint, including the first Test referee, Ian Gourlay — chosen by New Zealand because of his English-sounding name — who penalised All Black captain Andy Leslie for offside play in a maul! Of course, the All Blacks were threatening to score at the time.

Nevertheless, the failure of the All Blacks to win the series was as much a reflection of their own shortcomings as it was of the low standard of refereeing. Flawed selection pre-tour and on tour certainly played a part.

The defection of 1975 All Black fullback Joe Karam, and the consequent selection of Laurie

South Africa's political turmoil was experienced first-hand by All Blacks Ian Kirkpatrick and Bryan Williams when police fired tear gas at demonstrators in downtown Cape Town.

Mains (too slow) and Kit Fawcett (inexperienced), meant the All Blacks went on tour without a fullback they could trust. That both the selected players' goalkicking proved unreliable meant part-timers Sid Going and Bryan Williams were entrusted with the responsibility. Their 33 per cent success rate was not good enough by any standard.

Then there was the switching of first-five Duncan Robertson to fullback for the first and fourth Tests, a move that met with limited success. His missed tackle on Gerry Germishuys allowed the Bok winger to score in the first Test.

Fawcett proved to be the black sheep of the touring party, and despite obvious ability never played for New Zealand again. Whether he deserved the criticism that painted him as lacking in maturity is for those who were there to comment on and for him to counter. It is unforgivable, however, that he has taken all the responsibility for the try that gave South Africa the crucial lead in the third Test. That he has been blamed for dropping a pass that allowed Johan Oosthuizen to score is certainly more to do with personality than fact.

Fawcett's culpability can be questioned on two counts. Firstly, what were the All Blacks thinking of when they called a move to be executed wide out more than 60 metres from the opposition line? They were leading just 7–6, and had a left-winger — Grant Batty — whose knee was so badly damaged there was no way he could cover for the fullback.

Secondly, Fawcett might have dropped the ball, but the pass from second-five Joe Morgan was what I would term a 'floater'. By that I mean the ball wasn't guided in a spiral motion in front of Fawcett, who was running right. Instead it was flicked from the hands, wavered in the air and dipped back high and into Fawcett's left shoulder.

Why dwell on this incident? Certainly not to criticise Joe Morgan, who played above himself throughout the tour and scored a memorable try in the second-Test victory. Rather, there were other players involved in the decision to make the move — players far more experienced than Fawcett. If they regarded him as so erratic, why involve him in such a tactic?

Great player that Grant Batty was, there is no way he should have been able to command a Test position given the serious knee injury he carried throughout the tour. Unfortunately there was no ready alternative in the back-up, because Neil Purvis and Terry Mitchell didn't possess the speed needed for South African grounds.

Meanwhile, at home, players like goalkicking Bay of Plenty fullback Greg Rowlands, and big, fast wingers such as Brian Ford and Terry Morrison, or elusive types like Peter Goldsmith watched on television.

Coach J. J. Stewart's on-tour decision-making also bordered on the bizarre at times. After winning the second Test, he dropped first-five Doug Bruce and flanker Kevin Eveleigh, both of whom had performed mighty deeds. Bruce had dropped a goal and directed operations with skill and composure, while Eveleigh had been all-purpose, especially on defence, where he'd rattled Bok first-five Gerald Bosch and, in one memorable moment, cut Morne du Plessis' legs from underneath him with such ferocity one feared amputation.

Then there was the prop crisis. Illness had debilitated Kerry Tanner, while Brad Johnstone, a hero of the second Test, was sent home with an injury, only to play a short time later. Johnstone's replacement was Manawatu's Perry Harris, who was then drafted into the third-Test team after just one appearance. Admittedly Bill Bush was struggling with an ankle injury, but many believed he should still have played. For the entire 80 minutes Harris was collapsed to the ground by Bok strongman Johan Strauss, once again with nary a peep from Bezuidenhout. Instead the referee hassled Going about his putting-in, urging him to feed collapsed scrums.

Great moments in the series for New Zealand were few, but the second-Test heroics of halfback 'Super Sid' Going (eight points from his goalkicking, a reverse pass to set Morgan free and a between-the-legs pass for a Bruce drop goal) and lock Peter Whiting were special. Wasn't it strange, therefore, that both were rucked on their heads in the third Test? At least Going only lost his temper — Whiting almost lost an ear.

All Black second-five Joe Morgan scores the crucial try of the second Test at Bloemfontein.

This time New Zealanders had watched on television, and there was discontent at the method of defeat. There was a belief that the All Blacks' inability to win in South Africa had more to do with sinister Afrikaner forces than anything else. And those forces were steeled by the world's increasing impatience with South Africa's apartheid system. Rugby was that nation's way of fighting back, and the All Blacks simply had to be beaten.

Bezuidenhout is alleged to have declared as much. It is said he told the All Blacks it was all very well for them to be upset, but he had to live in the country.

It is incredible now to contemplate that the 1976 All Black tour to South Africa closely followed a day (June 16) when 176 mostly young protestors who wanted school subjects taught in English, not Afrikaans, died as the result of police gunfire in Soweto, Johannesburg. By the end of the tour some 3000 black and coloured people had been killed or injured in the escalating violence.

It is also incredible to contemplate that New Zealand's continuing desire to play rugby against South Africa could interfere with an event as great as that year's Montreal Olympic Games. But it did, with 28 countries boycotting the event.

Remembering back to 1976 is not difficult. It was a time when sport was all to me. That year John Walker won an Olympic gold medal in the 1500 metres. It was a great achievement, but I would have preferred Tanzania's Filbert Bayi on the dais beneath him. I don't need to guess what my other hero, Muhammad Ali, would have thought about the All Blacks tour to South Africa.

There was one last lesson to be learnt before the protest groups finally won their battle, but the All Blacks would not return to South Africa for 16 years.

1981

WHEN SPORT AND POLITICS MIX

NEW ZEALAND	14	SOUTH AFRICA	9
NEW ZEALAND	14	SOUTH AFRICA	9
SOUTH AFRICA	24	NEW ZEALAND	12
NEW ZEALAND	25	SOUTH AFRICA	22

CHAPTER TEN

1981

WHEN SPORT AND POLITICS MIX

THE FIFTH SPRINGBOKS IN NEW ZEALAND

by Grant Harding

IT WAS EARLY one Sunday morning in Wellington, several months before South Africa's 1981 tour was to commence, that I got my first taste of what the winter would bring. As I turned from Cuba Street into Crosby Terrace, where I shared a grubby student flat, I came across a group of policemen gathered underneath the drive-in area outside Preston's Wines and Spirits.

At first I walked on, but like a moth to a flame I was drawn back to the surreal sight before me. An officer stood to the left of the others, who were lined up in two columns like a pair of rugby teams about to take the field. All had face shields, all had batons drawn, all were looking straight ahead. I asked the officer, 'What's up?' Without answering he told me it would be better if I moved off home. The next morning I heard they'd raided the Black Power headquarters in the street directly opposite ours.

'Warming up for the Springbok tour,' was a flatmate's sharp assessment.

Sure enough, the Springboks' arrival would soon make such sights commonplace, and for the duration of their visit New Zealand would be a country divided.

Years of protest, first under the slogan 'No Maori, No Tour', and eventually 'No Contact with South Africa' because of the apartheid policies of that nation's white government, had had no impact on the New Zealand Rugby Football Union. It was therefore predictable that the NZRFU, led by chairman Ces Blazey, would proceed with the 1981 tour, and all the more so when Prime Minister Robert Muldoon said the National government would not stand in its way (although, at the same time, he cunningly advised that the tour should not proceed, so as to be seen to have acted in accordance with the Gleneagles Agreement, a document signed by Commonwealth heads of state favouring censure of sporting contacts with South Africa).

The Springboks duly arrived on July 19, having flown via the United States because of an Australian ban on providing transit facilities. Included in their ranks was the first-ever coloured

The dress and demeanour of these Wellington protestors highlights the gulf that emerged between police and protestors at the height of the 1981 tour.

Springbok, utility back Errol Tobias. Tobias had played two Tests against Ireland before the tour, and was destined to play four more as a 34-year-old in 1984, two against England and two against South America. It was a disappointment of the tour that his abilities as a midfield back or first-five were not seen to best effect. The wet conditions did not suit his natural attacking game, and it wasn't long before he was viewed as a token non-white selection. Such an assessment was unfortunate, and anyone who saw his form in 1984 will have realised it was also flawed.

But perhaps the South Africans themselves should shoulder the blame for Tobias' difficulties on tour. I know of at least one hotel worker at the time — my wife — who states categorically that Tobias cut a lonely figure in the dining room throughout his stay in Napier, and there were rumours of other instances of poor treatment.

Protests at the airport and at the venue of the first game, in Gisborne, were controlled by police, but it was not long before the threat of civil disorder, which had led Labour Prime Minister Norman Kirk to cancel the 1973 tour, was realised.

In Hamilton several hundred protestors broke through perimeter fences and made their way onto the ground. Eventually the match was abandoned, although that had more to do with the knowledge that a light plane had threatened to crash-land at Rugby Park.

What followed set the scene for the tour. When the protestors finally left the field, they were pelted with objects by angry spectators, and there were reports of brawling for several hours afterwards.

There is no doubt, also, that some within the police were annoyed at commissioner Bob Walton's handling of the situation. They felt the protestors should have been forcibly removed, and that by holding back the police had shown weakness. The battle lines were now drawn not only between protestors and supporters, but between protestors and police. It became common to see protestors as well as police wearing protective gear.

After Hamilton, consideration was given to calling the tour off, but the government decided it could not back down in the face of violence, especially in an election year. Undoubtedly the disorder brought out the worst in some police, just as it attracted criminal elements to the protest movement, leading to some of the most turbulent scenes in New Zealand history outside Eden Park on the day of the third Test.

For many ordinary New Zealanders, the majority of whom had favoured the tour when it had started, the scenes at Hamilton had come as a great shock. Some wanted the Springboks to go home, others wanted the police to keep the peace. The polarisation of views meant few families, communities or workplaces were immune to the emotional tempest whipped up by the tour. Not even all All Black families were united.

Through all the disturbances the Springboks stuck stoically to their task, and by the time of the first Test they had won six matches. However, the selection of their first Test team raised eyebrows. Omitted was long-serving winger Gerrie Germishuys, captain Wynand Claassen and other players viewed as first-choice when the tourists had arrived. Another veteran of 1976, Theuns Stofberg, was named captain. The pack appeared to be chosen for size rather than mobility, and the team featured four new caps, including winger Darius Botha, brother of dominant first-five Naas Botha.

The All Black team featured just one survivor of the 1976 tour to South Africa, flanker Ken Stewart. He owed his place to the absence of All Black captain Graham Mourie, who had made himself unavailable for the series because of his views on apartheid and on the damage he believed the tour could do to New Zealand. Strangely enough Mourie admitted he might have gone to South Africa if the All Blacks had been touring there, and almost definitely would have gone had he been selected in 1976.

Brilliant centre Bruce Robertson had also made himself unavailable, ending his career. He had visited coloured and black communities during the 1976 tour and had not liked what he had seen, including a lack of effort to develop rugby among the disadvantaged majority.

New Zealand nevertheless fielded a powerful combination, featuring just one new cap, Northland winger Fred Woodman. New captain Andy Dalton had several experienced lieutenants in support, including Gary Knight, John Ashworth, Andy Haden, Stewart, Murray Mexted, Dave Loveridge and Stu Wilson.

Because Christchurch hotel workers refused to service the Springboks, the visitors prepared for the first Test in Invercargill before transferring to the Linwood rugby club on the Friday before the game. This pattern was repeated for the second and third Tests, the tourists preparing in Napier for the Wellington game and in Whangarei for Auckland, then sleeping under the Athletic Park and Eden Park grandstands the night before the match day. Somehow one expected the Springboks to be unaffected by this, reasoning that the laager mentality would steel them against such adversity and make them even more difficult opponents. In reality it was tough for them.

Just prior to kickoff at Lancaster Park, a group of demonstrators burst through the barbed wire erected around the playing field and scattered numerous sharp objects across the muddy field. It took some time for protestors and objects to be removed, but the start of play was delayed by only five minutes.

For the first 25 minutes of the game South Africa's giant forward pack and the boot of Naas Botha threatened to sweep the All Blacks away. Botha kicked a drop goal, and New Zealand's lightweight fullback, Allan Hewson, was left crumpled and concussed after fielding yet another 'Botha bomb'.

It wasn't until a defensive scrum yielded a tighthead that the All Blacks were able to ease the pressure and begin to turn the match with powerful driving play. In time, the All Black loose-forward trio of Mexted, Mark Shaw and Stewart achieved total domination, and a Shaw punch sat flanker Eben Jansen on his backside every bit as firmly as Jansen's brother Joggie had sat All Black opponents down with his ferocious tackling in 1970.

Tries to first-five Doug Rollerson (from a powerful blindside dash) and centre Stu Wilson (from a brilliant run from broken play, although it did appear Ken Stewart was accidentally offside during the movement) gave New Zealand a 10–3 lead at halftime. This was extended 11 minutes after the break, when Shaw drove over after irresistible lead-up. The All Blacks continued to dominate, peppering the goal posts with three drop goal attempts, until the Springboks, as is their way, came back with a try to giant lock Hennie Bekker two minutes from time. Botha converted from the sideline, upping the heart rates on both sides, but the All Blacks withstood a last attack to go one up in the series.

Despite the 5000 protestors outside the ground, the 2000 police and the barbed wire, it had been a match of quality. Most of the typical features of a New Zealand–South Africa Test had been on display, including an all-out brawl started when Bernie Fraser made a late head-high tackle on Springbok fullback Gysie Pienaar. During the ensuing scuffle Shaw was felled from behind by Darius Botha, and a Springbok clearly stomped an All Black on the ground. Players on both sides would have faced suspensions under modern citing procedures.

The All Blacks had found a way to win, but had no doubts that an improved Springbok team would face them in Wellington. Not that the build-up to that match was particularly fruitful for the visitors. The match against South Canterbury was cancelled as the police, whose tactic was now to meet the protestors well away from the ground, were concerned about the ease of access to Fraser Park. Then Nelson Bays were easily defeated, before a titanic clash against New Zealand Maori ended in a lucky draw, Colin Beck being awarded a dubious late drop goal.

The Boks made seven changes to their Test team, six in the forwards (among them the

All Black lock Andy Haden leads the charge into Springbok territory in the first half of the deciding third Test at Eden Park.

inclusion of Claassen, as captain, at No. 8), while New Zealand made three, two forced on them late in the week. Incredibly farming duties ruled out Gary Knight, while lock Graeme Higginson broke his ankle during training. Auckland prop Greg Burgess and Frank Oliver, who had played the fourth Test in 1976, were called in.

The outcome of the match can be traced to Dalton's decision to play upwind, for in the first 10 minutes South Africa raced to a 12–0 lead. An orthodox passing movement created a try for reinstated winger Germishuys, and Naas Botha's unerring boot did the rest of the damage.

By halftime the score was 18–3, and with the Springbok forwards in top form there was to be no escape by the All Blacks. By fulltime Botha had contributed 20 points to his team's 24–12 victory, from a conversion, five penalty goals and a drop goal — at that time an all-comers' record in a Test against New Zealand.

The All Blacks were now feeling the pressure of the tour. While their guests had enjoyed reasonably comfortable accommodation in the Athletic Park lounge, they had been housed in a

PLAYER OF THE DECADE

ANDY DALTON
BORN: 1951
POSITION: HOOKER
PLAYED SOUTH AFRICA: 1981 (3 TESTS)

At a time when New Zealand–South Africa rugby relations were threatened by the ever-growing anti-apartheid movement in New Zealand, Andy Dalton stood firm to his principles of sport for sport's sake. His attitude was typical of the rugby mentality, which believed politics should be kept out of sport.

In 1979 Dalton experienced the consequences of involvement with South Africa when he toured the republic with a World XV. He was forced to take unpaid leave from his job in the civil service and while he was away, his wife received several anonymous and abusive phone calls.

Dalton made his captaincy debut for the All Blacks in the tumultuous 1981 series, when preferred choice Graham Mourie made himself unavailable by opposing the tour. While often under police protection, and

saddened by the barbed wire that surrounded Test grounds, Dalton regarded the series victory as a triumph. He also maintains his stand would be the same today.

In 1985 Dalton was to captain the All Blacks to South Africa, but a court injunction obtained by two Auckland lawyers destroyed his goal, leaving him 'psychologically and mentally destroyed'. The son of 1949 New Zealand vice-captain Ray Dalton, his aim after becoming an All Black was to win a series in South Africa, and thus avenge the whitewash his father's team had suffered.

The following year he led the rebel New Zealand Cavaliers to the republic, but was rendered a non-participant in the second game when his jaw was broken by a vicious punch from Northern Transvaal forward Burger Geldenhuys.

cold dungeon-like dressing room for several hours before kickoff to outwit the protestors. Huddled in blankets, they had not enjoyed the experience.

After three more provincial victories for the Springboks, the series decider at Eden Park arrived.

The enormity of the occasion did not stop the New Zealand selectors from introducing four new Test caps. The silky skills of Southlander Steve Pokere were recruited at second-five, moving Lachie Cameron (who had replaced Andy Jefferd for the second Test) to centre, and Wilson to his best position on the right wing, ahead of Fred Woodman. Young Auckland lock Gary Whetton and Bay of Plenty flanker Frank Shelford, who had played superbly for New Zealand Maori against the tourists, replaced veterans Oliver and Stewart, while Geoff Old stepped in for injured Manawatu team-mate Shaw, and Knight returned from his farm.

Injuries forced three changes to the Springbok pack, hooker Robert Cockrell, lock Bekker and flanker Rob Louw replacing Willie Kahts and second-Test standouts Johan de Villiers Visser and Stofberg.

As a series decider, the ensuing encounter had everything. As a moment in history, it had even more. Vicious battles between police and protestors raged outside the ground, injuries occurring on both sides, while inside a rugby Test like no other was fought. An unforgettable occasion was ensured by a low-flying Cessna that dropped flour bombs, leaflets and flares throughout the

Will it? Won't it? All Black fullback Allan Hewson is anxious, referee Clive Norling is all concentration, and Springbok prop Okkie Oosthuizen can hardly bare to look. Moments later it was Hewson punching the air in triumph after his controversial penalty goal succeeded and ultimately won the 1981 series.

match. In the second half a flour bomb knocked All Black prop Knight to the ground, causing him to suffer headaches for months afterwards.

But it was not just the antics of protest gone mad that should be remembered, for the rugby Test played at Eden Park that day was as dramatic, as tension-filled, as controversial and as skilful as any in the memorable history of New Zealand–South Africa rivalry.

Given first use of the wind New Zealand was 16–3 ahead by halftime, courtesy of tries by Wilson and Knight, and goals from the left-footed Hewson and right-footed Rollerson.

Wilson's try was the most spectacular of the series. From a midfield ruck, Pokere's and Rollerson's quick hands had Hewson flashing towards the line. With the defence streaming across, the fullback threw a visionary pass, centimetres in front of the retreating Botha, into the hands of Wilson, who distanced Botha and stepped inside Ray Mordt to live up to his reputation as a consummate finisher.

With the All Black forwards on top, it appeared a New Zealand victory would be a formality. The Springboks, however, had other ideas. Twelve minutes into the second half Mordt chased a kick and bustled Hewson out of the way for one try, then chipped ahead and took the bounce in front of Hewson and Pokere for another. Botha converted both and kicked a penalty goal, leaving the tourists trailing by just one point (18–19) with 22 minutes remaining.

A wonky Rollerson drop goal extended the All Blacks' lead, until with a minute remaining on the clock, the Springboks mounted an attack just outside the New Zealand 22. A heavy tackle saw the ball jolt loose, but Botha was first to react, toeing it onwards and giving Mordt the chance to crash through Loveridge and complete a hat-trick.

Everyone present believed Botha would now win the series for South Africa. It was not an easy kick, however, perhaps eight metres in from the right-hand touchline — and the delay caused by the removal of the senseless Loveridge didn't improve matters. To All Black relief and Springbok dismay, the ball drifted outside the right-hand upright, but there seemed some fairness in the prospect of a 22-all draw.

As the sole judge of time, Welsh referee Clive Norling knew there was at least five minutes to play. He would later claim stoppages caused by the Cessna, which had once again buzzed the ground as Botha had prepared for his vital kick, had been added on with the agreement of the two captains, Dalton and Claassen.

At a scrum in Springbok territory, halfback Divan Serfontein caused his hooker, Robert Cockrell, to strike early by baulking the feed. Both actions were offences, and Norling gave New Zealand a free kick. Replacement halfback Mark Donaldson surged forward, only to be tackled by players who were ruled to have not retreated 10 metres. A penalty was duly awarded, and Hewson stepped forward. From 40 metres out he kicked the goal, and an agonising minute later the final whistle sounded on an incredible afternoon's events.

I remember with remarkable clarity where I was that day. I watched the final Test on television leaning against the wall in a small, packed lounge in a student flat. Most of those in the room were rugby-loving people, but some were anti-tour. Others I sensed just didn't want to

DEFINING MOMENT

Three Part Drama
THIRD TEST, AUCKLAND, 12 SEPTEMBER, 1981

Was the defining moment of the troubled 1981 Springbok tour of New Zealand outside, above or inside Eden Park on 12 September, 1981? In truth, the unprecedented violence on the streets, the manic flight pattern of the light plane (and the flour bombs it dropped onto the park and players) and the sheer theatre of Welsh referee Clive Norling's penalty award, late in injury time, which allowed Alan Hewson to snatch a series victory for the All Blacks, all provided defining moments. They were the three parts before the final curtain was drawn on a real-life drama that art could only imitate.

talk about it. I recall purposefully controlling my emotions, and slipping away soon after Allan Hewson had kicked his winning penalty goal. I was pleased, not thrilled, that New Zealand had won. At least we'd got something from the tour, I reasoned. For — I won't sit on the fence — I was pro-tour, which was not a comfortable stance at a university known for its liberal politics.

As the months passed, however, I came to the realisation that I could not support future contact with South Africa, and certainly not in New Zealand. Sport and politics had mixed to create a volatile cocktail that most New Zealanders could not stomach. The protestors had won, and in the end they were proven correct. Without New Zealand's support, without the Springbok tours, change would happen more quickly in South Africa.

New Zealand rugby would not fully recover from the ructions of the tour until the 1987 World Cup. For some New Zealanders the experience had been intensely personal; for all, it had been an issue.

Thankfully nobody was killed in the 1981 protests.

1981

THE SOUTH AFRICAN RESPONSE

THE FIFTH SPRINGBOKS IN NEW ZEALAND

by David Williams

THE 1981 SERIES is remembered with a unique mixture of pleasure, resentment, sadness and shame. Perhaps it was just as well Naas Botha failed to convert Ray Mordt's equalising try in the third Test. If the Springboks had won the series, too much comfort would have accrued to the defenders of apartheid at home. Wynand Claassen's team would been placed on the same pedestal as Philip Nel's 1937 giants, the ruling National Party would have basked in the warm glow of achievement and taken the credit, and that would not have been right. It would have been vulgar and distressing to see South Africans gloating over a defeated New Zealand team whose society had also been torn apart by two conflicting impulses of decency: the desire to host the ancient rivals in the national game, and the desire to express moral outrage at the evil policy of apartheid.

Of course, there was hypocrisy and confused thinking. It was difficult to understand or respect the thinking of a Graham Mourie, who did not want to play against the Springboks in New Zealand but was prepared to tour South Africa. And not a few liberal white South Africans were morally against the tour but could just not resist getting up in the middle of the night to watch the matches on television.

In the broader scheme of things, justice was probably done by the All Black series win. Many white South Africans were becoming increasingly uneasy about apartheid. Young men were spending more and more time in the military and resenting it deeply, with steadily rising casualties in occupied Namibia and Angola. The advent of television in 1976 had broadened perceptions, despite state censorship, and brought home just how isolated the country had become. White families were told repeatedly what they were fighting against — communism and revolutionary chaos — but they were less confident about what they were supposed to be defending. The country had not really appreciated the feeling behind the demonstrations that made the 1969–70 Springbok tour of Britain a miserable failure. In 1981, thanks to TV, South Africans watched an inherently peaceful country tearing itself apart because of the Springboks' presence. Our desire to enjoy the rugby was constantly qualified by unease and shame.

That said, the actual route to defeat remains a source of anger. South African rugby men still believe referee Clive Norling deliberately engineered a New Zealand victory in the third Test.

RIGHT:What a pity it was that Danie Gerber's appearances against the All Blacks came 11 years apart. Here the brilliant Bok midfielder (middle) stops All Black No. 8 Murray Mexted with the help of Burger Geldenhuys.

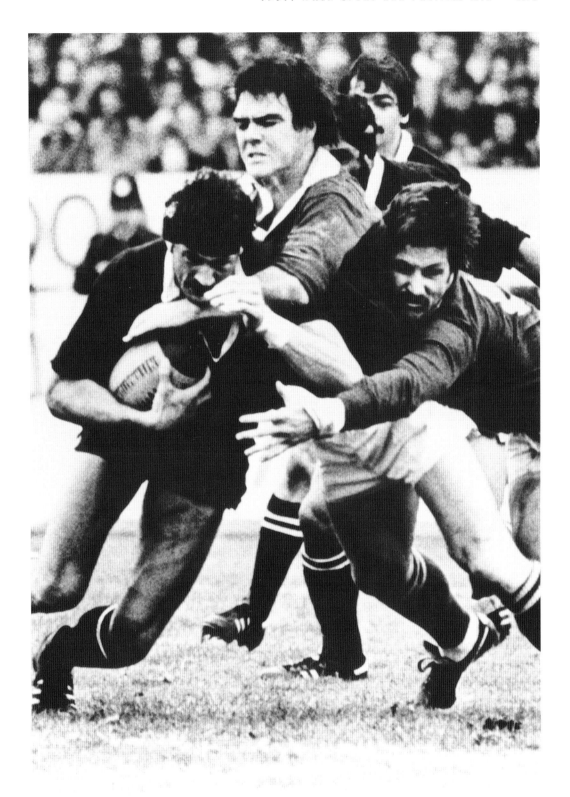

The more charitable view, apart from the exceptionally forgiving assumption that his watch must have stopped, is that Norling's interpretation of the laws was wrong, or at least unduly harsh, when he awarded the final penalty that was converted by Allan Hewson. He turned a Springbok scrum into a free kick to the All Blacks on the grounds that hooker Robert Cockrell had 'flashed' at the ball. Wynand Claassen wrote later that Cockrell had simply moved his feet because the scrum was wheeling and could hardly have been foot-up before the scrum had been fed. The free kick then became a penalty, because the Springbok backs, in Norling's words, 'were not making any effort to retire'. Claassen used the video evidence of the match to back his claim that his backs had indeed retired and that Doug Rollerson was tackled after he had run 10 metres.

What puzzled Claassen most was that the match continued after Ray Mordt's try. Just before this Norling had said it would be the last move of the game. If Botha's conversion had succeeded, Claassen speculated, Norling would have blown the final whistle for a 24–22 Springbok win. Norling is reported to have told two old Springboks, Jan Pickard and Dave Stewart, that 'nobody wanted a draw'. The fact that he also happened to be a showman referee did not help. Claassen, normally measured in his opinions, regarded Norling as bossy, arrogant and a seeker of controversy.

Claassen also admitted that, in the desolate Bok changing room after the third Test, his thoughts turned to the 1976 All Blacks and how they had failed to draw a series in South Africa because Gert Bezuidenhout had not awarded them the penalty try they deserved. 'I realised how they must have felt,' said Claassen, 'and slowly gathered the resolve to go out and face everyone with my head held high.'

Remembered pleasure from the tour comes from Ray Mordt's great try-scoring performances and the explosive release of Springbok talent in the second Test, which must be regarded as one of the great victories of all-time, sparked by one of the greatest individual performances from Naas Botha. It was not fully realised at the time, but man for man the 1981 Springboks were one of the most prodigiously talented touring sides ever. The pity was that this fact was undermined not only by the practical difficulties of touring in a social firestorm, but by an insensitive management team that got neither the politics nor the selection right, notably when they omitted Claassen from the first Test.

1986

MERCENARIES FOR THE CAUSE

SOUTH AFRICA	21	NZ CAVALIERS	15
NZ CAVALIERS	19	SOUTH AFRICA	18
SOUTH AFRICA	33	NZ CAVALIERS	18
SOUTH AFRICA	24	NZ CAVALIERS	10

CHAPTER ELEVEN

1986
MERCENARIES FOR THE CAUSE

THE NEW ZEALAND CAVALIERS IN SOUTH AFRICA

by David Williams

SOUTH AFRICAN WHITES were stunned with disappointment when the 1985 All Black tour was cancelled almost at the last minute, following the unexpected success of what had seemed an eccentric New Zealand court application. Fans were not interested in the legal niceties but they were outraged at being deprived of the opportunity to watch their beloved Boks prove they were the best in the world. One of the old enemies, England, had been thrashed in two Tests the year before; now it was time for the real thing. The fact that the country was heading for a political abyss, with a state of emergency in force as President P. W. Botha tried to crush black opposition, seemed to make the rugby deprivation all the more acute.

If New Zealanders traditionally defined themselves in relation to the All Blacks, so white South Africans at that time increasingly projected their national aspirations onto the Springboks to escape the more disturbing political realities of their country.

Ironically, the fans were justified in one respect. The Springbok side of the mid-1980s was arguably one of the best in history, if not the best. It was one of those rare periods when several truly great players reached their peak at the same time. Many international teams (including, sadly, the 1999 Springbok team at the World Cup) would count themselves fortunate to have just one backline player of the calibre of Naas Botha, Michael or Carel du Plessis, Johan Heunis or Danie Gerber. Yet these players were all available in 1985 and in their prime, having cut their teeth on the 1981 tour of New Zealand. Jaco Reinach was a newcomer on the right wing but he was the holder of the national 400-metres track record.

Luckily for South Africa, all these men were also available in 1986, when 28 of the 30 All Blacks selected for the 1985 tour defied world opinion and came anyway, as the New Zealand 'Cavaliers'. Louis Luyt's Transvaal union organised the 12-match visit to protect the national body from having to sanction a rebel tour. Danie Craven, ruthless as always, promised an inquiry

New Zealand Cavaliers' captain Andy Dalton takes his leave from the tour with a broken jaw in his first outing. The culprit, Northern Transvaal's Burger Geldenhuys was ruled out of the 'Test' series as a result.

that everyone knew would be token. The presence, as Cavaliers' manager, of Colin Meads, regarded in South Africa as the quintessential All Black, added further legitimacy. South African fans were happy to pretend the 1985 cancellation had merely been a postponement, that the absence of John Kirwan and David Kirk was of no consequence, and that the Springboks would in fact be playing the All Blacks for the unofficial world championship.

Tensions caused by the tour were not only political. Senior South African players knew the New Zealanders were paid handsomely to tour — one estimate was $US100,000 each, paid via Hong Kong into a promotion company run by lock Andy Haden. John Robbie, the former Irish and British Lions scrumhalf who had been favourite to play for the Boks in 1985, wrote: 'A lot of money was involved . . . people have told me, people who were involved.' The fact that the fees were in flagrant conflict with the amateur regulations was of no interest, because everyone knew South African provincial players earned big money on the quiet. But the hypocrisy deeply upset the Springboks, who were paid relative peanuts and felt their patriotism was being exploited. Rumbles over money disrupted the Bok squad throughout the tour, with frequent talk of mutiny.

If South Africans were grateful to the New Zealanders for coming, they never showed it. If these were really the All Blacks, it was legitimate to nurture the ancient enmity. But even hardened local fans were shocked when, during the second tour match, Northern Transvaal flanker Burger Geldenhuys cynically and openly hit Cavalier captain Andy Dalton, breaking his jaw and putting him out of the tour. Geldenhuys, another 1981 veteran, had been a certainty for the Bok team, but Danie Craven was appalled and insisted he must not be selected. 'I would say a man like that should be suspended for life,' he said later. 'There is no room in my vocabulary for incidents like that — no room — no mercy.' And Geldenhuys did not play for South Africa again.

In the event the Springboks may actually have been strengthened. The loose trio of Gert Smal, Wahl Bartmann and Jannie Breedt proved to be exceptionally efficient, complementing one another's strengths and matching the Cavaliers' Mark Shaw, Jock Hobbs and Murray Mexted.

The first international game at Newlands was regarded as a full international in all but name. The Cavaliers were expected to do well on a ground that was soggy after heavy rain. Their forwards dominated the first half, but with 20 minutes to go in the match they were leading only 15–12. Botha was able to make it 15–all with ten minutes to go, and a draw seemed the likely result.

Then Botha showed his genius. Taking a difficult pass from a lineout inside the Cavaliers' half, he kicked carefully towards the corner flag, but the ball stayed in and skidded across the greasy turf towards the deadball line. Carel du Plessis was able to round Kieran Crowley and won the race to the ball, which had stopped with a metre to go. It was one of the greatest tries seen at Newlands, and Botha's masterful conversion, with Gerber holding the ball for him, was added to the 15 points he had piled up through three penalty goals and two drop goals.

PLAYER OF THE DECADE

NAAS BOTHA
BORN: 1958
POSITION: FLYHALF
PLAYED NEW ZEALAND: 1981, 1992 (4 TESTS)

If Morne du Plessis, of Western Province, was the man Northern supporters loved to hate, balance was neatly restored when Naas Botha, of Northern Transvaal, became the favourite villain of the coastal fans. The two men's Test careers overlapped briefly in 1980. Like 'Morne', 'Naas' became and remains a household name; and like Morne, Naas had to overcome strong initial prejudice. Now he is acknowledged as one of the greatest flyhalves ever to have played the game.

The 1981 All Blacks and the 1986 Cavaliers experienced the genius of Botha. His match-winning ability as a kicker is legendary. When Jannie de Beer put over five drop goals to sink England in the 1999 World Cup, there was wild astonishment. If Naas Botha had done that, there would have been only mild surprise.

What is acknowledged less often than Botha's kicking prowess is his all-round flyhalf skills. Under a sympathetic coach, and when the time was right, he could conjure a perfect break and capitalise on it with speed and finesse. His tactical kicking was a powerful attacking weapon and his touchfinders broke the hearts of opposing packs. If he had a weakness it was his tackling, but as Buurman van Zyl, the legendary Northerns coach, pointed out, he'd rather somebody else did the tackling if Naas was winning the match.

Of all the Springboks whose careers were limited by their country's political isolation, Naas Botha is probably the one who would have made the greatest impact on the world game over the longest period.

Fox had also done well: 11 points from three penalty goals and the conversion of a penalty try. But Naas Botha had confirmed he was one of the greatest match-winners in the history of the game. Better than that, in his first game as Springbok captain he had scored a victory over the All Blacks — for by now the newspapers had given up pretending that the tourists were anything else.

However, on the same front page of the *Sunday Times* that trumpeted the Springbok's victory, the secondary headlines were less cheerful. There had been a 'massive raid' by more than a

Grant Fox had played just one Test when he toured South Africa with the Cavaliers, but South Africans viewed his battle with Naas Botha as the decider on who was the world's best first-five.

thousand police and army troops on the black township of Alexandra, near Johannesburg, and the 'unrest toll' of those who had died in civil disturbance and political violence 'now tops 1559'. By this time it was more than a tiny minority of whites who felt the presence of the New Zealanders had not only condoned P. W. Botha's policies, but had also exacerbated their disastrous effects.

Yet the rugby itself remained irresistible. Remaining true to All Black tradition, the Cavaliers won the second Test the following Saturday in Durban by 19 points to 18. Jock Hobbs came back into the side as captain, and they were altogether more convincing. Naas Botha had a rare off day, missing six penalties and a conversion in the awkward wind at King's Park, while towards the end of the game he missed a drop goal the home fans would normally have taken for granted. The Springboks' solitary try was scored by Reinach, more than matched by scores from Warwick Taylor and Murray Mexted.

Botha was determined to regain his form for the third Test, to be played at Pretoria's Loftus Versfeld, his home ground. Bok coach Cecil Moss, a winger in the 1949 side, had realised that his men were conceding too many penalties at the lineout. With Welsh referee Ken Rowlands appointed for all four Tests, Moss decided to use short lineouts for at least the first 20 minutes, in the hope that Rowlands would be more likely to notice the New Zealanders' barging.

Several days before the match, the Cavaliers employed some gamesmanship by arriving for practice at Loftus Versfeld at the same time as booked by the home side. The Boks stood their ground. That evening, Botha, worried his side had been discourteous, phoned Danie Craven and was immediately reassured: the All Blacks had tried exactly the same trick in 1937.

With the third Test under way, South Africa scored first after Rowlands duly penalised the Cavaliers for barging, but Botha and Fox were to trade goal kicks all afternoon, and soon the score was 6–6. Then the Springbok backs began to play to their potential, with Heunis and Carel du Plessis doing the creative work for hooker Uli Schmidt to go over for a try (12–6).

Fox pulled it back to 12–9, and the Cavalier forwards then set up excellent second-phase possession for Kieran Crowley to score in the corner (15–12). But the Cavaliers were missing too many touches. Reinach fielded one of these and sent a long pass inwards to Botha on the halfway line. Botha chipped ahead, Mexted failed to gather under pressure from Heunis, and Botha was able to snap up the ball and score his first try in international rugby (18–15). Fox replied with a drop goal (18–18).

With only 10 minutes to go, Botha made it 21–18, then Carel du Plessis and Danie Gerber combined in classic style to produce a try between the posts (27–18). Gerber followed that up with a blindside sprint and a try-creating pass to Reinach (33–18). The Cavaliers' sensible strategy of trying to tame the Boks up front had failed, and they had no answer to the genius of the South African backs. What might this Springbok side have done if it had not been restricted to only 15 Tests between 1981 and 1988?

In the fourth Test, at Ellis Park, the tourists seemed determined to use their backs to save the series, but again there was an extended kicking duel. The New Zealanders did score a try, by scrumhalf Andrew Donald, but got much the worst of the penalty count (a total of 21 infringements to South Africa's seven). There was a brief but dreamy debut for Helgard Muller, who came on for Jaco Reinach near the end (one Free Stater, it was alleged, had faked an injury to give another Free Stater his Springbok colours). Muller received the ball for the first time and chipped it down the right touchline. Scrumhalf Garth Wright nipped in to score, with Botha providing another touchline conversion.

At the function after the 24–10 loss Andy Dalton was publicly rude about Ken Rowlands, accusing him of dishonesty. Botha was sharp in reply: 'Now you know how we felt in 1981.' But a poignant moment, amidst the acrimony, was the simple ceremony of awarding national colours to Muller. He had been on the field for only a few minutes, but of course that was enough to make him a Springbok. He went up, bursting with pride and shyness, to receive his blazer from Danie Craven, who had made his own debut more than 55 years before. Several of those watching wondered aloud if Muller might be the last of all Springboks, so gloomy did South Africa's prospects seem of ever being accepted back into the fold by the rest of the world.

DEFINING MOMENT

No Longer All Blacks in Disguise
FOURTH 'TEST', JOHANNESBURG, 31 MAY, 1986

In a visit dominated by political drama, it is appropriate to go beyond the matches themselves to choose a definitive incident. It came just before the fourth Test, at Ellis Park, when the Cavaliers thrilled the 77,000-strong crowd by performing the traditional haka for the first time on tour. Clearly the New Zealand players felt they needed inspiration before attempting to level the series, but they were also making an important statement about their identity. Before the three other internationals and the eight other tour games, the Cavaliers had implicitly accepted their status as an unofficial invitation side and had avoided the haka. Now, when all was at stake, they felt the need to draw on the warrior exhortation that is reserved for only one team: the All Blacks. It was a statement that was welcomed by South African players, administrators and spectators, because it legitimised the contest and placed it in a great historical framework.

The Cavaliers went home to a slap on the wrist and a token condemnation by Prime Minister David Lange. Meads was fired as an All Black selector and the players were each banned for two Tests. Several retired but many went on to play a major part in New Zealand's 1987 World Cup triumph. Their punishment was obviously tempered by the knowledge that the All Blacks could not win the trophy without them.

New Zealanders seem to suffer from complete amnesia over the fiercely contested 1986 series. They don't like to talk about any aspect of it. Perhaps their mythology prevents them from accepting that their beloved All Blacks behaved like defiant mercenaries and were seen to be condoning a rotten, racist regime that all other sporting codes and even rugby nations had ostracised.

South African rugby men are convinced that if the Cavaliers had won the series, it would have been loudly acclaimed in New Zealand as the first-ever All Black series win in South Africa. Certainly the rugby played was of the highest quality — and the players thought it was the real thing.

1986

THE NEW ZEALAND RESPONSE

THE NEW ZEALAND CAVALIERS IN SOUTH AFRICA

by Grant Harding

LET'S GET ONE thing straight — the New Zealand Cavaliers were not the All Blacks, and would not have returned as conquering heroes had they beaten South Africa.

The All Blacks are a team that enjoys the support of all New Zealand. The All Blacks are a team that proudly wears the silver fern on the chest. The All Blacks are a team that does not have to soul-search before deciding to do a pre-Test haka. The All Blacks are a team selected from all available fit players in New Zealand.

The Cavaliers did not qualify in any such respect. Besides, the 1981 experience had been so traumatic that many people who had previously supported keeping sport out of politics had now decided that wasn't a sensible viewpoint.

Of course, the New Zealand Rugby Football Union didn't agree. It tried to launch a tour to the republic in 1985, only for it to be abandoned when the High Court granted a temporary injunction against it after action was brought by two Auckland lawyers. Just five days before the players were to leave, the High Court ruled that the tour 'would be contrary to the Rugby Union's statutory commitment to promote and foster the game'. There was no time for a defence to be mounted.

From that decision, and subsequent comments by New Zealand prime minister David Lange about the rights of individuals to travel where they want, were sewn the seeds of the Cavaliers' tour. After earlier moves had been thwarted, a squad of 30 players and a management featuring All Black legends Ian Kirkpatrick and Colin Meads were all abroad by mid-April the following year. Some had been harassed by protestors at airports as they left, while others arrived from International Rugby Board centenary matches featuring South African players, and other overseas commitments. Of the originally selected 1985 squad only John Kirwan and David Kirk were not on tour.

Of course, both unions denied knowledge of the tour. It's possible the NZRFU's Ces Blazey did not know about it, but Danie Craven was definitely lying. Lange said: 'Dr Danie Craven is probably the most dishonest person in politics or sport.'

Eventually the Cavaliers, an aging team, would share the fate of all New Zealand teams that had gone before them — defeat in a Test series, this time played over four consecutive weekends. They would complain of the pressure of proving what they had done was right, they would complain about the refereeing, and, quite rightly, they would complain about Andy Dalton having his jaw broken.

News-media coverage was negligible and almost entirely political. I tuned into the radio just once during the tour to find the Cavaliers leading 10–3 in the fourth Test before a succession of penalties led to them falling behind. Eventually the game ended with the referee being harangued by Jock Hobbs, Wayne Smith and Murray Mexted, before Hika Reid leant an unfriendly shoulder. So the Welsh referee, Ken Rowlands, was either unfair or incompetent. Did that really surprise anybody? This was a privately organised tour, not a tour sanctioned by the New Zealand Rugby Football Union, after all.

And the Cavaliers were also paid for their pain — probably legally — from a larger than usual tour fund. Fifty thousand dollars a player was the figure confirmed by Andy Haden in 1999.

While there is much about the tour that is disputed, it is beyond question that South Africa had a fine team. It is also clear this tour, finally, and forever, made New Zealanders realise South Africa would have to clean up its act before it could expect to play us on the rugby field again.

Rugby's image had suffered; but every cloud has a silver lining. The Cavaliers' subsequent two-match ban brought many new players to the Test arena, and when the All Blacks lined out in the 1987 World Cup final, just eight of them were veterans of the rebel tour. Teamed with them were John Gallagher, Kirwan, Joe Stanley, Kirk, Michael Jones, John Drake and Sean Fitzpatrick. Not a bad list of names, don't you think, Naas?

By the end of 1987 New Zealand were world champions. The Cavaliers were just a painful memory. South Africa was a country with problems, which, without New Zealand solace, might be solved more quickly. In the eyes of the rugby world the Springboks did not play an official Test between 1984 and 1992.

RIGHT: Springbok speedster Jaco Reinach scores the decisive try in the third Test of the series against the New Zealand Cavaliers, with Danie Gerber in attendance. Andy Haden's body language says he knows the dream of a series victory in South Africa is just that.

1992–1995

THE RAINBOW NATION ARRIVES

1992			
NEW ZEALAND	27	SOUTH AFRICA	24
1994			
NEW ZEALAND	22	SOUTH AFRICA	14
NEW ZEALAND	13	SOUTH AFRICA	9
NEW ZEALAND	18	SOUTH AFRICA	18
1995			
SOUTH AFRICA	15	NEW ZEALAND	12

CHAPTER TWELVE

1992–1995

THE RAINBOW NATION ARRIVES

1992

THE DESPERATE PRODIGAL

THE SIXTH ALL BLACKS IN SOUTH AFRICA

by David Williams

FOR NEW ZEALAND, the one-off Ellis Park Test against the Springboks on 15 August 1992 was clearly important. It was the climax of the first visit to South Africa by an official All Black side since 1976. But, for white South Africans, the excitement threatened to be overwhelming.

The Springboks had not played a full series against anyone since their troubled tour of New Zealand in 1981, and their last official contest had been the two-match demolition of England in 1984. Since then, they had had only a couple of games against weak invitation sides and the limited, sour satisfaction of a 'series win' against the New Zealand Cavaliers in 1986.

Danie Craven, now past 80 and in his 37th successive annual term as president of the South African Rugby Board, was unashamed in his emotion and deeply conscious of history. 'After the long and trying time we suffered,' he wrote in the match programme for August 15, 'we are now meeting the might of New Zealand. It is such an important encounter that winning or losing is less important than the encounter itself . . . Tears will flow today, and they introduce a new era and a new life in our relationships which have been built up over many years.' In a sense, Craven personified the ancient relationship: he recalled that he had first heard the words 'All Blacks' when he was 11-years-old, during the first series in 1921.

This big match at Ellis Park was ignored by most black South Africans, but the black élite understood very well its huge significance for whites. The ANC made it very clear that the Springboks were in action again only because the ANC was prepared to allow it, and that the privilege could easily be withdrawn if the ANC was not satisfied with broader political developments. Indeed, there were many black leaders who felt no international sport should be allowed until South Africa had elected a democratic government. But Nelson Mandela knew his Afrikaner very well — and he knew that South African whites, if they had to choose, cared far

Springbok hard men — Ian McDonald and Jannie Breedt on the run in 1992.

more about their rugby than they did for President de Klerk. If the threat of mass action was the stick, the restoration of international rugby and cricket links was the very juicy carrot.

On the ground, though, if there was appreciation of Mandela's concession, it was grudging in the extreme. There was an aggressive, often ugly mood in the decaying suburban streets around the giant Ellis Park stadium on the day of the match. For many white fans, this was an opportunity to show their defiance of the ANC and their visceral, reactionary loyalty to a South African order that had in fact disappeared forever. Other white spectators, never supporters of the old regime but equally keen on their rugby, were deeply embarrassed as they made their way to the ground. This was war, not a celebration.

Of course, the rugby reality was inconvenient and therefore ignored. The Springbok side could muster only 60 caps, none of them won in the previous four years. Naas Botha and Danie

Gerber (both aged 34) had played 42 Tests between them, each more than the other 13 players combined, and no other backline player was capped. Collectively, the All Blacks were five times more experienced, with a total of 316 appearances between them; many of them had known the heat of the World Cup; and they had played regular, competitive international rugby. Naas Botha's total of 23 Tests was exceeded by six All Blacks. The impact of isolation really hit home when it was pointed out that Grant Fox was four years younger than Botha but had nearly twice as many caps, and that Ian Jones was 12 years younger but had already played more Tests.

Leaving aside the minimal international experience of the 1992 Springboks, they happened also to offer far less natural talent than the great sides of the 1970s and 1980s. Apart from the veterans Botha and Gerber, the only truly world-class player was the Northern Transvaal hooker, Uli Schmidt. The side lacked the authority of the 1986 team that had defeated the Cavaliers, and bore no comparison to the stellar class of '81. It contained too many provincial journeymen,

Naas Botha about to gather, protected by Danie Gerber.

toughened on the Currie Cup but not quite of the required standard. The only men who would go on to make a memorable impact in the Bok teams of the 1990s were rookies James Small and Pieter Muller. In the backs, there was nobody to compare with the Du Plessis brothers, Carel and Michael, or winger Ray Mordt or fullback Johan Heunis. The forwards looked more solid, with Transvaal No. 8 Jannie Breedt the most impressive, but most of them seemed to fall somewhere between good provincial and international class.

As the price for allowing the tour to take place, the ANC and its allies had demanded that 'Die Stem', the national anthem traditionally sung in Afrikaans (although there was an English version, 'The Call of South Africa'), should not be performed at Ellis Park. The rugby authorities gave a reluctant undertaking: they warned they could not stop the crowd singing 'Die Stem', but it would not be presented officially. This caused fevered discussion and enormous resentment, even among more liberal rugby fans: how could the Springboks be expected to watch the All Blacks perform their haka and offer absolutely nothing in return? Did the ANC not understand this cultural imperative?

In the event a political storm was caused when 'Die Stem' was played over the public-address system after all. The official story was that this had been done on the spur of the moment because the crowd's mood was becoming ugly as kickoff approached. In fact, the word was out in the press box at least three hours before the kickoff that Louis Luyt, then president of the host union Transvaal, had already decided to play 'Die Stem'. The ANC was furious and felt it had been betrayed. To make matters worse, large sections of the crowd disrupted the agreed observance of a minute's silence, perceived as an ANC imposition, to honour all those who had died in political violence.

The recriminations were to be so intense they would threaten the Test scheduled for the next Saturday against the Australians. But, for the moment, every South African rugby fan's attention could be focused, at long last, on the 38th Test match between the Springboks and the All Blacks.

The All Blacks had the advantage of having played and won several warm-up games on tour, with the victory against a strong Natal side the most significant. They were clear favourites and looked set to take firm control of the Boks, establishing a lineout dominance that would last throughout the game. The South Africans found it hard to break the habit of lifting, still illegal. But the home side, playing with courage and passion, were not overwhelmed. Gerber looked impressive and the Bok forwards were solid, despite a tendency to play the ball on the ground. (Perhaps it was inevitable, with hindsight, that the match began with Sean Fitzpatrick punching Naas Botha.)

Fifteen minutes into the game a high tackle on scrumhalf Ant Strachan enabled Fox to put the All Blacks in the lead (3–0).

With only seven minutes to go to halftime, the score was still 3–0, Botha and Fox having both missed penalty attempts. After a period of sustained All Black pressure, with Frank Bunce prominent, the Boks were offside just a few metres from their own line. As they retreated and milled about, waiting for Fox to kick the points, their lack of international sharpness was exposed. Zinzan Brooke took a quick tap, and before the Boks knew what had happened he had dived over to create a seven-pointer.

The impression that the match was tilting towards New Zealand was reinforced as the referee gave a stern lecture to Botha about dirty play. Botha looked mystified and may still have been unsettled when he failed soon afterwards with a reasonable drop goal opportunity. But there was an inspiring Springbok surge just before halftime, with Gerber almost getting over the All Black line, but losing the ball, followed by a forward drive that was halted just short.

Halftime saw New Zealand still leading 10–0. What was clear was that the Springboks' tactics had been too conservative. They had been mostly on the back foot, but they had also looked dangerous when they had broken free. Whenever they had sent the ball wide, the All Blacks had looked vulnerable — and like New Zealand teams before and since, the visitors hated to be kept moving back.

As if to exploit this weakness in the All Blacks' armour, the Springboks took the initiative at the start of the second half. A huge punt by Botha took them to within five metres of the All Black line. A try was missed when Muller lost his bearings and passed into touch, as was another when Gerber came desperately close again. There was consolation when Botha was able to punish a lineout infringement five minutes into the half (10–3).

Provoked, the All Blacks showed their pedigree for the first time in the game. Bunce cut inside after getting the recycled ball, straightened, unloaded to John Kirwan, who wrong-footed the Springbok backs to thunder in at an angle for the try. Ellis Park was silent: the Boks had threatened on occasion but produced nothing like this. It was 17–3 after 10 minutes in the second half.

Just as New Zealand had raised the stakes, so now did the South Africans. More settled, and thinking more quickly than in the first half, they surprised their opponents with a quick lineout, which resulted in a long advance down the left flank, with good work by Jannie Breedt, Theo van Rensburg and Wahl Bartmann. Eventually the ball was fed back and reached Gerber, who shed a decade as he smashed the All Black defensive line with a try no less impressive than Kirwan's (20–10).

Three minutes later, John Timu slid in for a try that was the result of good driving down the centre by the New Zealand forwards, followed by fast passing and excellent linking. Gerber looked older again as he tried and failed to catch Timu. With about 20 minutes to go, it was 27–10 and the match was receding for South Africa.

It was then that Botha finally decided to adopt the necessary tactics. His backs got more ball and spread it wide, and for the first time the All Blacks looked stretched. With Robert du Preez playing like a loose forward, the Boks, driving with ball in hand, created more space. A South African try was stopped only when Jon Preston took Small into touch as he dived for the line. After more pressure, Muller, after getting the ball from the tank-like Bartmann, crashed through three tackles to score, bringing the score to 27–17 with four minutes to go. Muller's try had in fact followed a knock-on by scrumhalf Du Preez, missed by the referee, but this was

DEFINING MOMENT

Tearful Respect for the Green Jersey
READMISSION TEST, JOHANNESBURG, 15 AUGUST, 1992

Even though James Small was new to Test rugby, he had already developed a reputation as something of a wild man. When playing club rugby at the University of the Witwatersrand in the late 1980s, he had delighted in taunting Afrikaner opponents by pulling faces. Yet as he had moved up to play for Transvaal, where English-speakers had traditionally found it difficult to break into provincial rugby, it had become clear he had talent, ball skills, self-confidence and big-match temperament. His selection for South Africa was regarded as courageous but not controversial. His mixture of aggression, patriotism and eccentricity was of the kind understood by Danie Craven, who believed players with complex, artistic temperaments should be allowed to express themselves.

Small played sensibly and with occasional flair in his first Test. But perhaps the most cruelly memorable incident came when he knocked on a routine pass with the New Zealand line at his mercy. The match was at that late stage when a Springbok try would have won the match for them. Although there was nobody marking Small directly, the replay does show the All Black cover defence might have intercepted him. But in the heat and confusion of the moment, it appeared to all who saw the incident that he had thrown away the game. It seemed to sum up the day: an inexperienced side had played with passion and increasing flair, but had failed at the crucial moment.

After the final whistle Small was filmed crying freely, cheeks wet and chest heaving. Those who did not know rugby may have been surprised at this naked emotion, but the old Springboks present nodded with dour understanding. After all, the boy had just played his first Test match against the All Blacks. That unashamed public display might not have too many precedents in this man's game, but it proved Small's respect for the green jersey. That was what counted. The passion of the leaping Springbok had not been extinguished by isolation and politics.

compensation for Sandy MacNeill's earlier ruling that Gerber had lost the ball going over at the corner flag when in fact the score was good.

Now, for the first time in the game, the Boks were playing with real confidence. The All Blacks looked worried as the pressure was piled on, and were visibly relieved when Botha took his only wrong option of the second half and dropped for goal when he had men to spare lined up, deep in the New Zealand half.

The Boks continued to throw everything into attack while maintaining discipline, and were rewarded with Gerber's second try (27–24). But their resurgence had come too late, and even in the several minutes of injury time, despite some close calls, there were no more scores. In the end it was close, but arguably because the All Blacks had lapsed into complacency when they were 27–10 ahead.

The lingering impression was that once the Springboks had got over their nerves and their instinctive conservatism born of long exile, they had done very well. Their lineout technique was clearly obsolete, their habit of going to ground was a handicap, and they were clearly unaccustomed to varying running angles to break up defences. But their basic skills were impressive, despite the eight new caps in the side, and many try-scoring opportunities were created. It could not have been imagined at the time, but Botha's mixture of rusty and green Springboks played better rugby against the All Blacks that day than many of their successors were to do in the 1990s.

It was also true that the genius of Gerber and Botha proved more influential than anyone had predicted — and the two players were virtually on pension. Few of the youngsters had come through to dominate, and the team's limitations were fully exposed the following week, when the Wallabies, put on full alert by the Boks' late surge at Ellis Park, handed out a crushing defeat at Newlands. Thus was shattered the South African dream of beating the 1987 and 1991 World Cup champions on successive weekends. Politically, it was probably just as well the Boks lost both games: certain elements of white South Africa needed the corrective to help them face a broader reality.

Springbok rugby was not to recover its self-confidence for another three years. But perhaps the last word should go to New Zealand rugby boss Eddie Tonks, writing in the programme for that Ellis Park match in 1992: 'In 1995 when the World Cup is held in South Africa, we will know the true World Champion.'

1992

THE NEW ZEALAND RESPONSE

THE SIXTH ALL BLACKS IN SOUTH AFRICA

by Grant Harding

THE EVENT AND the outcome were equally important to the All Blacks when they ventured to Ellis Park, in Johannesburg, on 15 August 1992.

Certainly the opportunity to play in an official Test against South Africa in South Africa for the first time in 16 years, and in a first Test against the Springboks for every member of the All Black team, made for a momentous occasion. And as anyone who has attended a packed Ellis Park will tell you, the atmosphere of the place could only add to the theatre. Statements about the validity of previous World Cup tournaments by Louis Luyt and Springbok captain Naas Botha also needed a response, and that response had to be an All Black win.

The All Blacks had come out of the 1991 World Cup in bad shape, and new coach Laurie Mains had set about rebuilding them. Series against a World XV and Ireland were won before a tour to Australia, which was to be immediately followed by a five-match tour of South Africa.

In Australia the team made real progress, and with an ounce of luck could have come out on the right side of a 2–1 series loss. That progress manifested itself in three superb tries at Ellis Park. The All Blacks also had a decisive edge at lineout and among the loose forwards.

Grant Fox, the only survivor of the New Zealand Cavaliers, also outplayed Naas Botha, while inside him halfback Jon Preston was a special hero, giving a faultless display after coming off the bench in the 16th minute.

The All Blacks used captain Sean Fitzpatrick and winger Va'aiga Tuigamala to run powerfully off the rucks, often directly at the most fragile target, Botha. Fitzpatrick remembers an initial tangle got Botha's mouth working overtime.

It was only in the latter stages of the game, when the physically taxing combination of heat, altitude, two months on the road and playing the ninth Test of the year kicked in, that South Africa closed the gap.

It was New Zealand's first Test victory at Ellis Park since 1928, and the first time it had ever won a first Test in South Africa.

Botha, winger Pieter Hendriks and hooker Uli Schmidt had played in New Zealand for the World XV earlier in the year, while Botha and the brilliant centre Danie Gerber, who showed his skills were still superb with two tries, were survivors of the 1981 tour to New Zealand.

South Africa's return to the rugby scene had come earlier than expected and followed the establishment of a new, unified, multiracial rugby body at a meeting in Kimberley in March. The All Blacks were promptly invited and accepted — to the disappointment of some veterans of the

Back in the international fold . . . Springbok James Small (right) enjoys the chance to get up close and personal with All Black first-five Grant Fox after the first post-isolation Test, at Ellis Park, in 1992.

protest movement. These people believed a resumption of sporting relations with South Africa had come too early in the process of political change in the republic, and the behaviour of some Springbok supporters at Ellis Park that day certainly gave credence to such a view. Nevertheless, South Africa was back in the fold, and progress would be made. By the end of the year Naas Botha was gone, and the Springboks could go about modernising their style of rugby as well as their image.

1994

STRANGE DAYS? INDEED

THE SIXTH SPRINGBOKS IN NEW ZEALAND

by Grant Harding

NELSON MANDELA HAD been South Africa's president for more than a month by the time the Springboks touched down in New Zealand on Tuesday, 21 June 1994. That fact ensured the black days of 1981 were, in the main, consigned to history.

Nevertheless, the impact of the events of 13 years before were always going to play a role in shaping the tour. Black days gave way to bland and colourless days as the Springbok team went about proving, in an almost apologist manner, that the metaphorical nose of their new rainbow nation was truly squeaky clean. They were almost too nice as they tried to fit into a modern world which was both suspicious and demanding of them.

That Television New Zealand assigned a current affairs reporter and crew to the tour was symptomatic of a lack of trust in post-apartheid South Africa. Yet there was not even a hint of scandal surrounding the Boks' treatment of their sole coloured player, Chester Williams, despite the best efforts of some who suggested he was a token selection when he missed the opening three games of the tour. Those misguided souls were obviously not aware of the compulsory stand-down for concussion, such as that suffered by Williams against England. Of course, the best response came from Williams himself, who quickly established himself as the tourists' top winger and went on to play all three Tests. In many respects he was the player of the tour. The TVNZ reporter's post-tour item, meanwhile, lacked any impact whatsoever: testament to the success of the Boks' public relations exercise, at least off the field.

Yet adding to the greyness of the occasion was the fact that the tourists had yet to reassert themselves as a top rugby-playing nation. Since losing their comeback Test to New Zealand at Ellis Park in 1992, they had won just five of 13 Tests, although among their spoils of victory were the scalps of defending world champion Australia, France and England. Isolation had caused rugby cancers that South Africa had been slow to recognise. World rugby was in the process of cleaning up its act, and the 'anything goes' mentality was no longer deemed valid, even in a man's game. If that was to be the attitude of players, the only thing likely to go was them, from the field. Three Springboks had received their marching orders in 1993, although to be fair two had been marched at Tucuman in Argentina, a venue renowned for intense provocation. That said, the Boks still had a penchant for rough play, as had been evidenced in their brutal series-squaring second-Test victory against England just prior to the tour.

Another cancer wrought by isolation was parochialism. Starved of Springbok action, provincial rivalries had replaced Test-match rivalries, with the result that there was an uneasy relationship between the leading unions. It became an open secret that coach Ian McIntosh had not got the team he wanted, and that a number of injured and otherwise unavailable players had been left behind.

McIntosh, a Zimbabwean, not a former Springbok, and from English-speaking Natal, was himself under pressure. It seemed he believed nothing less than a series victory would allow him to continue on to the World Cup, and the harrowing presence of Louis Luyt throughout much of the tour served only to heighten his anxiety.

Selection aside, McIntosh was still battling to convince players of the merits of the 15-man game. Forwards and backs had for some time been separate entities in South African rugby.

Naturally the Springboks' mediocre record was not a cause for concern in New Zealand, especially since the home side's fortunes had also plunged. When the Springboks arrived in the country, the All Blacks were about to start a two-Test series against France that would lead to a first-ever series loss to the Tricolores. Following on from a dreadful defeat at the hands of England at Twickenham at the end of 1993, this confirmed the widespread view that rugby in New Zealand was in crisis.

Certainly the New Zealand Rugby Football Union added to the atmosphere of doom and gloom by refusing to confirm Laurie Mains as All Black coach through to the 1995 World Cup, which was to be played in South Africa the following May and June. They also sacked Peter Thorburn, a member of Mains' selection panel, and replaced him with former All Black halfback Lin Colling who had never coached beyond club level. As far as Mains was concerned such moves were the manifestation of an Auckland conspiracy aimed at promoting his nemesis John Hart to the top coaching position for the World Cup.

Indeed, the Springboks' arrival for their first tour in 13 years was muted owing to the presence of the French and the damage they did to All Black reputations, including that of beleagured coach Mains. By the time Jean Luc Sadourny touched down for his historic try at Eden Park, the Boks had completed four matches and were just six days away from their first date with the All Blacks at Carisbrook. Such an itinerary for the home side certainly supported Mains contention that the NZRFU were doing nothing to help him. He later commented that during the French series he struggled to focus his players on the job at hand such was their excitement about the Springboks. The result was that from the beginning the South African series was cloaked in desperation.

The Boks had lost their inspirational captain Francois Pienaar to concussion against Wellington, thus ensuring he became the fifth Bok tour captain from just six visits to miss the first Test of a series. Just two of their team, feisty winger James Small and centre Pieter Muller, had played in the 1992 Test against New Zealand, while winger Chester Williams became the first coloured player to represent South Africa against New Zealand. Fullback Andre Joubert had played for the World XV against New Zealand in the 1992 centenary series. In the absence of Pienaar, Tiaan Strauss was chosen to lead the side from the unfamiliar position of openside flanker.

Just eight of the All Blacks had appeared against South Africa in Johannesburg two years earlier, and there were three changes from the team that had lost to France at Eden Park six days earlier. Former Samoan international Alama Ieremia replaced Matthew Cooper at second-five, Graeme Bachop returned to international rugby for the first time since 1992 to replace Otago's Stu Forster, while John Timu moved back to winger after 13 consecutive Tests at fullback to replace Jonah Lomu, allowing Shane Howarth to make his Test debut.

A pre-match organisational blunder served only to inspire the Boks. Since the inauguration of Nelson Mandela's presidency, it had been policy that South African sporting teams honour two national anthems — the Xhosa 'Nkosi Sikelel' iAfrika' ('God Bless Africa') and the Afrikaner 'Die Stem' ('The Call of South Africa'). Unfortunately the Otago RFU failed to play 'Die Stem', which led to the bizarre sight of the Springboks in full voice accompanied only by the All Black haka.

Complaints aside, the Springboks came at the nervous home team with such ferocity that they threatened to win the match inside the first quarter. With the Bachop brothers, Graeme and Stephen (the eighth set of brothers to play Test rugby for New Zealand) giving a nightmare kicking performance and the backline struggling for cohesion, it was South Africa who made all the early running, three times coming close to a try. The All Blacks also had to contend with the loss of Ian Jones with a hairline fracture of the cheekbone, leading to a complete reorganisation of the pack.

As it was, all the visitors got for their early pressure was an Andre Joubert penalty goal. When New Zealand finally broke free of the siege, Bok infringements and mistakes aided their cause, as did the departure of prop Balie Swart with concussion.

The referee, Ireland's Brian Stirling, played a major role in the home team's recovery to lead 12–3 at halftime, courtesy of four Shane Howarth penalty goals, by awarding penalties and free kicks 12–4 in their favour. This incensed Ian McIntosh, who, during the break, instructed Strauss to query Stirling.

Whatever else was said it appeared to be working when the Boks closed to within one point just four minutes after the resumption of play, thanks to Joubert's second penalty goal and a try by big flanker Rudolf Straueli. However, the Boks continued to botch opportunities, Joubert missing the conversion and a penalty goal. Conversely All Black pressure led to Howarth's fifth success.

Indiscipline proved to be the decisive factor. South Africa was awarded a kickable penalty in the 23rd minute, only to concede a penalty when a touch judge intervened to identify prop Johan le Roux for a stomping offence. New Zealand swept on to the attack from the resulting lineout, winning ruck after ruck until finally John Kirwan was given space down the blindside to run in a record 67th try for the All Blacks (and his 35th in a Test). With Howarth's conversion, the tally from just a few minutes' play rose to 10 points.

The visitors fought back, but fierce New Zealand defence and Bok errors, ill-discipline — frustrated halfback Johan Roux stomped All Black captain Sean Fitzpatrick — and bad luck saw the host side home with the concession of just one more Joubert penalty goal.

In the final analysis it was a Test that New Zealand simply couldn't afford to lose. Captain Sean Fitzpatrick had told the players before the Test that it was either a case of winning the game or being issued with razor blades — and not to shave with!

There was nothing pretty about the match. Nerves, emotion, intensity, pressure, mistakes, over-vigorous play, courage and commitment were its principal components. At the post-match conference, Ian McIntosh bared his teeth. Inconsistent interpretation of ruck and maul laws and allegations of All Black illegalities — barging at the lineout, the collapsing of scrums — were on the agenda.

It was difficult not to feel some sympathy for him, especially when one considered Stirling's credentials. Rated just third in his own country, here he was in charge of the most intense Test rivalry in world rugby. The pace of the match was unfamiliar to him, and afterwards he was seen slumped, completely exhausted, in the referee's room. Still, that was how appointments were made by the International Rugby Football Board at the time.

Hero of the day was undoubtedly Shane Howarth. A few years previously he'd broken his neck in a diving accident. But at Carisbrook, in front of a crowd of 41,000, the only breaking he did was of the hearts of the Springboks and their supporters. In a dream debut he had contributed 17 points with his goalkicking, his successes including a mighty 46-metre effort just before halftime.

Before the second Test a foul-play citing against James Small by Waikato completely took the gloss off a quality win over the Ranfurly Shield holder. Initial rejoicing at the sight of Springbok backs and forwards combining superbly turned to contemplation of a disrupted Test build-up. Small had made a reckless charge at the ball as it was being gathered by Waikato lock Steve Gordon, leaping into the air, where his knee collided with Gordon's head, knocking him unconscious. Some of Small's actions later in the match probably didn't help his cause. The 'McEnroe of rugby' blew a kiss to Waikato halfback Simon Crabb as he scored one try, and gesticulated rudely to another player after a long chase back on defence.

Broadcaster Murray Deaker got in on the action, claiming on national television that Small was a 'nutter', before adding, 'What would you expect from a bloke who says he's used dope?' This was a reference to an interview given by Small in which he'd admitted smoking marijuana as a teenager. Small and the South African management were justifiably upset, and at one stage considered legal action. Considering Deaker was a reformed alcoholic, it was a cheap shot.

As it was, the NZRFU judiciary decided Small's actions didn't deserve a penalty, although it was easy to suggest rugby had once again closed ranks and the reasoning behind the judgment had more to do with ensuring the good of the tour than arriving at a punishment to fit the crime.

Springbok lock Adri Geldenhuys contributed further to the mid-tour blues by being sent off for punching just four days before the second Test, in a match against Manawatu that saw worse acts of violence. He was subsequently banned from playing for one week.

It may have been coincidence, but television replays appeared to be excellent at pinpointing Bok transgressions, less so at highlighting All Black infringements. However, such problems were

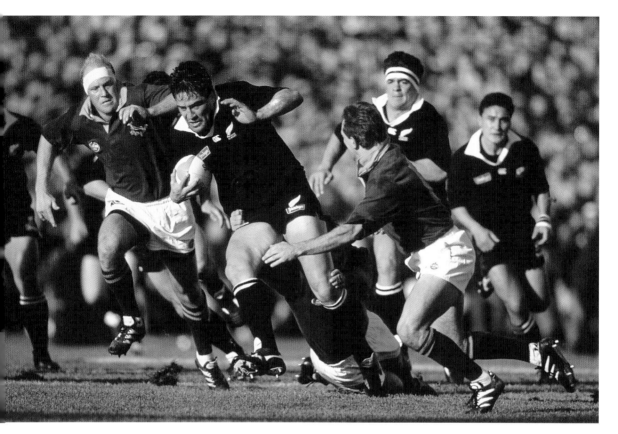

All Black No. 8 Zinzan Brooke's dynamic form during the 1994 series is clearly illustrated by this run during the first Test at Carisbrook.

to pale into insignificance following the second Test, at Athletic Park in Wellington.

New Zealand made just the one change to their team, a fit-again Robin Brooke coming in for Ian Jones, to give the home side two sets of brothers in a Test match for the first time since Don and Ian Clarke and Colin and Stan Meads had taken on France in 1961.

Meanwhile South Africa made four changes. Theo van Rensburg replaced Andre Joubert at fullback in the hope that he would prove a more successful goalkicker; tour reinforcement Japie Mulder came in for Pieter Muller, who had returned home because of a neck injury suffered in the first Test; and Guy Kebble, who had replaced Swart at Dunedin, was now in the starting line-up. The most significant change, however, was the return of captain Francois Pienaar, who had proved his fitness against Manawatu. Pienaar went to the openside flanker position, forcing Strauss onto the blindside in place of Rudolf Straeuli.

Perhaps because the All Blacks had yet to win back their public's confidence, pre-match talk focused on Springbok desperation rather than the likelihood of the All Blacks closing out the series. Within the confines of the All Black camp that situation was skilfully exploited.

Former All Black No. 8 Murray Mexted was invited to speak at the team meeting on Friday night. He had played in the corresponding Test in Wellington in 1981, when the All Blacks had been beaten 24–12 after trailing 18–3 at halftime. Mexted's message was that 'the game was all over in ten minutes' as the All Blacks, playing into the wind, had been 'hit with a steamroller'.

The tactics, the history, the bloody-minded attitude needed to succeed — the 1994 All Blacks took it all on board. They won the toss, played into the wind — a not-too-stiff breeze — and earned a 10–6 lead in a fast and furious first half. Then, in a heroic second half, they kept the Springboks at bay to win both the match, 13–9, and the series.

Both the home team's tries were classics of their kind. The first came after a lineout had been won and the ball moved as far as Ieremia, who hit the advantage line. No. 8 Zinzan Brooke, who gave an astonishing performance, was on hand to take it on further before the pack came in behind and drove forward. The Bachops instinctively knew the blindside was the way to go, Frank Bunce slipped into a gap and away from the defence before off-loading to Blair Larsen, who drew the last defender and ran Timu in for the try. Backs and forwards, set piece and second phase, good options and good finishing.

Joy is beating the Springboks in a series at home — (from left) Alama Ieremia, Zinzan Brooke, Mark Cooksley and Graeme Bachop enjoy the final whistle at Athletic Park.

While Zinzan Brooke's try was less spectacular, in psychological terms it was an even greater blow to the opposition. It came from a five-metre scrum after van Rensburg had been deceived by a wicked bounce and forced to run the ball dead. The New Zealand pack, clearly dominant after struggling at Carisbrook, went to work. Aided by a fatal error from the Springbok loose forwards, who detached to defend, the shove gained momentum, allowing Brooke to crash over. Technically it should not have been a try, the ball emerging and re-entering the scrum, before emerging again for Brooke to score, but the effort was worthy of five points.

While the South Africans reasserted themselves in the second quarter it was not until they faced the wind that they became dangerous with the ball in hand. Heroic tackling was now the All Blacks' duty. The pressure continued to be applied, but the visitors' forwards were guilty of taking the backs' ball far too often. When they didn't, the defence swarmed, none more so than Zinzan Brooke and Bunce. The cut and thrust continued until the final whistle, the Boks being denied at least two tries by desperate defence.

When the final whistle came it had never sounded sweeter for the All Blacks in 199 previous Test victories. For the fourth time New Zealand had won a series against South Africa in New Zealand.

All Black coach Laurie Mains summed up the mood perfectly when he admitted his first reaction had been, 'Thank Christ for that.'

Unfortunately, another story was about to overtake the series victory. A TVNZ camera had captured Springbok prop Johan le Roux biting All Black captain Sean Fitzpatrick's ear. Even before he had come to New Zealand Le Roux had brought the game of rugby into disrepute, having been suspended for returning a positive drugs test, and his Springbok debut against England, prior to the tour, having been memorable for its brutality. During the first Test at Carisbrook he had caught the referee's attention on three separate occasions, and had cost his team a crucial penalty reversal.

Although the Springbok management moved swiftly, it was not quick enough to head off a believe-it-or-not situation. Rival managers Colin Meads and Jannie Engelbrecht had agreed that the two teams should get together socially after the match, and the All Blacks duly arrived at the Springboks' hotel. At the function Le Roux approached Fitzpatrick and shook his hand.

'He congratulated me on the win. But he didn't apologise for biting me,' Fitzpatrick said.

Later that night, after viewing videotape of the incident, the South African management pre-empted the judiciary deliberations and took the decision to send the 32-year-old Le Roux home. He stayed on in Wellington, where his disgrace was completed later that week when he was banned from playing rugby for 19 months, a penalty which was not reduced on appeal. After almost six hours of submissions and deliberation, the NZRFU appeals committee chairman, John Laurenson, QC, said the act of biting was not only foul play but 'incomprehensible in any reasonable terms'.

A cartoon in a South African newspaper took a lighter approach, claiming of Le Roux that 'actually he's a vegetarian — he only chews cauliflower ears', while other slogans, such as 'If you can't beat 'em, eat 'em', emerged. For most, however, the name of Johan le Roux was instantly demoted to the sporting hall of shame.

The Springboks' misery was compounded in their next match, in which Otago relieved them of their prized Bok head in wet conditions at Carisbrook.

The final Test, in Auckland, was to be refereed by Welshman Robert Yemen, a veteran of three minor Tests. Thankfully the series had already been decided.

Once again New Zealand made just one change, with fit-again Ian Jones replacing Mark Cooksley. South Africa's five changes were the return of Andre Joubert, the call-up of fullback Gavin Johnson — the sixth tour replacement — as a goalkicking winger, the dropping of first-Test captain Tiaan Strauss for Fritz van Heerden, the return from injury of Balie Swart to replace Johan le Roux, and the inclusion of Keith Andrews in place of Guy Kebble. Strauss had been tagged 'the Lion of Africa' before arriving in New Zealand but had failed to live up to his reputation. Possibly he was hampered by playing at flanker rather than in his preferred position of No. 8, an opportunity Ian McIntosh could have provided in the third Test given the ordinary ball skills displayed by his preferred choice Adriaan Richter.

McIntosh might also have gambled on halfback Joost van der Westhuizen, whose ability on the break could have ignited his dangerous backline. As it was, the personable South African coach, who had already told New Zealand journalists he would be dumped upon his arrival home, came within an ace of recording a Test victory.

Certainly his team's two-tries-to-nil tally offered them a moral victory, even though the scoreboard read 18–18 at fulltime thanks to faultless goalkicking by Shane Howarth. 'A draw is like kissing your sister,' was McIntosh's droll reaction. His point was beautifully made. Both teams had fallen short of their objectives. New Zealand had failed to wrap up a series whitewash with a stylish victory, and South Africa had failed to return home with a face-saving Test win.

South Africa should have won. There were missed try-scoring and goalkicking opportunities, and indiscipline once again was costly.

Perhaps it was this Test that saw the South African public's view of Sean Fitzpatrick turn from dislike to hatred. The All Black captain's gamesmanship had already irked the Bok faithful, and some believed he was not blameless in Le Roux's disgrace. An elbow here, a jersey tug there, the use of an opponent's face to help himself off the ground were all Fitzpatrick trademarks, and his disbelieving face when retaliation ensued was convincing. So while Brendan Venter's flailing fists were provoked by Fitzpatrick pulling his jersey, the result was three points to New Zealand. Unfair? It really depends who you support and how you view violent acts.

South African writer Paul Dobson wittily commented: 'There's an old rugby story about a wise referee who said to a player, "If I see anybody hit you again, I am going to send you off the field."'

The highlight of the second half was the return of Michael Jones to Test action, albeit wearing the coach's jersey, No. 23, his own having been misplaced. Sunday Tests and injury had previously ruled him out. His dynamic presence and speed added drive to a forward pack which was already

DEFINING MOMENT

The Johan le Roux Disgrace
SECOND TEST, WELLINGTON, 23 JULY, 1994

Who made the decision to bring Johan le Roux on tour? His indiscipline cost a 10-point score at a crucial stage of the first Test, and his biting of Fitzpatrick cost South African rugby its integrity. How good was he anyway?

dominant in set piece, and late in the match he came within inches of stealing an undeserved victory.

So the series ended and the post-mortems began. All tour the South African public had expressed concern about the penalty counts, the citings and why the tourists had not countered, and the decline of Springbok forward play. Now it was time for the political world of South African rugby to go into full swing. When the tourists arrived home, McIntosh, as he had predicted, was replaced by Kitch Christie. Engelbrecht, who was continually at war with Luyt over his interference in New Zealand, was eventually axed after much public bickering.

At this stage, therefore, few were predicting with confidence that the World Cup in South Africa in 10 months' time would see a New Zealand–South Africa final. Even fewer were suggesting the Springboks would enter that match unbeaten in their last 13 Tests.

However, the benefits of the 1994 tour were not lost on some within the Springbok camp. New Zealanders were to come to respect names such as Joubert, Williams, Small, Mulder, Muller, Hennie le Roux, Van der Westhuizen, Ruben Kruger, Krynauw Otto, Kobus Wiese, Mark Andrews, Swart, Ollie le Roux and James Dalton, all of whom were developed during the 1994 tour.

Mains became embittered by a lack of recognition for his team's achievement in becoming the first New Zealand side to win a series against South Africa without dropping a Test. While history tends to support his view, most critics believed the series hadn't been played by the two best teams in the world.

Only the second Test had produced rugby of a consistent quality, and the All Blacks' attacking back play hadn't been of the highest standard. It was only later in a desperate second-half comeback against Australia that they threw off the shackles of negativity. Even then, as he realised the 15-man game had to be mastered for the World Cup, Mains knew his 1994 team was not equipped or fit enough to deliver it.

His eyes had been opened.

Strange days? Indeed.

1994

THE SOUTH AFRICAN RESPONSE

THE SIXTH SPRINGBOKS IN NEW ZEALAND

by David Williams

A SIDE INTENT on playing dirty rugby could not have dominated as the Springboks did for the first quarter of the first Test. Tiaan Strauss nearly scored a try soon after kickoff, and in the first 20 minutes of play the Boks enjoyed a 75 per cent territorial advantage. Their mauling was disciplined and effective, while their backs were running confidently from within their own 22-metre area.

Ian McIntosh was right to be frustrated at halftime with the All Blacks' tactics and referee Stirling's failure to keep up. The first temper flare-up was caused when Robin Brooke openly played the ball with his hand in a ruck, with the Boks on the move in a good attacking position. Instead of awarding a penalty, Stirling embarked on one of his many schoolmasterly lectures. The South African players, more accustomed at that time to taciturn referees, were intensely irritated.

As the match moved to the second quarter with the Boks leading 3–0, the tension sharpened. The All Black backs responded to the pressure by frequently drifting offside, their forwards by mountaineering in the rucks and mauls. After one of these frightening pile-ups, Balie Swart began staggering around with concussion. Although the injury was not in fact caused by foul play or a New Zealand boot, its timing seemed to raise the temperature further.

Swart's departure after three minutes of on-field treatment signalled a shift in the balance of power. Now the New Zealand forwards began to dominate and the South Africans to concede penalties under pressure. Although Hennie le Roux was creative at flyhalf, cracks were showing elsewhere. At lineouts the ball always went to Mark Andrews, and the opposing forwards made life difficult for him. Worst of all, South African frustration turned to ill-discipline. Johan le Roux was twice penalised for obvious offences, having earlier got away with taking out Sean Fitzpatrick at the side of a ruck.

In the second half the Boks' inexperience began to tell. They seemed unsure about the offside law and Stirling's fussy interpretations generally. Instead of playing as the referee saw it, they became distracted. Even so, at 12–11 South Africa was more than back in the game. If Joubert had goalkicked more accurately, the tide might have turned.

But the scrum count at that stage was running 10–3 in favour of New Zealand, a sure sign of steady pressure. The next goal kick came from Howarth, after a penalty for offside, followed by that reversed penalty and Kirwan's try. Suddenly it was 22–11 to the home side, whereas five minutes before it might easily have been 16–12 to the Boks. It did not help the Springbok mood that the original penalty had been given against Zinzan Brooke for playing the ball while on the ground.

Springbok coach Ian McIntosh became so concerned by the mounting penalty count against his team that he instructed debutant Test captain Tiaan Strauss to approach Irish referee Brian Stirling at halftime.

The margin was too much to make up in the remaining quarter of an hour, and the Springbok's focus was lost. Clearly Le Roux and Fitzpatrick had been grating each other from the start. With nine minutes to go Le Roux suddenly reeled back from a ruck in pain; the replay showed that Fitzpatrick, lying on the ground, had kicked his boot up hard and deliberately. Yet Stirling, whose performance bordered on the hysterical in the last 10 minutes, saw fit to warn only Le Roux that he would be sent off if he wasn't careful.

In the end, the scoring was a true reflection: one try each from genuinely creative play, but too many goalable penalties conceded by the Springboks. And the All Blacks were just too streetwise.

A pattern had been established for the series — and, indeed, the rest of the tour. The inexperienced Springboks tried to be creative but they were unable to rise above their suspicion of and uncertainty over refereeing interpretations. South African frustrations led to physical outbursts, which in turn attracted the righteous anger of the one-eyed New Zealand media. The All Blacks, by contrast, were more judicious and cunning, expert at constantly riding on the edge of the law and looking utterly innocent in the process.

In the classic second Test, the Springboks' courage and enterprise were once again under-mined by their own errors and well countered by the All Blacks' superb running, clinical skills and occasional gamesmanship. The first try for New Zealand happened so beautifully the referee overlooked the fact that the whole All Black pack had gone over the top in the build-up. Not long afterwards, with the score at 5–3, a scrum collapsed and Fitzpatrick stood up and openly punched Francois Pienaar, with not a murmur from referee or linesmen.

But South Africa was its own worst enemy. When leading 6–5, how did Theo van Rensburg contrive to carry the ball over his own line and into touch-in-goal? It wasn't a wicked bounce: the ball would have rolled out harmlessly for a 22-metre drop-out, or Van Rensburg could have just fallen on it. The ensuing pushover try was marginal but good. New Zealand had gone ahead 10–6, and those five points proved crucial.

For much of the game thereafter, the All Black pack did to its opposition what the Springbok packs of old had done to theirs. When Fitzpatrick called for a five-metre scrum instead of tapping a penalty or going for the posts, it indicated the kind of confidence Philip Nel had relished in 1937.

Even so, the Springboks managed to claw their way back and put together some good sequences. Johan Roux came agonisingly close to scoring, and the All Blacks were then penalised for collapsing the scrum on their line, but the obvious compensation, a penalty try, was not forthcoming, and Van Rensburg missed the kick. Absurdly, New Zealand then moved to 13–6 ahead from a penalty apparently awarded for sledging, while the referee had already overlooked several blatantly high tackles by the All Black three quarters. With the score at 13–9, Fitzpatrick wasted time expertly, and finally the referee blew the game a minute short. The fans at home could have been forgiven for asking where Clive Norling had been when they had needed him.

The Le Roux–Fitzpatrick biting incident was rightly condemned (although it was never made clear why biting, appalling as it is, should be considered a worse crime than gouging a man's eyes or kicking him in the groin). South African fans felt ashamed, but one grizzled old Springbok, while condemning the method, approved the choice of victim: 'That Fitzpatrick's been asking for something for a while now. In my time he would have been sorted out long ago.'

It remained for the South African fans back home to haul themselves out of bed one more time for the third Test, to watch Fitzpatrick continue his niggling and Frank Bunce make high tackle after high tackle. But such issues were now academic and the two Bok tries were small consolation. The series had been intense and closely fought, but it had been lost, and the draw in the last match was not even as good as kissing your sister.

1995
HISTORY IS MADE

THE WORLD CUP FINAL

by David Williams

IF THE SPRINGBOKS were destined to achieve a fairy-tale victory in the 1995 World Cup, it certainly didn't look that way before the tournament. South African fans are prone to unrealistic optimism, but even they were sober about their team's chances.

The 1994 tour to New Zealand was regarded as a failure, and there was no question that the All Blacks were favourites to regain the William Webb Ellis Cup. There had been four Tests between the old foes since 1992 and none of them had been won by the Boks. Although South Africa had enjoyed some memorable moments since readmission into the world rugby arena in 1992, there had been too many unsettling defeats, not only by New Zealand.

Continuity was visibly lacking: there had been three coaches in as many years, and the retirements of such great players as Danie Gerber, Uli Schmidt and Naas Botha. Indeed, uncertainty about the team for the World Cup caused speculation that new coach Kitch Christie would recall the 38-year-old Botha. Christie later admitted that, with six weeks to go, he'd seriously considered it. He was concerned at the lack of big-match experience in the squad.

Even the captaincy was not settled. Francois Pienaar had done well with Transvaal but he was not popular in other provinces; even some Transvaal fans thought him too flash off the field and too petulant on it. Tiaan Strauss, the popular Western Province captain, was seen as a man more likely to unite the team and country behind him, but of course Christie was the Transvaal coach. The old spectre of provincialism and the north–south rivalry appeared to be undermining South African rugby again at a time when unity was vital.

Christie not only went for Pienaar as captain, he controversially excluded Strauss from the squad altogether. His reasoning was not that Strauss wasn't good enough, but simply that there wasn't room for both. 'It had to be one or the other,' he said later. 'We had to unite behind one captain.' Naturally the decision went down badly, particularly in the southern provinces. Another desperately unlucky loose forward was Natal's Gary Teichmann, so there was hardly a national enthusiasm for the Springbok side.

The positive aspects of the team's build-up would only really become apparent with hindsight. Christie's self-confidence as a coach, his insistence on discipline and his palpable integrity united the players. He received superb management support from the intelligent Morne du Plessis, one of the great Bok captains, who had nothing to prove, and the visionary Edward Griffiths, serving as Sarfu CEO, but a man with a rare capacity to anticipate and head off problems. Griffiths was also a former journalist and sports editor, and his understanding of the media was to prove invaluable.

PLAYER OF THE DECADE

FRANCOIS PIENAAR

BORN: 1967

POSITION: FLANKER

PLAYED NEW ZEALAND: 1994, 1995, 1996 (5 TESTS)

Francois Pienaar was not assured of being Springbok captain for the 1995 World Cup. He was not close to being the kind of auto-matic choice, that ironically, Gary Teichmann later seemed to be for the 1999 campaign. But Pienaar and coach Kitch Christie had worked together at Transvaal, their success record had been exceptional, and that was that. There were many fans outside Transvaal, and not a few within that faction-ridden province, who were deeply sceptical. What favoured Pienaar, though, was the widespread belief in South Africa that the Springboks would not get far in the World Cup anyway, having gone down recently to New Zealand and France. He had nothing to lose, with Kitch Christie describing the in-heritance of the coaching role as an 'ambulance job'.

In the end Pienaar ended up winning every-thing. It must be one of the greatest images of sporting triumph ever captured: the South African captain receiving the William Webb Ellis Cup from Nelson Mandela before their home crowd, each wearing a no. 6 jersey. Pienaar somehow found the right touch on the field and the right words off it. If he enjoyed some luck along the way — well, nobody worked harder for his luck than Pienaar. He grew into the role of captain and is now an elder statesman of the world game.

It all began to come together. The Springboks' preparation suddenly turned into a campaign, and the country, excited at the scale of the event, was swept along and there was a new sense of togetherness behind the brilliant slogan 'One Team, One Country'. After a decade of unprecedented turbulence and violence, culminating in 1994 in the first genuinely democratic general election, South Africa needed something to take its mind off politics.

Rugby World Cup 1995 caught fire with the very first match, at Newlands on Thursday May 25: the world champions against the hosts, Australia versus South Africa. The Wallabies were clear favourites and they knew it. South Africans talked resignedly about losing the game and then possibly meeting New Zealand in the semi-final. But the Springboks drew on a hundred years of passion, achieved the ideal focus in front of an ecstatic crowd, executed Christie's tactics to the letter and blew Australia off the field (27–18).

The following weeks were not easy. Lesser countries such as Canada and Western Samoa, with no chance of winning, resorted to cynical violence and dangerous tackling to unsettle the Boks. Floodlight failure in Port Elizabeth added to the tension. Hooker James Dalton and winger Pieter Hendriks (who had gone round David Campese to score the decisive try at Newlands) were banned for poor discipline. The semi-final against France was nearly abandoned because of freak monsoon-style rains in Durban — there were fears that men might drown under the rucks — and in the end the Boks scraped through (19–15) after a climax of utterly draining tension.

Even then, New Zealand was regarded as firm favourite. Jonah Lomu had electrified the tournament with his humiliation of defenders such as England's Mike Catt, and the All Blacks had looked composed throughout. If Australia could be beaten so well by England, who then in turn were brushed aside by New Zealand, what chance could South Africa have in the final? But the underdog status suited Christie perfectly, even though he had injuries to worry about (notably Andre Joubert's broken hand and Joel Stransky's damaged eye).

Christie shocked the already pessimistic home fans when he again asked Mark Andrews to play at No. 8 instead of lock. It may have worked in the slush of King's Park against France, but Ellis Park's surface would be hard and fast. Christie, though, was implacable, and his confidence again rubbed off on his players. 'He instilled this idea that we could not lose,' said Andrews later, 'and he made it all seem somehow very personal.'

*

Johannesburg produces a perfect highveld day for the final on Saturday 24 June 1995. The sour tension of that 1992 readmission Test here against New Zealand is a vague memory, soon forgotten. From about noon the crowd gets high on an ecstatic cocktail of tension, colour, song, dancing (a 'World in Union') and the awesome, unexpected sight and sound of a South African Airways Boeing 747 roaring just a hundred metres above the stadium.

But the undisputed climax, in a build-up full of climaxes, is the appearance of President Nelson Mandela, not in the usual presidential suit and tie, not even in one of his famous African shirts, but in a No. 6 Springbok jersey. The largely white crowd cheers in delight and then begins spontaneously to chant: 'Nelson! Nelson! Nelson! . . .' People are seen to cry and not to hide it. It is part of a healing process, and no sport but rugby could have provided such a moment. And there is still a match to watch!

As if to confirm Mandela's over-the-top patriotism has unsettled them, the All Blacks reveal vulnerability immediately after the kickoff. First the ball doesn't carry 10 metres, then New Zealand is penalised for offside. Ellis Park roars as if a try has been scored. Stransky misses touch but Glen Osborne kicks out and it is a Springbok lineout. The ball is tapped back to Joost van der Westhuizen, who also kicks into touch. Even now, the All Blacks fail to impress: they lose their own lineout and Stransky comes motoring through, but the Boks concede the put-in after the ball goes to ground. This is frantic, unplanned, exploratory stuff by both sides.

Then the All Blacks start exerting control. Zinzan Brooke deftly feeds from the back of a scrum to Bachop going blindside; on to Osborne, whose jinking running eludes first Stransky

Nelson Mandela's appearance at the Rugby World Cup final united the Rainbow Nation. The implacable Louis Luyt (middle) and Steve Tshwete (left), Minister of Sport, stand to the left of South Africa's president.

and then the desperately galloping Andrews, who is trying to be the covering No. 8 he is not. Now there's trouble. Osborne has the crowd shrieking as he makes another 30 metres down the far touchline, closing now on the Springbok 22. It's time to spread back wide, and there comes Lomu, steaming down the centre as he has been doing all week in a hundred thousand South African nightmares, with the Bok defence stretched and going backwards.

But the long pass bounces short of Lomu, and Ellis Park sighs with relief — although the All Blacks still have possession. Now Walter Little charges in and crashes towards the 22-metre line. But the moment has passed. Osborne's strained pass to Lomu has given the green jerseys time to get back and organise themselves. Little is steered briskly into touch on the quarter-line. Lots of action for New Zealand, but no ground gained.

The All Blacks take a fresh grip. Mehrtens kicks high, his forwards drive. Little and Frank Bunce link up neatly, and the pressure causes the Boks to concede a penalty for joining the maul from the wrong side. It's 15 metres in from touch and 27 metres out, which means the posts look fat and inviting. Mehrtens breathes nervously but his kick is smooth: 3–0 after six minutes.

That's bad for the crowd — but not as bad as it might have been. Lomu hasn't run through anyone yet. What is encouraging is that the Bok backs are coming up very fast on defence.

After 10 minutes' play the Springboks have still not got beyond the All Blacks' 10-metre line. But after a period on attack, with good driving and recycling, they get a penalty 15 metres in and about 26 metres out from the All Black goal-line. Stransky puts it over with more coolness than Mehrtens displayed, and after 12 minutes the score is 3–3. As if to confirm South Africa refuses to be intimidated, Small takes the ball from the kickoff and achieves a brilliant touch.

But now Jonah Lomu threatens at last to get into the game. After a clean lineout ball from Ian Jones and a neat scissors movement by Frank Bunce, Lomu has the ball and straightens his run. He powers through Stransky and Pienaar and makes 20 metres. But Van der Westhuizen has covering back, takes Lomu neatly round the ankles, and down he goes like a felled tree. The Bok try-line is still vulnerable, but, as Lomu tries to pass, Mark Andrews gets back fast to intercept. The All Blacks immediately ruck Andrews away ruthlessly, but there is no advantage, and Ed Morrison calls the players back for a New Zealand penalty just outside the 22-metre line in the middle of the field. The Springboks just couldn't absorb the pressure without going offside. Mehrtens puts it over — 6–3 after 14 minutes. But at least a try was prevented.

Mehrtens kicks an astonishing 22-metre drop-out, creating a lineout just one metre from the Springbok line. It has happened so quickly touch judge Derek Bevan has to guess the point of exit. But the Boks weather the pressure again, and Stransky clears to halfway. Now the flow is in the other direction. The crowd roars as Chester Williams dumps the bigger Jeff Wilson, then Stransky gets a huge touch from a penalty and for the first time the Boks are within 10 metres of the All Blacks' line — and it's a Springbok throw-in.

Beautifully taken by Hannes Strydom. Out to the backs, who try a decoy run followed by a scissors, but the move breaks down. Ball recycled, and Chris Rossouw charges for the line and the crowd screams. New Zealand's defence holds, but it's a scrum to South Africa, just five metres out. Andrews picks up at the back after a partial wheel and, charging low, gains two metres. Van der Westhuizen collects and makes another two metres, slips it back to Ruben Kruger, who goes over and scores . . .

But the referee's signal is emphatic: Kruger was held up, no touchdown, so it's another five-metre scrum. It seems the try was good but the scoreboard says otherwise. The crowd seethes with discussion and outrage. Then New Zealand are blown for breaking up the scrum as they go backwards over their line, and there are appeals for a penalty try. No such luck. The Boks' attacking momentum is lost, but at least there are another three points from a Stransky penalty goal. That makes it 6–6 after 22 minutes. As South Africans pause to think, they realise they are very much in the game — but the statistics show ominously that New Zealand has enjoyed 66 per cent of the possession in the first quarter.

Francois Pienaar changes tactics. Instead of those deep, probing kicks, he keeps the ball with the forwards, who drive with the discipline Kitch Christie has demanded so uncompromisingly in practice. Soon the All Blacks are under pressure again when Osborne and Wilson get confused

Referee Ed Morrison is well positioned to award a try to Springbok flanker Ruben Kruger. Unfortunately for South Africa, Morrison's eyes played a trick on him.

by an awkward stab kick from Van der Westhuizen, who follows up and almost collects to score. Again it's a five-metre scrum, and again there are futile cries for a penalty try as the All Blacks collapse under pressure. But this time Stranksy misses the posts.

South Africa maintains the pressure. Stransky rewards his forwards' hard work with a low but successful drop attempt. South Africa leads for the first time (9–6). Now the All Blacks are looking rattled. Halftime is not far off and the script has not been followed. Sean Fitzpatrick has been very quiet, and Jonah Lomu is again tackled convincingly by Small. Suddenly the first 40 minutes are gone.

The second half starts and the crowd jeers confidently as Lomu completely misses a pass. The Boks drive forward superbly, keeping control with short kicks and careful passing. For the third time, the All Black scrum collapses. When the Boks are penalised for going over the top, Mehrtens goes for the posts, even though the mark is inside his own half and just 20 metres in from touch. He misses, and it seems only just, given the ascendancy of the Springboks.

It is as if the first 20 minutes of the game belonged to New Zealand and the next 30 to South Africa. Now the tide turns again in favour of New Zealand. Lomu receives the ball out wide on the left and he's clear! He is chased by Joubert, but as Lomu gets to the Springbok 22-metre line it is Japie Mulder who takes him low and hard from behind in a textbook tackle. A try is averted but the All Blacks have built up enough pressure to give Mehrtens space in an ideal position — in front of the left upright, on the 22-metre line — to drop for goal. After 15 minutes of the second half the score is 9–9, and now the excitement is turning into raw tension. Two minutes later, Mehrtens misses another drop attempt.

Now the match becomes attritional again. As in the first 20 minutes, both sides become cautious: nobody wants to concede the match-winning penalty or miss a vital tackle. Garry Pagel, one of the iron men of South African rugby, is a shrewd substitution at prop for Balie Swart. Both sides surge close to the try-line, but each time there is someone to get the defenders out of trouble. With only five minutes to go, Lomu, now looking merely human and almost meek, is given space by his team-mates but is taken again by Van der Westhuizen.

With three minutes to go, New Zealand, in heart-stopping action, almost seals the game. Bachop's grubber puts them eight metres out from the Bok try-line, and the Springbok forwards fail to clear. The All Blacks get the ball back and run straight and hard. Frank Bunce almost edges through but is eventually retarded by green-jerseyed arms clinging desperately to his leg. But he gets his pass away and the ball slips back to Mehrtens, again perfectly positioned near the middle of the field for the drop attempt. The World Cup is heading for New Zealand . . . but this time Van der Westhuizen gets up in time to pressurise, and the kick veers to one side.

Stransky drops out deep — anything to get away from the danger zone — and Osborne's unhappy match continues. He fields well but kicks out on the full from his own 10-metre line. The nerves are getting to everyone. A minute later, good work by Andre Joubert and Chester Williams forces substitute Marc Ellis to concede a lineout just five metres from the New Zealand line. But the Boks, absurdly, don't even challenge for the ball and suddenly it's fulltime.

First blood in extra-time goes to the All Blacks, when they get a penalty almost on the centre spot for offside. Mehrtens goals superbly in the still, thin air, and it's 12–9. The South African dream seems to evaporate further as Bachop kicks across the field into space and only an unkind bounce prevents the galloping Ellis from collecting and scoring what would surely have been the World Cup-winning try. Instead, Chester Williams gathers from the bounce, evades Ellis, and puts Van der Westhuizen away. He passes to Small, who makes 20 metres, and now the Boks are flying with nearly all the New Zealanders trying to catch up with play. Small passes to Stransky with 40 metres to go and no All Black can catch him.

But Ellis Park howls with dismay as Ed Morrison blows for a marginal forward pass. Now men are beginning to drop with fatigue and cramp. Bachop is nowhere to be seen and Mehrtens feeds the scrum. The ball goes straight back to Walter Little, whose hard running is supported by Bunce and then Lomu, who is stopped again by Small. The All Blacks simply cannot find space to move, and the Springboks are searching desperately for a way to get three points.

They get them at last when the All Black forwards fall over the top at a ruck and Stransky goals from 35 metres out. The score is 12–12 with a quarter of an hour to go, in the longest rugby match ever played and the most important in Springbok history. Shadows lengthen over the ground but the spectators are oblivious to the settling highveld chill. They spend more time looking at the electronic clock than at the play.

Rudolf Straueli comes on for Mark Andrews — an inspired substitution — and he's almost immediately in action. Joubert drives the ball over the deadball line for a 22-metre drop-out. Straueli fields the kick neatly and mauls forward in concert with Kruger. Now the Boks are 35 metres out. Van der Westhuizen gets the ball, back to Stransky — will he go for the drop? No, it's a masterful up-and-under, dropping just outside the All Black 22-metre line. The great Zinzan Brooke is under it but he fumbles.

Every Bok team needs a Jewish player. Joel Stransky turns away in the knowledge that his second drop goal must surely have put the World Cup in South Africa's grasp, while Andrew Mehrtens, Josh Kronfeld and Walter Little watch and hope for a change of flight path.

What sweeter moment is there for a rugby player? The Boks revel in their status as world champions.

    Scrum to South Africa, 26 metres out and 15 metres in from the Boks' right touchline. Morrison battles to get them settled. They wheel through 90 degrees and the scrum must form again. The All Blacks are playing for time and you can't blame them: if the final score is a draw, they will win because James Dalton was sent off against Canada. As the exhausted men go down again, each willing himself to stand his ground, TV commentator Gavin Cowley says: 'It's interesting how Stransky is positioning himself, far back and just wide of the scrum . . .'

    This time the Bok front-row manages to hold the scrum square and the ball comes back, where it is held by Straueli. Control, control . . . then back to Van der Westhuizen, who rockets it back to Stransky. Everyone knows instantly that the drop is on, but they don't yet appreciate the awful reality for New Zealand: Mehrtens and Josh Kronfeld have simply too much ground to cover. Stransky has just enough time to settle and be perfectly balanced. Head down, swing, follow-through . . . the kick is beautifully timed and it soars. Only the spectators behind the posts can really see whether it has the direction, only those to the sides know if it has the distance. Their combined roar soon tells the story. And there can be no dispute: the ball travelled so high Ed Morrison had time to get almost beneath the crossbar to signal the goal.

DEFINING MOMENT

Mandela becomes the extra Bok no. 6
WORLD CUP FINAL, JOHANNESBURG, 24 JUNE, 1995

When Nelson Mandela appeared before the match with a Springbok No. 6 jersey (discreetly requested by his personal assistant that morning), the All Blacks knew they were playing against an extra man. It was the central image of the 1995 World Cup. The odds stacked up further with the ritual of introducing the president to his players as if he had never met them before.

First his captain, Francois Pienaar. Mandela takes both Pienaar's hands in his own, especially warmly. Then an ordinary handshake for each of the front-row: Os du Randt, Chris Rossouw and Balie Swart. Now it is Kobus Wiese, who is the first to give a special two-handed clasp in return, and fellow lock Hannes Strydom. Then the other loose forwards, Ruben Kruger and Mark Andrews. An extra shake of the hand for Joost van der Westhuizen, and a two-handed clasp for the flyhalf and centres: Joel Stransky, Hennie le Roux and Japie Mulder. Now there are just the wings and fullback. Mandela puts a fatherly arm round the shoulder of James Small, who must stop Jonah Lomu today, and gives a gentle pat to the shoulder of Chester Williams, the only player in the side who is not white. Finally a brief handshake for Andre Joubert, expressionless with tension as always.

The All Blacks look stunned by the atmosphere; they seem dulled and unhappy, staring ahead. Mandela greets Sean Fitzpatrick casually ('How are you? Nice to see you.') then uses the same words to Jonah Lomu. Mandela's beaming demeanour must be subtly shocking and undermining. The All Blacks look very far from home. Everyone knows they are starting at an extreme disadvantage and there is nothing anyone can do about it.

South Africa is ahead 15–12, with eight minutes to go. The courageous All Blacks try to create chances but the Springboks are swarming everywhere, tackling and spoiling and crowding. Little is clearly battling. Ellis concedes a scrum by knocking on a Bunce pass. Osborne and then Zinzan Brooke get the ball to Lomu, who drops it and is slung into touch by Small. Kronfeld collapses with the ball and concedes another scrum. A promising run by Bunce, Ellis and Osborne ends with a penalty to South Africa for obstruction.

Stransky's touch is safe. As the lineout forms, Brendan Venter sprints on for James Small, who has hauled himself with his hands to the touchline, his legs paralysed with cramp. There's another penalty to South Africa when Kronfeld and Richard Loe (on for Craig Dowd) go offside. It's kickable, and Stransky almost scrapes the right upright as he misses. But that's fine — it's used up some time.

Now the All Blacks are desperate. They attempt a quick drop-out, back through the legs. Little gets the ball and is driven back. The Springboks are just 10 metres out and Morrison is looking at his watch. The scrum forms, breaks up. They go down again . . . but Morrison turns away, looks down, waves his hand, and the impossible has happened. The final whistle is drowned by a joyous roar.

Pienaar screws up his eyes and sinks to his knees. He waves his team-mates closer. They had leaped into the air; now they pray. The All Blacks walk slowly to the tunnel, their faces drained and bleak.

After the celebratory milling about, some formality is restored. David van der Sandt, the TV interviewer, cannot disguise his own emotion. His voice husky, he thrusts the microphone at the Springbok captain: 'Francois Pienaar, you are the captain of the world champions!'

'David, I don't know what to say . . . it's very emotional. The team has played superbly. It's been the greatest six weeks of my life. And too many people to thank at this stage . . . The All Blacks played brilliant rugby — they kept in there for the extra 20 minutes and I want to take my hat off to them. Well done, Sean, you and your men.' This produces a roar of appreciation from the crowd.

'We had 65,000 people here today,' says Van der Sandt. 'It was tremendous support.' Then an inspired Pienaar gives perfect expression to the mood: 'David, we didn't have 60,000 South Africans here today, we had 43 million South Africans . . . I told my guys to keep calm, keep discipline . . . and Joel Stransky, you beauty!'

Pienaar finally receives the William Webb Ellis Cup from his president. It could only have happened in South Africa, this tortured country with its endless capacity to surprise and delight.

1995
THE NEW ZEALAND RESPONSE

THE WORLD CUP FINAL

by Grant Harding

WHEN ED MORRISON blew his whistle for the last time in the World Cup final at Ellis Park in Johannesburg on 24 June 1995, New Zealanders had no reason to cry foul. They did have reason, however, to be disappointed. An All Black team that had thrilled them over a period of four weeks had played well below its best standard.

That the match went to extra-time was fortunate for the All Blacks. From memory — I haven't watched the match since, and have no desire to — Springbok flanker Ruben Kruger scored what appeared to be a legitimate try.

So, at their first attempt, the Springboks were world champions. Naturally they were excited. Naturally examples of both good and bad winner behaviour followed.

Few had expected a Bok victory. The All Blacks had dominated and entertained throughout the tournament, collecting a Grand Slam of victories over Ireland and Wales in the pool matches, Scotland in the quarter-final and England in the semi-final. In addition, a team made up of mostly second-string squad members had produced an astonishing display against Japan to win 145–17.

Along the way Jonah Lomu exploded onto the world stage. If his two tries, blockbusting runs and sheer physical freakishness against Ireland had the world's media in raptures, as the tournament progressed his reputation took on almost mythical proportions. Certainly his performance against England in the semi-final was god-like, and without doubt the greatest individual performance at any World Cup to date. In the second minute he gathered in a bouncing ball from a poorly directed pass, turned, fended off his marker, Tony Underwood, accelerated round England captain Will Carling and recovered from a stumble to plough over the top of Mike Catt for a surreal try. Further tries followed in the 24th, 41st and 70th minutes.

Incredibly, at one time it appeared Lomu would not even be selected for the World Cup squad. At a pre-season training camp his fitness was found wanting, and coach Laurie Mains was concerned he would be incapable of performing in the all-action game that was being planned. It was only in April that Lomu began to convince the selectors of his worth. By June, South Africans were running sweepstakes on who could tackle him. But the performance against England featured much more than Lomu, as the All Blacks, playing unconventional rugby, went ahead 25–0 after 24 minutes, then 35–3 early in the second half, before eventually easing off to win 45–29.

Brilliance was displayed throughout the team. In fact the try of the match, later voted the try of the tournament, was scored by Josh Kronfeld, who supported a break by Walter Little and Glen Osborne from the All Black 22. Then there was a massive drop goal by No. 8 Zinzan Brooke, and the performance of a lifetime from halfback Graeme Bachop.

In every phase, all over the park, the All Blacks played astonishing rugby. That was why few believed the Springboks, who had clearly been lucky to beat France in their semi-final, could live with them. South Africa had talented individuals, but it was a one-dimensional team. These All Blacks were 'fast, dynamic and direct', according to England captain Carling, with a 'freak' on the wing.

As I've already said, New Zealanders had nothing to cry foul over at the final whistle of the World Cup. After the match, however, it was revealed several of the team had been struck down by a mystery illness in the days leading up to the final. Mains alleged that a kitchen hand, 'Suzy', had been sacked from the team's hotel after admitting she had been paid to put a substance in the tea and coffee in the players' dining room. By whom she was supposed to have been paid has never been ascertained. Mains' information came, via a reliable source, from the hotel manager, but the manager later denied the 'Suzy' story.

Despite the poor timing of the revelation, and the unproven allegations, there is no doubt illness and the after-effects of illness played a part in New Zealand's defeat. There is merit in Mains' contention that the All Blacks had lost the metre of pace which had given them an advantage throughout the tournament. Against a team as determined and well supported as the Springboks it made all the difference.

My initial reaction to the defeat was that Mains' intensity could have strangled the team. During his time with Otago he'd never won any of the big prizes. Sure, there was an NPC victory in 1991, but that owed much to the fact that Auckland ended the competition without 14 World Cup-bound All Blacks. Ranfurly Shield challenges had come and gone, with his team performing disappointingly on most occasions. Excellent coach though Mains was, his intensity could sometimes get the better of him.

In their book *Turning Point: The Making of a Captain*, co-authors All Black captain Sean Fitzpatrick and Duncan Johnstone more than hinted at this quality: 'Mains had become paranoid, perhaps justifiably so. But it was rubbing off on his players, who had to wait to have the team room swept for electronic bugs each session in case the South Africans were recording the All Black talks and tactics. Mains had ordered a separate dining room, too, to get the team out of the public glare. "It was all just adding to the pressure," remembers Fitzpatrick.'

So the All Blacks lost a game their talent demanded they should win. On another day the result would in all probability have been different. But that is rugby.

For the Springboks, it was the first time they had beaten their old foe post-isolation. It was a great day for the so-called Rainbow Nation.

Personally I would have preferred it if the All Blacks had rained on their parade and taken the pot of gold. As it was they left the tournament not as world champions, but as the best side in the world, a mantle they would wear proudly for the next two seasons. Lomu, Mehrtens and Kronfeld had emerged. The All Blacks had earned admiration for their style, but there was no cigar.

Bugger!

1996–1999

ENTER PROFESSIONALISM

1996 Tri-Nations in New Zealand
NEW ZEALAND 15 SOUTH AFRICA 11

1996 Tri-Nations in South Africa
NEW ZEALAND 29 SOUTH AFRICA 18

1996 The Seventh All Blacks in South Africa
NEW ZEALAND 23 SOUTH AFRICA 19
NEW ZEALAND 33 SOUTH AFRICA 26
SOUTH AFRICA 32 NEW ZEALAND 22

1997 Tri-Nations in South Africa
NEW ZEALAND 35 SOUTH AFRICA 32

1997 Tri-Nations in New Zealand
NEW ZEALAND 55 SOUTH AFRICA 35

1998 Tri-Nations in New Zealand
SOUTH AFRICA 13 NEW ZEALAND 3

1998 Tri-Nations in South Africa
SOUTH AFRICA 24 NEW ZEALAND 23

1999 Tri-Nations in New Zealand
NEW ZEALAND 28 SOUTH AFRICA 0

1999 Tri-Nations in South Africa
NEW ZEALAND 34 SOUTH AFRICA 18

1999 World Cup
SOUTH AFRICA 22 NEW ZEALAND 18

CHAPTER THIRTEEN

1996 1999
ENTER PROFESSIONALISM

1996
SIEGE MENTALITY RULES

TRI-NATIONS IN NEW ZEALAND

by Grant Harding

IMMEDIATELY FOLLOWING the 1995 World Cup, the world's top players forced the game to go professional. Of course, rugby hadn't really been amateur for a long time. Players in the northern hemisphere had received so-called boot money for many years, and the exodus of southern hemisphere players to European destinations in the off-season was not simply a reflection of their love for the game.

But the situation had become dire. In New Zealand any number of players listed their occupation as 'coaching co-ordinator', a term that often meant 'lowly paid professional rugby player', and they were becoming increasingly bitter. They were filling stadiums year round, the World Cup was a booming commercial event, and yet amateur regulations meant they lived in the shady world of 'shamateurism'. Frustrated by the out-of-date amateur regulations, and with the third World Cup behind them, their mood became revolutionary.

Of course there was league, or rugby in Japan, neither of which required players to endure year-round match play. However, another option had suddenly appeared during the World Cup. Under the World Rugby Corporation's scheme (supposedly funded by Kerry Packer), All Blacks were initially offered up to $500,000 to play in a global series of competitions, a figure which was later increased to in excess of seven figures for some players.

On the eve of the World Cup final, Rupert Murdoch's News Corporation struck a $760 million deal for television rights to international and provincial rugby in New Zealand, Australia and South Africa. The only problem was that none of the players was contracted, and the WRC was hovering. Incredibly, player payment details had not even been discussed.

Eventually, the NZRFU said it would pay players $150,000 each over three years. This was clearly not enough.

During July and early August, the future of rugby hung in the balance, until one key

All concentration and determination … Springbok No. 8 Gary Teichmann leads the charge against the All Blacks at Lancaster Park, with captain Francois Pienaar (partially obscured) in support. Within weeks Teichmann had succeeded Pienaar as Bok captain.

happening suddenly changed the course of history. South Africa Rugby Football Union chairman Louis Luyt simply bought the affections of his World Cup-winning Springbok squad; and their failure to commit to the WRC deal in a video hook-up featuring All Black and Wallaby representatives effectively ended the breakaway.

While the NZRFU revised its offers upwards, the best news it could have got came in the form of the signatures of Jeff Wilson and Josh Kronfeld. Within a week the signatures were rolling in for the guaranteed money, and by the end of the month the dear old IRB announced that rugby was now an 'open' game.

The new alliance created by the Murdoch deal, SANZAR (South Africa, New Zealand, Australia), announced two new competitions: the Rugby Super 12, featuring five regionally selected New Zealand teams, four South African provincial teams and three Australian provincial teams, and the Tri-Nations, an annual home-and-away competition between New Zealand, Australia and South Africa. The sceptics were many, but the Rugby Super 12 was a hit from day one.

At the end of 1995 Laurie Mains had stepped down as All Black coach, allowing his nemesis, 50-year-old John Hart, to become the first-ever fully professional All Black coach. The approach

Springbok hooker John Allan (centre right) should have been sent off for headbutting Sean Fitzpatrick in the early stages of the Lancaster Park Test.

of the new man was totally different from Mains'. Media-friendly or manipulative, depending on your outlook, Hart promised to produce stylish, winning rugby, improve the All Blacks' public profile and aid the successful introduction of the professional game.

Hart inherited a team at the top of its form. But his mission in 1996 seemed to be a 'mission impossible'. The All Blacks were to play 10 Tests in 13 weeks, including five against South Africa, of which four would be in the republic over 21 days in August. The first Test in South Africa was the final Tri-Nations match, and the next three a Test series, giving the All Blacks an opportunity to become the first-ever New Zealand team to win a series in South Africa.

The season started promisingly, with the Auckland Blues winning the inaugural Rugby Super 12 title and the All Blacks comfortably dealing with Samoa and Scotland twice. Then, in the first Tri-Nations clash, New Zealand produced an astonishing wet-weather performance to thrash Australia 43–6.

Meanwhile, the Boks' reign as world champions had continued relatively smoothly, although illness had removed coach Kitch Christie. His replacement was Andre Markgraaff, a dour Afrikaner. A reserve for the Springboks against the New Zealand Cavaliers in 1986, Markgraaff had since turned Griqualand West into a leading province. As a member of the SARFU executive he was viewed as a Luyt man.

Before arriving down under, the Boks had unconvincingly beaten Fiji to continue a winning streak of 15 matches. Then, in their Tri-Nations debut against Australia, they were beaten 21–16, creating excitement among New Zealand supporters desperate to see the All Blacks avenge the World Cup final defeat.

In my *Rugby News* editorial at the time I wondered if New Zealand could finally break out of the siege-like mentality that had enveloped the 75-year history of the game between the two nations. I wrote:

'A funny thing happens to New Zealand rugby folk when it comes time to play South Africa. Suddenly instead of talking about such matters as "accuracy" and "imposing the game plan on the opposition", the statements become far more emotional. All Black coach John Hart was no different last weekend when the spectre of South Africa once again began to loom. Terms like "foe" and "challenge" again came to the fore. The reason I raise this matter is not to criticise, but because I've long held a theory that South Africa is the only rugby nation in the world that creates an element of doubt in the New Zealand psyche. Of course tradition — the Springboks are the only team to enjoy a better win-loss record against the All Blacks — plays a major part in that. But it is my contention that we have, at times, struggled to produce our best form against South Africa not only because of the quality of the opposition, which of course is outstanding. On occasion New Zealand has failed to play the rugby it is capable of because of a kind of siege mentality caused by the mere mention of South Africa. The World Cup final last year was a classic example. Enter South Africa, and sometimes it appears, the All Blacks lose their heads.'

Such concerns proved well founded.

The Springbok team that took the field in Christchurch was seven places different from that which had started the World Cup final. The inside-back pairing of Joost van der Westhuizen and Henry Honiball had been dumped after the loss to Australia for the more conservative combination of Johan Roux and World Cup hero Joel Stransky. The Boks were preparing for another battle of attrition based round their traditional power and kicking game.

Inheriting a settled team, Hart made changes that were cosmetic by comparison. The only new player was brilliant Wellington Hurricanes fullback Christian Cullen, who had starred in the 1996 Hong Kong Sevens. Restored to the team was the legendary Michael Jones, whose powerful physique was despatched to the blindside, an area that had become increasingly important owing to changes in regulations relating to loose forwards remaining bound at scrum time. Halfback Justin Marshall, who had been introduced to international rugby at Paris in late 1995 by Laurie Mains, was the only other player who had not appeared in the World Cup final.

South African intentions became clear inside two minutes, when, at the first scrum, hooker John Allan head-butted All Black captain Sean Fitzpatrick. The fact that the incident came so early in the game was probably the only reason Allan escaped being sent off by Scottish referee Ray Megson. It was obvious that while the players were there for a great spectacle to ensue, the spirit was not. It took New Zealand a full 30 minutes to recover from the intimidation. After 80 minutes it was the All Blacks who claimed a 15–11 win, but most of the talking points had a negative slant.

Certainly a victory against the World Cup holders was not to be scoffed at, but New Zealand, once again, when faced with the physical and uncompromising style of South Africa, failed to deliver the rugby of which it was capable. Error-free against Australia, and committed to keeping the ball in hand in conditions many times worse than those prevailing in Christchurch, the All Blacks were error-prone and lacking in composure. Their scrum had also been pressured.

Then there was the questionable Springbok defence. Midfield backs Brendan Venter and Japie Mulder lived in the All Black backline to such a destructive extent that, in the absence of the sin bin, one or other of them should have been sent off.

The All Blacks got home on the back of an improved second-half effort aided by Springbok indiscipline, which led to a favourable penalty count and the opportunity for Mehrtens to

All Black second-five Walter Little breaks the line during the 1996 Tri-Nations Test at Christchurch with Frank Bunce in support. But there was to be no try for the All Blacks in this dour clash.

Tough Penalty Sinks Boks
CHRISTCHURCH, 20 JULY, 1996

The Springboks were denied a match-winning situation when they were penalised for collapsing an attacking scrum five minutes from fulltime. Behind by just one point and in control of the game at the time they were victims of a harsh decision.

showcase his goalkicking skills, the brilliance of lock Ian Jones at lineout, and great defence. The visitors' inability to finish sealed their fate. Why did the Boks not pursue attack with ball in hand after Andre Joubert scored a superb try in the first quarter?

Both coaches were united on the refereeing performance. Megson awarded 37 penalties and free kicks in the match, while his touch judges, fellow Scotsmen Jim Fleming and Ken McCartney, intervened six times. Hart renewed his call for the International Rugby Board to institute a merit-based panel.

Privately, Hart also took pleasure from the Springboks' confidence that they would turn the tables on the All Blacks in South Africa by scrumming them into the ground. Hart knew his team could play much better.

1996

THE SOUTH AFRICAN RESPONSE

TRI-NATIONS IN NEW ZEALAND

by David Williams

THE SPRINGBOK DEFEAT in Christchurch probably had its origins in early July, when tens of thousands of South African rugby fans got up to watch the All Blacks win the very first Tri-Nations match. Seeming to relish the wind, rain and mud, the old enemies were awesome as they achieved a record 43–6 thrashing of Australia.

It would have been only human for the world champions to underestimate Australia after that match, while thinking ahead about the obvious competence of New Zealand. But to blame complacency would be charitable, because the next week the Springboks were utterly outplayed. In fact, Australia's 21–16 win in South Africa's first Tri-Nations outing might just have represented the biggest thrashing by a five-point margin in rugby history.

Springbok confidence was therefore low by the time the Boks got to Christchurch. Whether they took the field intending to be negative is debatable, but there was certainly something wrong with their minds. Allan's attempted head-butt on Sean Fitzpatrick (who made the most of it, as usual) was not the only regrettable incident. Pieter Hendriks' bizarre shoulder charge on an opponent who was already in touch; James Small's scalp-high tackle on Jonah Lomu; Brendan Venter openly playing a man without the ball — these were more than indiscretions.

But they were not the work of evil men. More plausibly, they were symptoms of a deep, collective loss of confidence. Australia had splintered the Springboks' spirit and now the All Blacks swept away the shards. That quiet steeliness in coach Kitch Christie's personality, which had previously covered his team like a blanket, had gone. Faces looked too anxious in adversity; shoulders drooped too quickly. There was a reluctance to seize the match and control it.

It did not help that referee Megson blew the match a minute short, and awarded that mysterious penalty when the last thing the Boks would have done was collapse a scrum. But Megson couldn't be blamed for the defeat. He didn't let the game flow, but that hindered the All Blacks as well. In any case, the previous week against Australia the Springboks had been awarded two dozen penalties and hadn't known what to do with them. No, the Springboks' problems were in their heads — and the distressing thought was that new coach Andre Markgraaff would not be able to solve them.

1996

START OF THE ROT

TRI-NATIONS IN SOUTH AFRICA

IT SEEMS ABSURD that, after the glory of the World Cup victory, 1996 and 1997 turned out to be two of the most miserable years in the history of Springbok rugby. The retirement of the great Kitch Christie as national coach was not, in itself, a shock. There was great sadness: he had been fighting cancer for years, and his departure was handled badly by the South African Rugby Football Union, creating a widespread feeling that the man who had won the World Cup had been treated ungraciously.

by David Williams

Christie's successor, Andre Markgraaff, had a dour image, but was respected for his knowledge of the game. He did not make things easy for himself by leaving out World Cup hero Joel Stransky for the warm-up Fiji Test before the inaugural Tri-Nations tournament. Stransky was one of the few players in the Bok squad with the vision to dictate a game. The All Blacks, by contrast, seemed to be crammed with such players.

The Fiji game was not helpful. Then, in their two away Tri-Nations matches, the Boks seemed strangely lacking in direction and leadership. Francois Pienaar seemed unable to lift his team and concentrate minds when the drift set in; there was a lack of composure that verged on panic when penalties were taken. Apparently only one tactic was available: give the ball to a surprised tight forward, wait for him to charge and hope for the best. The Boks were shaky in the lineouts, appearing easily intimidated and producing low-quality ball even on their own throw. The drive in the loose came in fits and starts: several times the ball appeared and nobody knew what to do with it. Stransky was brought back for the Christchurch game but his confidence had been shaken.

Edward Griffiths (who had been sacked in February 1996 as CEO of the SARFU but remained closely in touch with the players) later described the impact of the first two Tri-Nations defeats: 'The notably fragile Springbok management structure was starting to splinter . . . Markgraaff was privately blaming Pienaar and the captain was blaming the coach.' Scrumhalf Joost van der Westhuizen recalled that 'the squad was starting to divide: you were either a Markgraaff man or a Pienaar man'.

It made matters worse when New Zealand, by beating Australia a second time, won the Tri-Nations with two fixtures still to run. True, there was a revival in confidence when the Springboks beat the Wallabies 25–19 (all the points being scored by Stransky), but the victory was tarnished by a dispute over the SARFU's apparent endorsement of the old national flag, which was waved in great numbers in conservative Bloemfontein.

An unsettled mood seemed to dominate South African rugby, which now had to face four

Tests on successive Saturdays against what was clearly the best team in the world. Still, this was the ancient rivalry, and the first official home Test series against the All Blacks for 20 years. Excitement mounted as the return Tri-Nations game at Newlands approached.

At first it seemed the Springboks would justify their world-champion status. Stransky again performed superbly, controlling play by taking the right options with the ball fed to him by an impressive pack. The pressure resulted in two Springbok tries, by Japie Mulder in the 13th minute and Os du Randt in the 25th. With Stransky's boot in action, the score had reached 18–6 with about half an hour to go.

It was only then that the All Blacks finally managed to get into the game. They recieved the ball from a 22-metre drop-out and mounted a sustained attack on the Springbok line. They recycled at will, back and forth across the field, with the ball going from man to man more than 40 times. The Bok defence held, but the players must have been shell-shocked. Some kind of moral high ground was taken by the All Blacks at this point in the game: they were suddenly

A brilliant All Black backline move is given final expression by Glen Osborne, as the All Blacks take the lead for the first time in the final Tri-Nations match.

persuaded they could win. Significantly, during this four-minute attacking spell, Francois Pienaar was already injured and groggy from the concussion that would force him off the field 15 minutes from the end.

That period of all-out New Zealand attack, combined with two impressive tries in the last 10 minutes, left the impression that the second half belonged to them, that the Boks had been engulfed by a black tidal wave. On the contrary, the Springboks probed several times deep into All Black territory in the second half, but were let down badly by mistakes and exhaustion, not a defensive attitude or a lack of courage.

In the first 30 minutes of the second half, the Boks had close on 20 opportunities to use the ball, almost all from scrums, lineouts and kicks awarded. That statistic revealed two things: the Springboks were getting little loose ball, but the All Blacks were making mistakes as well.

Two of the six Springbok scrums in that half-hour came during a sustained period of Bok pressure, which culminated in a Stransky penalty goal. But the next scrum awarded to South Africa nearly resulted in a New Zealand try, as the clearance was charged down by Frank Bunce. Another two scrums were conceded as tightheads; the second was especially damaging, with the Boks deep in New Zealand territory, after good attacking work, and the score at 18–9 with only 17 minutes to go.

South Africa was awarded four lineouts in the first 30 minutes of the second half. From the first throw-in, Joost van der Westhuizen pressurised and forced another lineout 10 metres from the All Black line. But that was followed by a Bok knock-on, and then Justin Swart fielded an anxious All Black clearance and kicked out on the full. Another good lineout in an attacking position was negated by one of the lost tightheads; yet another was spoiled by a crooked throw.

In the last 10 minutes, after Pienaar had left the field, the All Blacks showed their worth and scored two excellent tries (by Osborne, the first in 370 minutes of rugby against South Africa, and Craig Dowd), which boosted the score from 15–18 to 29–18.

The consensus after the game, heavily influenced by stand-in captain Gary Teichmann's remarks in the post-match TV interview, was that the Springboks had tried to defend a lead in the second half instead of continuing to attack. I don't think this was true. The evidence shows that South Africa did continue to try to attack, but simply ran out of energy. The respected rugby correspondent of the Johannesburg *Sunday Times*, Daan Retief, argued that 'there was little doubt that the All Blacks would have won, even if Pienaar had not left the field'.

Markgraaff was delighted with Stransky's performance, but wondered afterwards: 'Why would we want to collapse the scrum when we were going forward?' He pointed out that in their two previous Tests the Springboks had conceded 13 penalties; now, against the All Blacks, they had conceded 24. Sean Fitzpatrick seemed to acknowledge an injustice after the final whistle when he said to Pienaar: 'Sorry about the referee.' But Markgraaff also confessed his team's discipline had not been good. The All Black camp alleged the Bok backs had been lying so flat they had been guilty of consistently and deliberately going offside. The truth probably lay somewhere in between: the Springboks had been pressurised into conceding penalties.

The All Blacks finished the inaugural Tri-Nations unbeaten thanks to an astonishing come-from-behind victory at Cape Town. Here prop Craig Dowd scores the crucial try.

The sad reality was that the Springboks had lost because they had made mistakes at vital moments. They had lacked sharpness and shrewdness in the loose, and they had been unable to last the full 80 minutes. In stark contrast, the All Blacks had shown themselves able to keep their nerve and absorb enormous pressure, before scoring points when it counted.

This was how I began my *Financial Mail* column in the week after the Newlands Test: 'And they don't even need Jonah Lomu . . . the aftertaste of that 29–18 All Black victory was bitter. We are a nation of extremes and the gloom-and-doom on Saturday night and Sunday morning was only to be expected.' Two weeks before, I had written that 'the All Blacks, to offer a paradox, are playing happy rugby as if their lives depended on it. This is why they are likely to beat us for the first time in a series in this country.' After the second Tri-Nations defeat, I saw no reason to change that view.

Even if Markgraaff could get the mental side right; even if Andre Joubert was recalled and James Small put back on the wing; even if the Bok forwards could match their commitment in the loose with a greater working knowledge of the ruck and maul laws — even if all these things could be done in the time available, and the side could recover from the loss of Pienaar, there was a growing sense that these All Blacks were just too good.

1996

THE NEW ZEALAND RESPONSE

TRI-NATIONS IN SOUTH AFRICA

by Grant Harding

THE ADMINISTRATORS said the Tri-Nations clash was separate from the three-Test series to follow. But there is no doubt the All Blacks wanted to win at least three of the four Tests they would play in the republic. By winning the Tri-Nations match they knew the lustre could not be taken off a 'mere' 2–1 series victory.

For much of the game it appeared mistakes and errors of judgment at crucial times would stop Sean Fitzpatrick's men from completing a clean sweep in the inaugural competition. Even during the early stages of the second half, by which time New Zealand had established a clear advantage in the forward battle, the Springbok defence held. At 18–6 down with just 20 minutes to play, achieving victory against the World Cup holders at home appeared to be if not 'mission impossible' then 'mission improbable'. Few teams would have had either the self-belief or the skill not only to get up and win, but to win going away. But the All Blacks knew, or at least hoped, that the continuous pressure they were bringing to bear by applying the most basic of rugby skills — winning the ball and retaining it — would eventually bring results. And so it proved, as they scored a remarkable 23 points in 18 minutes without reply.

Battered and bruised by wave after wave of All Black attack, the exhausted South Africans eventually had no answer, as personified by Os du Randt leaving the field on a stretcher through sheer fatigue.

One count had New Zealand winning rucks and mauls by a staggering 58–28, and the lineouts by 13–9, after trailing 7–5 at halftime.

Undoubtedly the All Black forwards were the architects of New Zealand's victory. Where they had creaked a little under Springbok pressure at Lancaster Park, this time, to use an unfortunate South Africanism, they murdered the home team. At the forefront was Craig Dowd, who made a meaningful contribution in all aspects of play and was rewarded with the try that sealed his team's win.

The All Blacks' two tries were their first against South Africa since the second Test of the 1994 series.

1996
THE GREATEST ALL BLACKS?

THE SEVENTH ALL BLACKS IN SOUTH AFRICA

by David Williams

THERE WAS SOMETHING deeply disconcerting about the 1996 series in South Africa. It was difficult for South African players and spectators to get to know these All Blacks. Four Tests on four successive Saturdays seemed on the surface to be exciting, but in fact the currency was in danger of being devalued. There was no time to savour the struggle, for the teams to lick wounds and plot properly. Finally, it was confusing to have to accept that one of the four Tests didn't 'count' because it was part of the Tri-Nations. Intense would have been the arguments indeed if the All Blacks had won two matches and the Boks two — but happily for New Zealand that blurring never arose. Whether you said the final tally was 2–1 or 3–1, the All Blacks had prevailed.

Going into the first Test of the three-match series in Durban on August 17, Springbok confidence was low after the Tri-Nations defeats, and Francois Pienaar was out because of concussion. To make matters worse, Markgraaff did not seem to be concerned about losing his captain. It was also a sad comment on the instability of South African rugby that only six Springboks had survived from the 1995 World Cup final. One of those dropped was Van der Westhuizen, regarded by many as the best scrumhalf in the world. The happy atmosphere around the team also seemed to have evaporated.

Markgraaff seemed to represent a throwback to an older, more conservative management style. There had been a surprising period of enlightenment, starting when Ian McIntosh was appointed coach in 1993 and culminating in the 1995 World Cup. During that triumph Edward Griffiths was CEO of the national body, with Kitch Christie, Morne du Plessis and Francois Pienaar in charge of the Springbok team. Barely a year later, that team had almost gone. Griffiths had been fired, Pienaar was out with injury, Christie was sick and had retired, and Du Plessis was about to give notice.

Both Griffiths and Du Plessis could fairly be described as liberal visionaries, which might explain their fall from grace. Pienaar was a hero and a powerful personality. Christie was less easily categorised. In some ways, he came across very much in the mould of old-style coaching legends like Northern Transvaal's Brigadier Buurman van Zyl: non-committal, ruthless with discipline, treating his men like boys, military in approach rather than earnestly motivational. That said, Christie offered much more than Van Zyl. He came across as direct, authentic and original — rare qualities that were backed by unusual technical expertise. His rugby philosophies may have been simple, but they were seldom obvious. It was Christie who pointed out, for instance, that the real Test of rugby knowledge lies not in coaching but in getting the selection right. He also knew how to get the best out of his players, and when to treat a team as 15 individuals or as a collective tribal entity.

In mid-1996 Markgraaff was still enjoying the media honeymoon that tends to be allowed a new national coach. In the end, of course, he too would be judged on results, not personality. And his honeymoon was cut short when the All Blacks duly dominated the first Test with the kind of rugby that had been expected from them the year before at the World Cup.

Markgraaf had brought in several new caps: the Northern Transvaal centre pairing of Andre Snyman and Danie van Schalkwyk, the Free State flanker Andre Venter and the Northerns hooker Henry Tromp. Two of these selections (Snyman and Venter) would prove to be inspired; the other two were unremarkable. Justin Swart stayed on the wing after James Small (who had played fullback in the Tri-Nations game at Newlands) was dropped ahead of a disciplinary hearing for being out late at a nightclub.

In the first half there were sharp, confident tries from Jeff Wilson and Christian Cullen, to which the Boks could only reply with penalties from Stranksy. Those tries resulted from the kind of flawed play the Springboks produced that year: enterprising but careless. The Boks ran two free kicks, but then went over the top at a ruck and conceded a penalty for backchat. That gave Osborne a chance to run down the blindside touchline before the ball was fed back across field to Wilson, who beat the cover defence to score in the corner. Du Randt was penalised for stamping, enabling the All Blacks to create an attacking lineout, advance up the middle and force a kickable penalty (8–0). Ian Jones then stole a Bok lineout and Zinzan Brooke hung out on the right to make space for Cullen to score in the corner (15–3).

Stransky missed two penalty attempts but still managed to get the score back to 15–9, and the All Blacks benefited again from South African indiscipline when winger Justin Swart tackled Sean Fitzpatrick without the ball (18–9). The New Zealanders were not angels — they went over the top professionally to thwart a good Springbok drive and were happy to concede the three points (18–12). But there was no argument with the quality of their next try. From deep in All Black territory, Walter Little kicked ahead and the ball was followed swiftly by Wilson, who flicked to Fitzpatrick. The All Black captain was able to feed Zinzan Brooke, who sustained the pace to score in the corner (23–12). It was the kind of try South Africa never looked like scoring.

Although Van Schalkwyk managed to narrow the gap with a fine effort, forcing his way through the tackles of Robin Brooke and Cullen after 60 minutes (23–19), the Springboks proved incapable of playing error-free rugby and there were no more scores.

Small was later found not guilty at his disciplinary hearing. He had told the newspapers he could not bear to attend the match as a spectator and had gone down the coast instead to sit on the beach. 'I would die for that team,' he said, and nobody thought it an absurd statement. South African rugby fans felt let down.

The second Test provided the All Blacks with arguably the greatest moment in their history.

After beating Danie van Schalkwyk, Jeff Wilson assesses time and space before moving on to complete a remarkable second try in the historic series-winning Test at Pretoria.

Sean Fitzpatrick's men became the first New Zealand team to win a series in South Africa by taking the game 33–26, with the added satisfaction of recording their fourth successive victory over the old enemy. Fittingly enough, it turned out to be one of the great Test matches.

After 37 minutes the Springboks were trailing by 13 points and seemingly dead and buried. But the return of Joost van der Westhuizen in place of Johan Roux was paying dividends, and when Kobus Wiese came on for another 1995 World Cup veteran, Hannes Strydom, the Bok pack was suddenly galvanised.

There was a superb eight-minute period of rugby from the 56th minute. Gary Teichmann, who was starting his second match as captain, was off receiving attention for a cut, and Ruben Kruger called a lineout throw to Mark Andrews, who had been inexplicably neglected and had been therefore kept quiet. From his clean take there followed six mauls in a row, forcing a penalty. The Boks went for the try and got it. Suddenly the score was 24–18 and New Zealand was looking nervous. Simon Culhane fluffed the kickoff, and Wayne Fyvie (on for Teichmann) picked up at the base of the scrum, worked his way forward and fed back. Van der Westhuizen chipped into space ahead of Cullen, darted forward, collected and sprinted in for a great individualist try (24–23).

But again the Springboks let themselves down. They went over the top in a dangerous position, and Jon Preston (on for Culhane) made it 27–23. Stranksy pulled the score back to 27–26, Preston replied for the All Blacks to move out to 30–26. Every South African fan knew that one score would do it, one interception — but such thinking was actually a reflection of the lack of a Springbok pattern or battle plan. The All Blacks had proved themselves able always to pull ahead when necessary, and now the final nail came from Zinzan Brooke. Outrageously, when he was expected to drive back to his forwards or link with the backs, he dropped for goal — and it was over (33–26). As if in acknowledgment of Brooke's genius, the crowd's reaction was one of resignation rather than surprise.

Unusually, South Africans were gracious in defeat. They thought their team had been weakened by the dropping of the passionate Small, and there was no affection for the dour Markgraaff. But there was also admiration for what was clearly a great All Black team. When Fitzpatrick embraced each of his men on the field after the final whistle, there was measured but genuine applause.

It was said at the time of the Springboks' World Cup final victory in 1995 that, while they deserved to win on the day, they would lose to this All Black side eight or nine times out of 10. So it proved: since the Springboks' return from isolation in 1992, they had won one and drawn one in nine contests with New Zealand. The All Blacks were the better side.

What was remarkable about the second Test was that South Africa came as close as it did to winning. If you had had to choose a backline from both sides, using the best man available for each position, all seven players would have been All Blacks. True, the Boks were missing James Small, Hennie le Roux, Henry Honiball and Japie Mulder. They had two green centres pitted against Walter Little and Frank Bunce, the best and most experienced partnership in the world, while our wingers Pieter Hendriks and Justin Swart were not in the same class as Jeff Wilson and Glen Osborne.

South Africa would have given much treasure to have been able to play a Jonah Lomu, but New Zealand could afford to do without that mighty star. Every time Cullen, Wilson or Osborne got the ball, one sensed danger was not imminent but already present. It would have been unfair to criticise Andre Joubert for not contributing more when there was such appalling disarray in front of him. As for the halfback positions, Joel Stransky and Joost van der Westhuizen had not enjoyed the coach's full confidence and it showed. Over the series, they should have looked better in comparison with Simon Culhane and Justin Marshall.

It was the Bok forwards, therefore, who took their team close to victory — so close that the All Blacks were mightily relieved and exhausted when the final whistle blew. For South Africa's players there was no dishonour in losing the series. They were simply outgunned by a better side.

With the series settled after two Tests, for the first time in 75 years of the great rivalry, the All Blacks could be forgiven if their minds were not quite concentrated on the third and final Test. But the biggest single factor in the Springbok victory was not heart or guts or determination, or any of the other wonderful qualities invoked when rational explanation is inadequate. It was the presence of referee Derek Bevan.

For the first time on the tour, the All Blacks were not allowed to get away with the shadowy little infringements at which they were such masters. When they realised how tough Bevan was going to be (the Australians had been through the same experience with him in the first game of the 1995 World Cup against South Africa), the New Zealanders were forced to let the game flow.

Of course, the Boks gave away their fair share of penalties, and they were lucky it was New Zealand's turn to miss a series of kickable goals. But they must have felt they would at last be rewarded for their efforts, instead of being thwarted by professional infringements and inconsistent refereeing. This probably helped the renewal of confidence within the side.

Most referees in the modern game (especially Australians) seem to become mesmerised when there is a flowing pattern of attacking rugby as played by the All Blacks. They tend to follow the ball, thus overlooking offside and other off-the-ball incidents. Bevan was wise and experienced enough to see the big picture, while at the same time knowing which details to seize on.

The biggest difference in the Bok side in the third Test was in midfield. Japie Mulder added enormous presence, and Henry Honiball's lethal tackling clearly shook the All Blacks, who normally make a point of appearing impervious to intimidation. With solidity restored in front of him, Andre Joubert was at last given the freedom to hunt for attacking opportunities.

The game was won well by the Springboks, and provoked wistful questions in South Africa. What if selection had been more sensible? What if we had kicked our goals and picked more of our 1995 World Cup veterans? Why didn't we turn the New Zealanders round more often and force them to chase backwards? What if we had had a referee like Derek Bevan in the earlier Tests, to penalise the New Zealand tendency to lurk offside and play men off the ball? But this was to avoid reality. As 'Boy' Louw had once said after a lucky victory: 'Just look at the scoreboard.' Fitzpatrick had emulated Philip Nel in winning a series away, and we knew it.

Consolatory talk of bad luck and fluffed kicks was misguided. Such was the command of this New Zealand side that one felt it would always be able to score if it needed to. If its players were streetwise enough to concede a few professional penalties without being properly punished, good luck to them. The best sides (remember the 1974 British Lions in South Africa) have always got away with pushing the laws to the limit.

Defensively, the All Blacks had taken over where the Springboks had left off in the World Cup final, and were never caught twice by the same ruse. That was how they held out so magnificently in the second Test. They were exuberant and dangerous runners, but they could also conduct a war of forward attrition if they needed to.

Before the Test series I wrote in the *Financial Mail* that 'rugby may be a religion in New

PLAYER OF THE DECADE

ZINZAN BROOKE

BORN: 1965
POSITION: NO. 8
PLAYED SOUTH AFRICA: 1992, 1994, 1995, 1996, 1997 (12 TESTS)

While Sean Fitzpatrick's gamesmanship loomed largest in the South African psyche, the one player who encapsulated the difference between New Zealand and South Africa in the 1990s was Zinzan Brooke, for it was he who blurred the boundaries between backs and forwards to devastating effect.

Who will forget the cheeky try at Johannesburg when, from a close-range penalty, Brooke tapped and charged past the napping defence to give the All Blacks a 10–0 halftime lead? And what of the 1994 series when he finally came of age as a great All Black No. 8? Playing with the freedom to which Eden Park crowds had already thrilled for many years, he now demonstrated an extra dimension to his performance: punishing defence. It came as no surprise when he was named New Zealand Rugby Player of the Year.

After damaging his Achilles tendon in a warm-up match in April 1995, just getting to the World Cup that year was a major achievement for Brooke. But there he was in the final against South Africa on June 24. Unfortunately, it was he who dropped the high ball in extra-time that led to the scrum from which Joel Stransky kicked his winning drop goal.

The next year Brooke atoned for that momentary lapse with outstanding performances in the Tri-Nations tournament and the first-ever series victory in South Africa. In the Durban Test he was involved in all three New Zealand tries, displaying a combination of quick thinking, fast hands and support play, and scoring the third himself. What is more, he also led the tackle count. In Pretoria he scored his team's third try just before halftime from a clinically worked scrum move, then, late in the match, with body aching, mind at breaking point and the outcome in the balance, he found the composure and confidence to execute a 30-metre drop goal to give the All Blacks a seven-point buffer. For the remaining few minutes he and his team-mates defended as if their lives depended on it, and, when the final whistle mercifully came, Brooke stood in triumph with both arms raised, the epitome of skill, power and competitiveness.

The All Blacks' record victory over South Africa at Eden Park in 1997 was his last outing against his favourite opponent. In 12 Tests he had savoured nine victories, and scored four tries and a drop goal. The Boks brought out the best in Zinny, and his best was sensational.

190   Toughest of Them All

DEFINING MOMENT

Zinzan Brooke: Greatest in a Great Team
Second Test, Pretoria, 24 August, 1996

There was general agreement that the All Blacks were potentially the best side at the 1995 World Cup — although they did not become champions. But New Zealanders could be extremely proud of their 1996 team. The combination may have peaked a year too late, but it did not crack under the strain of the fiercest Test of all: a series against the Springboks in South Africa.

No South African fan who knows the game begrudges New Zealand its first away series triumph. The All Blacks had more flair, talent, confidence and determination. They always had something in reserve. Their superiority was symbolised by the clinching drop goal produced by Zinzan Brooke. Just as the All Blacks had found against Hennie Muller in 1949, so the Springboks discovered against Brooke: you cannot play against such a man. When his drop goal was conjured from nothing, South Africans could only shake their heads and acknowledge greatness.

Zealand, but why shouldn't church be fun? Their lightness of touch probably has something to do with the vast confidence and experience of men like Sean Fitzpatrick, Zinzan and Robin Brooke and centre Walter Little . . . The All Blacks, to offer a paradox, are playing happy rugby as if their lives depended on it. This is why they are likely to beat us for the first time in a series in this country.' And so it proved.

Where did this leave the coach, Andre Markgraaff? A series defeat in itself was not sufficient reason to dismiss him, because the opposition had clearly been of such high quality. And it was not his fault he was not Kitch Christie: the succession was always going to be a poisoned chalice.

But Markgraaff did not do things he should have done. He failed to impose a pattern of play on the Springbok backs, both in attack and defence. While the forwards were admirable in winning ball, the backs were knocking it on and bumping into each other, to the point of embarrassment. Off the field, Markgraaff failed to express himself in a way that inspired confidence. He was needlessly prickly and defensive under criticism. He mishandled the James Small affair to the point of ridiculousness. Can you imagine the All Blacks finding reasons to leave out their best wing with a series-decider coming up?

An unhappy footnote to the series defeat was Markgraaff's decision to leave out Francois Pienaar from the Springbok team, although this was no reflection on the abilities of Gary

Teichmann. As Natal captain, he could surely take much of the credit for sustaining that team's ruthless, sparkling, efficient, happy brand of rugby. As national captain, he took over a beaten Springbok team and led them to an admirable and honourable victory over the All Blacks in the final Test. He had the kind of imposing presence that was never negotiable, but which Pienaar only really achieved at the 1995 World Cup, after some years of controversy over his playing and leadership qualities.

As players, the two men were not competing directly for the same position, but Teichmann revealed the classical features that elevate the great No. 8s from the rest: ball skills, strength,

It's over. The All Blacks have won a series in South Africa for the first time.

height, speed, vision, unusual anticipation on attack and defence. Like his Natal predecessor, Tommy Bedford, he seemed to be that rarity among captains: one who inspired both by ability and personality.

Pienaar was obviously a great player and captain, nobody questioned that: his record proved it. But he was also the kind of player who is more than the sum of his parts, and the biggest of those parts was sheer courage. He was fast and strong, but he could be clumsy when working with the ball in hand, while his kamikaze tackling impressed more for its guts than its timing.

There is no question that Pienaar gave South Africa its finest hour in the 1995 World Cup. But in Markgraaff's view, that hour was past. That was why it had to be all or nothing for Pienaar: he must either continue as captain or not at all. The fact that he was replaced by a man three years older was neither here nor there.

After the 1996 All Black series win, I wrote: 'Markgraaff's personal management style is clearly disastrous and he has so far shown little in the way of strategic or tactical vision. And it is hard to find coherence in his selections and he is in danger of losing the confidence of his players. In short, it is difficult to see how he can last in the job until the next World Cup. But on the question of leaving out Pienaar, Markgraaff should be given the benefit of the doubt. He has a duty not to be sentimental about past glories — and a duty to be iconoclastic if necessary, because everyone else is still reluctant to leave the warm glow of 1995. The looming irony is that his other inadequacies as a coach may more than cancel out this brave and defensible decision.'

For a time Andre Joubert was called 'the Rolls Royce of fullbacks', and one occasion he lived up to the billing was the final Test of the 1996 series in South Africa.

1996

THE NEW ZEALAND RESPONSE

THE SEVENTH ALL BLACKS IN SOUTH AFRICA

by Grant Harding

OCCASIONALLY — JUST OCCASIONALLY — the sport of rugby becomes something more than a game. The All Black victory at Loftus Versfeld in Pretoria on August 24, to complete a first-ever Test-series victory in South Africa, was definitely one of those times. It was the completion of a mission that had been 'mission impossible' on five previous visits to the republic.

To achieve success the 1996 All Blacks faced a closer examination of their inner qualities than ever before, and in their dressing room just moments after the final whistle they battled exhaustion brought on by altitude, heat, the pace of the game and the physicality of the Springboks. They had created history, yet had been made to understand why a series victory in South Africa was so highly prized. Achieving the previously unachievable had not come easily.

In time-honoured fashion the Springboks had tested their physical endurance to its limits with a bruising forward display. This time the All Blacks had withstood the challenge. It had been the stuff of legends.

Three brilliant tries before halftime — two to Jeff Wilson, the other to Zinzan Brooke — all converted by Simon Culhane, had New Zealand ahead 21–11. Culhane made it 24–11 with a penalty goal early in the second half.

Then, as if the weight of history had descended upon them, the All Blacks failed to capitalise. Mistakes began to be made, and in a flash it was 24–23. With 19 minutes remaining it was the All Blacks who now appeared to be on the ropes.

Enter Jon Preston for Culhane, forced off by a broken wrist. For the first time since 1993 Preston was in a Test match, for the first time since 1991 he positioned himself at first-five, and within a minute he had kicked a 35-metre penalty goal. Joel Stransky replied before Preston slammed over a 52-metre penalty goal!

With minutes remaining Zinzan Brooke gave the All Blacks a seven-point buffer with a drop goal. Unbelievable!

Time remained for South Africa to snatch a draw and head to Ellis Park with a chance of squaring the series. For a final time the Springbok forwards smashed at the All Blacks' defensive line. A penalty, followed by another for not retreating, raised fears of a penalty try. Fortunately referee Didier Mene of France remained consistent.

The whistle blew, the match ended. Players struggled to their feet. Mission accomplished. Brilliant attack and heroic defence had earned victory. The last holy grail for New Zealand rugby had been seized, the World Cup final defeat of the year before had been avenged.

It was of no small importance that this was the first-ever series in South Africa to be controlled by neutral referees. In fact, New Zealand has won 13 of 20 Tests between the two countries since the introduction of neutral officials.

But other factors also were involved. The New Zealand Rugby Football Union's decision to grant coach John Hart's request for a 36-man squad allowed the Test XV to take no part in the four midweek matches. This was crucial, considering the four Tests were on consecutive Saturdays and came at the end of a 10-Test programme over 85 days.

A relatively injury-free run also aided the All Black cause. In 10 Tests, just 18 players were used in the starting line-up. The forward pack remained unchanged all season, and when it ran on at Pretoria it was the most experienced All Black pack ever to take the field.

The series victory was set up in Durban, where the All Blacks scored three tries to one, and it was their ability to score tries of rare quality that proved most decisive during the tour. South Africa dominated possession, but with their one-dimensional game based on physical domination they rarely threatened to score.

The mobile game depended as much on the skills of the forwards as of the backs. And it was here that locks Ian Jones and Robin Brooke — who celebrated breaking the world record for a Test locking partnership by setting up a try for Jeff Wilson in Pretoria — and No. 8 Zinzan Brooke came into their own.

But many other players were also at the top of their form, including veterans Frank Bunce, Walter Little, Michael Jones, Olo Brown and captain Sean Fitzpatrick, none of whom was destined to take part in another World Cup campaign. Fitzpatrick became the world's most capped forward at Durban, and was an inspirational figure throughout the tour. Another special hero was halfback Justin Marshall, who had thrived on the physical confrontation.

Despite their success the All Blacks were frustrated by their inability to put the Boks away. In Durban, Little was denied a certain try, which would have put the All Blacks ahead 30–19 with 20 minutes to play, when Zinzan Brooke was correctly penalised for breaking early from a scrum. And in Pretoria the All Blacks tired noticeably early in the second half.

The opportunity to whitewash the Boks and avenge 1949 was missed in the third Test at Ellis Park, and for those who ventured to the All Blacks' midweek training this came as no surprise. Pretoria had demanded too much; the goal of a series win had been achieved, and not even Michael Jones's 50th Test could inspire the All Blacks to make one more giant effort. Besides, the roar of the Ellis Park crowd demanded the Boks win at least one Test against the old foe in '96.

Not that anybody at home was concerned. The All Blacks arrived back in Auckland to a Queen Street ticker-tape parade. They had done the business.

It happened on a warm winter's day — it was 25 degrees Celsius — in the rarified air of highveld Pretoria. There will be other days like it. Not in a million years, however, will there be another day like 24 August 1996 in the history of New Zealand rugby. It was a day to remember.

1997

PASSION WITHOUT CUNNING

TRI-NATIONS IN SOUTH AFRICA

TO UNDERSTAND THE Springbok disasters of the 1997 Tri-Nation tournament, you have to go back to the series against the British Lions earlier that year. The bell started tolling for new coach Carel du Plessis when old-fashioned Northern Transvaal, minus several Springboks, managed to thump the British Lions, and the 35–30 score was flattering to the losers. Du Plessis also seemed bent on fielding an understrength side in the first Test. How else could one explain the omission of Kobus Wiese and Hennie le Roux from the 27-man Bok squad for the Tests against Tonga and the Lions?

by David Williams

There was more than a whiff of provincialism about the choice of Western Province's Fritz van Heerden ahead of Kobus Wiese. Van Heerden had not played Super 12 rugby that season, and Wiese, as the incumbent, had done nothing to suggest he should be dropped. Certainly the British camp followers were trying to hide their delight, just as they had when the selectors had been suckered into dropping John Williams in 1974.

Leaving out Hennie le Roux was even more difficult to explain. The Lions had offered further proof that flexible, fast-thinking centres are the prime source of killer counter-attacks. It seemed Du Plessis was continuing the role of Markgraaff in dismantling the winning team of 1995. But enormous respect remained among the rugby brotherhood for Du Plessis, 'the Prince of Wings' as he was known in his playing days. As usual, the honeymoon would turn sour only when the Boks lost.

As with Markgraaff, the honeymoon was a brief one. In the first Test many of the Springboks allowed themselves to be physically intimidated. They seemed out of touch and unused to pressure. Du Plessis looked like an apprentice who needed to turn himself into a sorcerer. Then the series was lost in the second Test when enormous Springbok passion was cancelled out by the boot of Neil Jenkins. Du Plessis knew the enemy had state-of-the-art heavy artillery in Jenkins, but the Boks took the field without even a machine gun. The country that had produced such world-class goalkickers as Okey Geffin, Keith Oxlee, Piet Visagie, Gerald Bosch, Naas Botha and Joel Stransky took the field naked in that department. It could only be concluded that Du Plessis was so arrogant he thought his team could win on tries alone.

As a consolation the Springboks won the third Test, with Jannie de Beer brought in to kick the points, but it had been the worst sequence in the history of South African rugby: home series defeats against the All Blacks and the British Lions in successive seasons.

By the time of the first Tri-Nations game against New Zealand at Ellis Park, it was hard to distinguish passion from desperation. The Springbok forwards were dominated for long periods but a really good side would not have allowed the opposition back into the game. Francois Pienaar's 1995 team would not have permitted the soft tries that cost the Boks this Test. Japie Mulder, Pieter Muller, Hennie le Roux, Brendan Venter — these men were no longer in the side, and their replacements, especially Percy Montgomery and Danie van Schalkwyk at centre, were just not able to impose themselves.

To be fair, the supposedly limited De Beer came through with great credit. He complemented his reliable place-kicking with a reassuring composure in open play. And Russell Bennett at fullback showed that Andre Joubert was not the only player in South Africa with flair at No. 15. James Small continued to command respect from his opponents. But as a division, the Springbok backs were in disarray under Du Plessis. On defence they were not structured, which was unsurprising given the minimal experience on offer. There was a desperate need for the organisation under pressure that in the past would have been provided by a Michael du Plessis or a Joel Stransky. On attack there was even less comfort to be had. The main tactics, after winning good ball, seemed to be to kick ahead or move back into the forwards. Neither

Springbok hooker Naka Drotske scores a superb try during the home team's frenzied start to the 1997 Tri-Nations Test at Johannesburg.

approach suggested flexibility, enterprise or vision. At scrumhalf, Joost van der Westhuizen was proving both an asset and a liability. His kick that was charged down and turned into an All Black try would have been unforgivable from any other player, yet he often conjured tries from the most unlikely situations.

Van der Westhuizen's play at this time was perhaps symptomatic of the team's performance under Carel du Plessis. There was no shortage of passion and commitment, along with some thrilling instinctive work built on forward dominance. But instinct is not the same thing as vision; individual brilliance from players like Gary Teichmann, Ruben Kruger and Mark Andrews did not always add up to an effective pattern. The All Blacks won because their defence was better than the Springboks'. The most telling demonstration of this was Teichmann's decision, when his side was trailing 35–32, to ask De Beer to go for posts and a draw instead of a try and a likely victory. We cannot say he was wrong, but his choice reflected the strengths of the two sides when it mattered.

Burnt out, washed up. 'Not just yet,' said Frank Bunce with a two-try performance at Johannesburg. Here he prepares to confront the Bok defence on a 50-metre dash for his second try.

1997

THE NEW ZEALAND RESPONSE

TRI-NATIONS IN SOUTH AFRICA

by Grant Harding

WHEN FRANK BUNCE was injured during the 1997 Rugby Super 12, many were already saying the 35-year-old's Test career should be over. But six weeks later he played in an All Black trial, and was then given every opportunity to find fitness and form in 'easy' Tests against Fiji and Argentina and a Bledisloe Cup clash against Australia. Nothing he did offered a clue to how he would perform in the first round of the Tri-Nations against South Africa at Ellis Park in Johannesburg.

It was Bunce who tiptoed through the South African defence to get the All Blacks started with a try after a merciless 10-point opening by the home team, and it was he who produced a try of real quality to tie the scores after an hour. The second of these, from 45 metres out, ranks with the best of his 20 All Black Test tries. After breaking through the Bok midfield defence — as he had done all match — he took on James Small, stood him up, turned him, and then took him and two other defenders over for the touchdown.

This was vindication for coach John Hart and his selection panel. It brought the All Blacks level for the first time in a Test match they should never have won. It was a symptom of Bunce's love of the physical confrontation South Africa provided, his love of the big occasion.

The New Zealand national anthem had been booed, the haka drowned out by the vocal abuse of a hostile crowd, and fruit and a bottle hurled at Christian Cullen and Bunce, while the Springboks played as if their lives depended on it. In situations like that it's time for the tough to get going. Frank Bunce was tough. New Zealand won (35–32).

1997
A FUNNY OLD GAME

TRI-NATIONS IN NEW ZEALAND

AT THE END of 1996, New Zealand and South Africa had played 47 matches, winning 22 each and drawing three. The average score per Test re-emphasised the closeness, the Boks taking the decimal point victory in a 12–12 draw.

In keeping with the introduction of the five-point try and the game's evolvement, post-isolation scores had grown. Statistically speaking it was no great surprise, therefore, when the Tri-Nations Test in Johannesburg in July 1997 saw the All Blacks eclipse their previous highest total, achieved in Pretoria the year before. It was more of a surprise that the losing Boks equalled their highest tally against New Zealand, achieved in their victory in

by Grant Harding

The laager mentality shields the Springboks from the All Black haka at Eden Park. Or were the Boks shielding themselves from the inevitable?

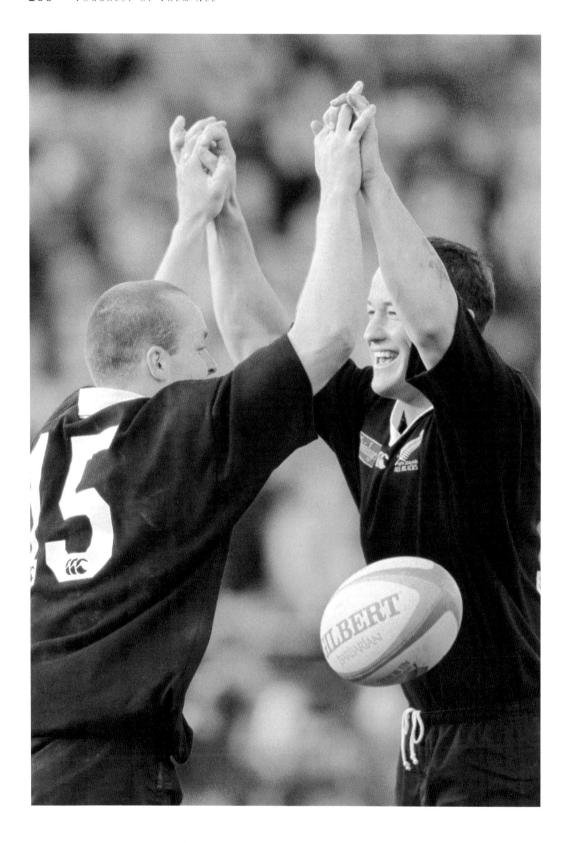

Johannesburg the previous year. The 35–32 scoreline meant that, before the Auckland Test, the average score in the 11 clashes since 1992 was 23–20 in New Zealand's favour — not a great margin considering New Zealand had won eight, lost two and drawn one in that time.

The All Blacks had clearly taken the majority of the honours — the World Cup being a highly regrettable exception — but not without a tension-packed struggle on each occasion. What transpired at Eden Park on August 9, therefore, had to be viewed — at the time at least — as an aberration. For the first time ever New Zealand took South Africa apart, a scoreline of 55–35 proving a statistician's dream and a Springbok nightmare rolled into one.

Strangely, it did not take a perfect performance from the All Blacks to achieve this result. As the managing editor of national weekly magazine *Rugby News* I headlined the match report 'All Blacks first, mistakes second, Springboks third.'

The All Blacks might have lifted themselves out of the siege mentality of previous contests to run in seven tries, many of them brilliantly executed, but they also conceded five to an opposition to which they were clearly superior. While the dream had been realised, the reality of the outcome did not live up to the prospect.

The unusual nature of the contest meant much post-match talk focused on the disappointing Springboks — their outdated attitude to the physical aspects of the game, their aimless kicking, their poor defence, their inferior fitness and their questionable selection — rather than the fabulous All Blacks. To the analysts, the Boks were an accident waiting to happen. Rumours had been circulating for some time that coach Carel du Plessis, who had taken over from the disgraced Andre Markgraaff, was not of international quality. A brilliant Springbok winger in the isolated 1980s, he had no coaching experience at first-class level to speak of.

The series loss to the British Lions increased the agitation. On the surface, the Lions — always respected by New Zealanders — had done well, while the Boks' form was a reflection of the moderate showings by their Rugby Super 12 teams. Only Natal, under former Springbok coach Ian McIntosh, had made the playoffs. The comfortable third-Test victory against the Lions, and the narrow loss to New Zealand at Johannesburg, where lady luck favoured the visitors, merely deferred Du Plessis's crucifixion until Auckland.

Another loss to Australia, in Brisbane, preceded the Boks' arrival in New Zealand, so by the time they hit Auckland there was an expectation they would prove easy-beats. On paper their team was a powerful combination, with only a few members new to the South Africa–New Zealand rivalry. The players were there, but the tell-tale signs of Du Plessis's inadequacies were in their positioning. International greenhorn Percy Montgomery was at centre and Henry Honiball at second-five, while, worst of all, Andre Snyman, a worthy rival for Bunce, was on the left wing. At first-five was Jannie de Beer, a player with a big boot and little imagination. Up front they had size and strength, but there were question marks about fitness and discipline.

LEFT: When you're hot, you're hot. Christian Cullen and Carlos Spencer celebrate another try in the record breaking victory at Eden Park.

DEFINING MOMENT

Venter's Shame
AUCKLAND, 9 AUGUST, 1997

When referee Derek Bevan sent off Springbok flanker Andre Venter for stamping on Sean Fitzpatrick's head early in the second half, the score was just 29–21. It was the first sending-off in the history of the rivalry, and a major blow for the Boks who had already lost brilliant flanker Ruben Kruger with a broken ankle after he had fallen within reach of his second try in just the ninth minute.

But the New Zealanders had little sympathy. They alleged the visitors' ill-discipline — winger James Small also received a yellow card after a crude attempt to foot-trip a try-bound Christian Cullen — was a result of their skill deficiencies.

It was not just the Springbok' poor form and internal problems that contributed to an air of confidence in the All Black camp. New Zealand's great escape act at Johannesburg had been followed by an emotional victory against Australia in the first-ever Test at the Melbourne Cricket Ground. A win at Eden Park would virtually assure the home team a second Tri-Nations trophy, and, after proving their resilience away from home, the All Blacks had seldom believed in themselves so strongly. More than that, this was a team that boasted quality based on experience and talent. It was the class act of world rugby.

Only five of the starting line-up had started their All Black careers post-World Cup, and only three — Tana Umaga, Carlos Spencer and Taine Randell — were in their first season of Test rugby. Selection was not really a debatable issue given the results. Even Spencer's elevation above Andrew Mehrtens could not be faulted. Initially, injury had opened the door for Spencer; however, he quickly closed it behind him, not only with his trademark attacking brilliance but with a previously unrecognised goalkicking talent. His 20 points in Johannesburg and 25 at Eden Park (the latter being the most by an All Black against the Springboks in a single match), gave him the highest total in a two-, three- or four-Test series by any player against South Africa.

As the crowd filed away pondering the reasons behind the decline of the Springboks, few considered the possibility that the match they had just seen signposted the beginning of the end of an era for the All Blacks. But it did. By the time New Zealand met South Africa again, the All Black careers of Sean Fitzpatrick (92 Tests), Zinzan Brooke (58 Tests) and Frank Bunce (55 Tests) had ended. In many ways this trio encapsulated the All Blacks' advantage over South Africa for most of the 1990s. Fitzpatrick's gamesmanship had annoyed the opposition to great advantage and its supporters to distraction, while his world-class hooking skills and winning attitude had been major bonuses to his leadership duties. The Springboks — or, for that matter anybody else — had never possessed a Zinzan. Brooke's class underwrote almost every major victory over the Boks. As for Bunce, he was a player who thrived on the collision of the great foes. The impact of these three players' departures could not have been more profound.

Only the statisticians were completely happy after the clash at Eden Park as they rattled off the milestones, of which some of those not mentioned above were most points conceded by South Africa in any match and highest losing score in an international.

Perhaps the game was best summed up by All Black lock Robin Brooke. 'It was a funny old game,' he mused. 'It never seemed to take shape.'

It's just possible — and that's all — that South Africa's stake in the game may have been greater had Ruben Kruger not fallen awkwardly and broken his ankle, with the tryline beckoning in the ninth minute. For in that short period — in which he had already scored a try — he had been inspirational.

1997

THE SOUTH AFRICAN RESPONSE

TRI-NATIONS IN NEW ZEALAND

by David Williams

SOUTH AFRICANS WERE so depressed by the 55–35 Springbok defeat at Eden Park, which came after a 33–22 thumping by Australia in Brisbane, that they could not bear to discuss rugby. Like one's brother-in-law being in jail for fraud, it was generally avoided as a subject of conversation, polite or otherwise.

It seemed that players selected for the Springbok side fell too easily into one of two groups: those who were being overpaid for winning the World Cup and those who were woefully inexperienced. Many genuine stars (such as Andre Joubert, Hennie le Roux and James Small) were ignored until it was too late, while others (the striking example was Joost van der Westhuizen) were apparently given no tactical guidance. These were classic indications of a coach lacking in confidence.

The record score piled up by the All Blacks did mask some small consolations and mitigatory excuses. After all, no other Springbok side apart from the 1937 tourists had scored five tries against New Zealand. Ruben Kruger had been removed from the game after a few minutes with a broken ankle. And it had been a harsh ruling when Andre Venter (not known as a dirty player in South Africa) had been sent off for stamping Fitzpatrick: the All Blacks had scored 34 points after he had left the field. Was it coincidence that Mark Andrews had also nearly got his marching orders for hitting Fitzpatrick? Whatever the reason, Springbok indiscipline had again cost South Africa dearly.

The Springboks did recover some pride in the last Tri-Nations game in Pretoria against Australia, running up eight tries in a remarkable 61–22 win. But this came too late to save Du Plessis. Victories against Australia were all very well, but only if he had done something comparable against New Zealand would he have lived to coach another day. Virtually before the sweat was dry at Loftus Versfeld, he was relieved of his command.

1998

MALLETT THE MESSIAH

TRI-NATIONS IN NEW ZEALAND

by Grant Harding

ON THE DAY the 1997 All Blacks beat England 25–8 at Manchester United's Old Trafford ground, the Springboks were in action against France. Now under the control of former Springbok No. 8 Nick Mallett, just three months after their humiliation at Eden Park, it was the South Africans who were doing the humiliating.

In the last Test ever played at the Parc de Princes, the Springboks spoiled what was supposed to have been an emotional farewell to the ground by adding flair, counter-attack, pace and precision ball-handling to their normal virtues of power and strength. So grand was their performance that the home crowd, who booed their own team, afforded the visitors thunderous applause as they enjoyed a lap of honour at the conclusion of the 52–10 demolition that sealed a series victory.

As 1998 rolled round, the significance of the Boks' win in Paris was not lost on All Black coach John Hart. After two magical seasons that balanced 20 Test victories against just one loss and a draw, he warned the public that an ill-wind might be about to blow in. Realism told him some of his players were tiring and rebuilding would have to be done, and against opponents like Australia and South Africa rebuilding could be painful.

He had also assessed Mallett's influence on the Boks. In fact Mallett had first entered Hart's orbit during the 1996 tour to South Africa when he had coached the feisty Boland XV that proved a tough opponent in the opening match.

Early in 1998 the Springbok coach came to New Zealand on a reconnaissance mission, and more than a few eyebrows were raised when Hart was openly friendly to him, even sharing a round of golf. Such camaraderie between international coaches caught New Zealanders short. Wasn't this the sworn enemy? Not until July 25 at Athletic Park, when the old foes would do battle for the 50th time. Until then Mallett was just good company. From the moment he arrived in New Zealand, he captivated the media's interest. Known for speaking his mind, he did not disappoint. And having majored in English, he was capable of doing it eloquently and with authority.

Mallett's passion for the game and for winning were evident, and his remarks were liberally dosed with humour. It's easy to laugh when you're winning, of course. By the time Mallett's Boks arrived in Wellington they had run up 11 consecutive Test victories, the most recent a fortuitous 14–13 Tri-Nations victory over Australia in Perth just a week before. That had been a historic moment — the Boks' first-ever Tri-Nations victory away from home.

Meanwhile, not all had been going well for John Hart. In two Tests against a woeful and understrength England, the All Blacks, now under young captain Taine Randell had played poorly. Then, in Melbourne, they had suffered their first-ever Tri-Nations defeat, losing to Australia for the first time since 1994. At first it appeared errors and missed opportunities were to blame. Had not the forwards won enough ball? The All Black selectors certainly thought so, Hart publicly laying the blame on first-five Andrew Mehrtens. Out went Mehrtens and in came Carlos Spencer, not only to guide the backline but also to kick the goals. Jonah Lomu came in for Joeli Vidiri on the wing, while Mark Mayerhofler returned from injury to replace Scott McLeod at centre.

The Springboks made just one change to the team that had beaten Australia, and that forced by injury, Andrew Aitken coming in for Rassie Erasmus. Nine of the team had been in the

A few frames on, this photographer might have proved Jeff Wilson scored a try for New Zealand at Athletic Park. But the scoreboard showed he didn't.

starting line-up at Eden Park nearly a year previously, although this time, tellingly, Percy Montgomery, Andre Snyman and Henry Honiball were in different positions.

Newcomers were Natal Sharks' winger Stefan Terblanche, Stormers' winger Pieter Rossouw, who had scored a try off the bench at Eden Park, second-five Pieter Muller, who had returned from rugby league, Aitken, and the props, former Zimbabwe international Adrian Garvey and Robbie Kempson.

Ultimately Spencer's inclusion cost the All Blacks dearly. By the time he was substituted by Mehrtens early in the second half he had missed five penalty goal attempts and failed to provide the authority for which Hart had said he had been selected. It was just one of many 'ifs' and 'buts' that threatened to cloud the real problems in the All Black camp. For example, what if Jeff Wilson had been awarded a try late in the first half when he forced the ball deep into the Springbok in-goal, instead of it being ruled to have gone dead?

The point was, success would only have led the All Black management to kid itself even further that this team was going to take New Zealand rugby forward. The facts were now clear to see. The great Michael Jones was no longer capable of immortal form. Other experienced forwards — Robin Brooke, Ian Jones and Craig Dowd — had not stepped up to support their young captain. Halfback Justin Marshall had come back from injury too soon. The midfield, featuring two second-fives, just couldn't find cohesion behind a forward pack that won the majority of the ball, though rarely when going forward. And Spencer and Mehrtens were now both struggling for form and confidence.

This Test proved to be a triumph for South African defence and Mallett's tactical nous. Perhaps the most crucial period of play was the last 15 minutes before halftime. In that period, trailing 3–0, New Zealand attacked relentlessly without reward.

Eventually the All Blacks did equalise, midway through the second half with a Mehrtens' penalty goal, but on this occasion it was the Boks who lasted the distance. Much credit for that went to the selection and use of an impact bench featuring Franco Smith, Bobby Skinstad and Ollie le Roux.

Montgomery's second penalty goal preceded the telling blow, a well-worked try to Pieter Rossouw with 10 minutes remaining. The All Blacks, with the ball, had been unable to break the grip of Springbok defence, and now, in the final quarter, they were in the grip of Springbok attack.

When flanker Aitken smashed Christian Cullen to the ground as he attempted to spark a counter-attack with five minutes remaining, and referee Ed Morrison awarded a penalty to South Africa, arms went into the air in triumph. The kick missed and play moved on, but New Zealand had been beaten.

It was the Boks' first Test victory in New Zealand since the Athletic Park game in 1981, and the players regarded it as the most important since the World Cup triumph in 1995.

DEFINING MOMENT

Rossouw's Smile Said It All
WELLINGTON, 25 JULY, 1998

Pieter Rossouw, whose try had made the difference, was one of the least quotable Boks following the match. His smile said it all. He did manage a 'yes' to the question as to whether or not the 16th try (of the previous 15, four had been against France the previous November) of his then 17-Test career had been his most important.

After all, it was a try that had decided a Test match, a try that effectively ended New Zealand's grip on the Tri-Nations trophy, and a try that had allowed a Springbok team, winless on the road in the first two Tri-Nations seasons, to go home with two away victories and the real possibility of overall triumph.

It was also a try that illustrated why the Springboks deserved to win the match. How so? Because their basic execution with the ball — and they had far less of it — was better than the home team's.

On this occasion, an attacking scrum close to the All Black posts saw halfback Joost van der Westhuizen move the ball to a flat-standing Henry Honiball, then move across field in an apparent attempt at a double-round. Not so. The rock-steady Honiball held on, turned his body infield to hold the defence, then passed across his body to Rossouw, streaking through on his outside, to score under the posts.

LEFT: Beautifully executed, professionally finished – Springbok winger Pieter Rossouw scores the crucial try at Athletic Park.

1998

THE SOUTH AFRICAN RESPONSE

TRI-NATIONS IN NEW ZEALAND

by David Williams

BEFORE THE MATCH at Athletic Park, Nick Mallett told a press conference that the Springboks would show respect for the haka. Now, it is never easy for the opposition to know what to do when that ritual is being performed. To ignore it looks childish and to try to imitate it with one's own war cry would be pathetic. By openly acknowledging the power of the haka in advance, Mallett was able to defuse it. It was typical of his original, impulsive, intelligent approach to rugby.

The Springboks proceeded to tackle like demons and wait for the few chances that might come their way. For the first time in many years, we had the spectacle of an All Black side looking bewildered.

Mallet's style of domination would come from picking fast, skilled tight forwards who could operate like flankers — hence Adrian Garvey at prop and Mark Andrews at lock. Mallett also liked robust backs who had the physique and temperament to get involved in mauling and rucking when necessary — witness Pieter Muller and Franco Smith. And his flankers — the model here was the swift and intelligent Bobby Skinstad — should be able to play like gifted three quarters.

Mallett characteristically added something else to the mix: his players were expected to enjoy themselves. Towards the end of the tight Test match in Perth, the camera settled for a moment on the Bok coach. He gave a brief smile, as if to say: 'Yes, I know you want to see how I'm taking the pressure. Of course I'm anxious, but it's not so bad I can't offer you a smile. After all, it's just a game.' That composure rubbed off on his team and was the main ingredient in the compelling 13–3 Athletic Park victory.

We've done it. The Springboks are delighted with their first post-isolation win in New Zealand, and their first since they beat the All Blacks at Athletic Park in 1981.

1998

GLORY AND ILLUSION

TRI-NATIONS IN SOUTH AFRICA

by David Williams

IT MIGHT HAVE been better for Nick Mallett's 1999 Springboks if the remarkable 1998 Tri-Nations match against the All Blacks in Durban had been lost. It really should have been, because the Springboks were down by 18 points at one stage and looking far less impressive, disciplined and cohesive than they had earlier in New Zealand.

But the Boks somehow managed three late tries, partly aided by the one weakness consistently displayed by the All Blacks under John Hart — a tendency to ease up when on top. Talisman Joost van der Westhuizen got the first try, darting through the defence, then Bobby Skinstad, playing to perfection his assigned game-breaker role, made an impossible victory seem merely improbable.

Two minutes from time, Jonah Lomu — showing again his deficiencies in all-round footballing sensibility and skills — was penalised for a late tackle on winger Stefan Terblanche. Another referee might not have awarded the penalty, but Lomu should not have allowed Peter Marshall any margin for error. Henry Honiball's corner kick was cool and accurate, setting up the lineout a few metres from the All Black line.

Scoring tries from such situations has always been difficult, because the defenders become intensely alert and have the advantage of knowing exactly where the *schwerpunkt* — the point of impact —will be: through the defending forwards. If the ball is dispersed down the line, defenders move up quickly in the knowledge that the attackers have little space and that stab kicks are likely to be unproductive.

But throughout 1998 Mallett had preached the importance of going for tries from the penalty-to-lineout sequence rather than kicking for goal. In a Bloemfontein hotel in 1998, before the first Test against the Irish, he told me a team should go for tries in all circumstances. He rejected the argument that consideration of context was better than blind faith in any particular tactic. In Durban he seemed to be vindicated. Mark Andrews soared to take the ball, his colleagues surged around him like demons, and James Dalton came round to burrow through a green and black mountain. Again, another referee might not have had the courage to award the try, but Marshall was convinced and the Boks were in a winning lead.

Thus an honourable season became an outstanding one. The Boks had won their 12th successive Test under Nick Mallett and were in the unfamiliar position of being able to look with confidence towards a Tri-Nations decider, at Ellis Park against Australia the following Saturday, and there was talk of South Africa being the favourite for the 1999 World Cup. The Springboks had also now levelled the overall head-to-head encounter with the All Blacks at 24 wins each.

Meanwhile, Gary Teichmann's stature as captain had grown further, prompted by the approving commentary of the way he had held his nerve towards the end of the month in Durban (before his loyal home crowd), kept his men disciplined and gone for the tries.

However, it was arguably in this game that Skinstad's spectacular potential saw him upstage the steadier, quieter Teichmann in Mallett's mind. A seed had been planted by the Wellington victory, with the shifting of Andre Venter from flank to lock when Skinstad had been put on the field for the last quarter. In Durban, Venter had again been moved to lock when Skinstad had come on (this time halfway through) for the injured Otto. Twice it had seemed to work perfectly.

Percy Montgomery had also staked a claim in Durban that made him a permanent fixture in Mallett's side for over a year. In particular, he had created the Boks' first try, passing to scorer Terblanche after receiving an apparent hospital pass from Andre Snyman, then unexpectedly bouncing out of Eroni Clarke's tackle.

The *Sunday Times* summed up the implications of that thrilling victory: 'With just six days to

In the first decade of the new millennium will Bobby Skinstad be to South Africa what Zinzan Brooke was to New Zealand in the 1990s? The All Blacks got their first look at the new wonder boy when he came on as a substitute in the 1998 Test at Athletic Park.

go, South Africa are handily placed to win a first ever Tri-Nations title. Passion and awesome self-belief have become the cornerstone of this team. And that, as New Zealand have come to discover, is awfully difficult to overcome.' Australia duly followed the script and succumbed at Ellis Park. South African fans were euphoric and began to talk of further glory in 1999. Dreams were made sweeter by revelling in the All Blacks' misfortune: Durban had given them their fourth successive defeat, a disaster which had happened only once before, in the 1949 whitewash.

In the week after the victory over Australia I also rode the wave of media enthusiasm, but could not help reminding *Financial Mail* readers that greatness had not yet been achieved: 'Is the present Springbok team the best in history? Such questions are inevitably being asked after our impressive annexation of the Tri-Nations trophy for the first time. To be taken seriously, a team must perform consistently by winning repeatedly against the best opposition, with the key requirement that it can also win the really big and decisive fixtures . . .

'Nick Mallett's Springboks are well on the way to meeting all the above criteria. Two things are missing on their CV, though, and both can be rectified. They need to maintain for at least two more seasons their new ascendancy over the All Blacks — and they need to win the World Cup next year. In fact, if they achieve the second, the first will not matter. Whatever you say about the relative merits of the 1995 Bok side coached by Kitch Christie — many people claim Mallett's 1998 model is superior, both man-for-man and as a team — the fact is that Christie's men won the matches that counted: Australia in the opening game, France in the semifinal and New Zealand in the final. Mallett's side must wait until next year to prove they also have what it takes to win at will.'

As all the world knows, they did not have what it takes. But if the Boks had lost the 1998 Durban Test, in which victory appeared to vindicate both Mallett's tactics and selection approach, it is doubtful that the images of Skinstad and Montgomery would have glowed as brightly in the coach's off-season mind as he considered his options for 1999. Skinstad's potential contribution at the World Cup might not have been taken so easily on trust after he ended up missing most of the 1999 season with a knee injury, while Montgomery might have seemed much less deserving of the coach's blind loyalty when he lost form and looked absolutely hapless.

If Andrew Mehrtens had converted just one of the two kickable penalties he missed in Durban, Mallett might have been less adventurous in 1999, and more likely to place his faith in established warriors like Teichmann and Andre Joubert.

1998
THE NEW ZEALAND RESPONSE

TRI-NATIONS IN SOUTH AFRICA

by Grant Harding

AFTER OPENING LOSSES to Australia and South Africa in the 1998 Tri-Nations, the All Blacks' season only got worse in the return encounter with Australia at Lancaster Park. At one stage they trailed 9–27, before two token tries narrowed the gap to 23–27. Nothing, however, could hide the fact that change was necessary.

Out went Walter Little (50 Tests), Ian Jones (75 Tests), Michael Jones (55 Tests) and Craig Dowd (45 Tests) for the return match against South Africa in Durban. In came centre Eroni Clarke (not wanted since 1993), No. 8 Isitolo Maka, lock Royce Willis and prop Carl Hoeft. Maka and Hoeft were starting a Test for the first time, while Willis was making his debut. Josh Kronfeld also returned from injury to replace Mark Carter.

For 67 minutes at King's Park in Durban the changes worked. The All Black forward pack gave its best performance of the season, both on the drive and in the scrum, and the visitors were well worth their 23–5 lead. Then, for the first time in memory, an All Black team, in the space of 13 minutes, threw away a winning lead.

On the face of it there were explanations. Maka, who had given the All Blacks power for the first time in the season, suffered a broken nose after a freak collision with Robin Brooke. Then Eroni Clarke, who, but for one early lapse, had brought all his maturity to bear on the midfield defence, fell lame. But these were just excuses.

A lack of communication on defence, or someone neglecting their defensive duty, allowed Joost van der Westhuizen to score, and from then on the Springbok attack grew stronger, the All Black defence became weaker and eventually, as it does, luck turned.

Nor was that all. What about the All Blacks' inability to come up with a constructive method of attack from a five-metre scrum late in the match? Call me old fashioned, but at 23–19 a drop goal from what was almost a midfield scrum wouldn't have been a bad option.

Then there was the substitution bench. It was difficult to understand why coach John Hart, who had agitated for the introduction of the seven-man bench, was so loathe to use it. By the end of the match several New Zealand forwards were struggling to keep pace with the substitution-revitalised Springbok pack.

Undoubtedly the Jonah Lomu late-tackle penalty call that led to the final try was marginal, especially when one considers Stefan Terblanche's kick ahead was out on the full before Lomu even touched him. Given the circumstances, surely a warning would have been sufficient.

As for James Dalton's try, which followed, this would never have been allowed by a video referee. New Zealanders, however, were not aggrieved by that. They were just stunned.

TIRED BONES

TRI-NATIONS IN NEW ZEALAND

by Grant Harding

ALL OF NEW ZEALAND'S rugby community rejoiced when England beat South Africa at Twickenham on 5 December 1998, for the honour of the 1965–69 All Blacks 17-Test winning streak had been protected. South Africa had a share of the world supremacy for consecutive Test wins, but the great All Black era was still in the record books.

The Boks had collected their 17 wins in little more than 15 months, eight victories coming in Europe on successive end-of-season tours. During the last of these, signs of tiredness were evident in a come-from-behind win against Wales followed by lacklustre triumphs over Scotland and Ireland, which saw the record equalled.

While New Zealand's best players — except for those involved in the New Zealand Maori three-match tour to Scotland — soothed their battered minds and bodies, the Boks were continuing the punishing schedule they'd set for themselves since their return from isolation in 1992. Between the end of the 1995 World Cup and the beginning of the 1998 season they had played 41 Tests, while New Zealand had played 34. South Africa's international players had effectively endured an extra season of international rugby. By comparison, in the year before the World Cup, the Boks had played 12 Tests to New Zealand's seven.

All Black coach John Hart expressed pleasure at the results when a 37-man squad assembled for a camp at the Special Air Services base in Hobsonville, Auckland, prior to the start of the World Cup season. Tired, unenthusiastic players had been replaced by fit, fresh and focused individuals determined to put the horrors of the previous year's five-Test losing streak behind them.

The Rugby Super 12 proved to be a New Zealand triumph, with the Canterbury Crusaders beating the Otago Highlanders in a rousing final; and while a similar scenario had been played out the year before, this time it appeared the players had more to give.

Hart also passed his first Test of the season, announcing a squad that caused few ripples of indignation. Because the selection panel had chosen on form, critics were comfortable to wait and see regarding Hart's more interesting calls, among which was his contention that captain Taine Randell was an international-class No. 8.

Meanwhile, Nick Mallett was starting his Test season without many of the previous season's stars. Halfback Joost van der Westhuizen did not play Super 12 because of a serious knee injury suffered against England, and many others had fallen by the wayside during that gruelling competition.

Mallett was also showing signs of taking his eye off the ball, or just getting a bit too clever for his own good. Experimentation, fine tuning and the odd gamble would characterise the Springboks' seven-match pre-World Cup campaign, he indicated. Unfortunately, he didn't count on a horrific run of injuries.

Still, two massive victories over Italy (74–3 and 101–0) offered only a subtle indication that the Springboks were not what they had been in 1998. To the keenest eye their game lacked shape. It was only when they played Wales, in the first-ever Test match at the Millennium Stadium in Cardiff, that the real extent of their problems was revealed. Graham Henry's team destroyed South Africa up front, defended strongly and goal-kicked superbly to beat the Springboks for the first time in 13 encounters since 1906.

By the time his team arrived in Dunedin to face an All Black side that had grown in confidence after consecutive wins against New Zealand A (22–11), Samoa (71–13) and France (54–7), Mallett was beginning to feel the cold wind of public pressure. The Tri-Nations now had a touch more importance for him. His problems started with captain Gary Teichmann, who was no longer the great player New Zealanders had always respected, and went from there. Side issues like race quotas strained his previously harmonious relationship with the media.

In addition to Van der Westhuizen, missing from the line-up for the Carisbrook Test were six other players who had triumphed in Wellington the previous year. Six players were also missing from the line-up that had started against Wales a fortnight before.

New Zealanders were bemused by the South Africans' sudden disintegration, but nobody was crowing too loudly. The pain of the previous year, followed by the ease of the All Black victories over Samoa and France, meant the Blacks' early-season form, while encouraging, was to be treated with suspicion. Everyone was waiting for a sign, and that sign was to be a victory over the Tri-Nations champion.

The All Black team that ran onto Carisbrook on July 10 featured three players new to the great rivalry — Canterbury second-five Daryl Gibson, Canterbury lock Norm Maxwell and Otago prop Kees Meeuws. Three-quarters Tana Umaga and Alama Ieremia were back for the first time since 1997, while Andrew Blowers was making his first start against South Africa, having appeared as a replacement in 1996. Christian Cullen, fullback in nine previous Tests against South Africa, had been converted to a winger, while Jeff Wilson, a winger in 10 previous Tests against South Africa, was now at fullback.

A capacity crowd of 41,500, most dressed in black thanks to a marketing masterstroke, welcomed a new-look All Black team on to the park. Now the property of sports-apparel company adidas, the All Black jersey was completely black, apart from the numbers, the silver fern and the adidas logo. To mark the occasion the home team made some subtle changes to their haka, the impact of which was intensified by a speaker system relaying it to the crowd at full volume.

For the next 55 minutes, two nervous teams failed to make the most of perfect conditions, butchering opportunities against, admittedly, committed defence. At halftime New Zealand led 6–0 courtesy of two Andrew Mehrtens' penalty goals, but try-scoring opportunities had gone begging, the most obvious from an unfortunate knock-on by Cullen after a splendid kick and chase. The Boks had also failed to capitalise from a lineout near the All Black line, and first-five Gaffie du Toit had been astray with a penalty goal and two drop goal attempts.

Immediately after halftime, the visitors' hooker, Naka Drotske, crossed under the bar, only to have referee Peter Marshall correctly rule that the final pass from Teichmann had been forward. Continuing to apply pressure, both Percy Montgomery and Du Toit missed drop-goal attempts, and Cullen stopped a dangerous attack with a near intercept.

Finally, New Zealand laid waste to the siege with a strong counter-attack, and the decisive

Jonah Lomu has never scored a try against South Africa, but in a superhuman run at Carisbrook he went close.

Them's The Breaks
DUNEDIN, 10 JULY, 1999

With the score just 6–0 early in the second half, a still not completely confident All Black team might have capitulated if a try had been awarded to Naka Drotske soon after the break. However, a knock-on by Gary Teichmann was ruled, and the 1999 All Blacks finally found their confidence with a try from a midfield scrum in the 55th minute.

moment was not long in coming. From a midfield scrum in the 55th minute, Justin Marshall ran strongly. Then, from the ensuing ruck, Mehrtens produced a visionary chip over the Springbok defence for Cullen to provide a visionary chase and regather on the full to score a game-breaking try. A Mehrtens penalty goal soon increased the lead to 16–0.

South Africa fired their final shot when Breyton Paulse was held up over the line after a period of excellent continuity. When a penalty was awarded and Teichmann opted for the scrum, only to have his own team penalised in the ensuing phase, the game was all but over. Indeed, in the final quarter, the Springbok forwards, who enjoyed a five-kilogram advantage per man, began to struggle.

All that remained was for New Zealand's confidence to be given further encouragement through tries to Wilson and Marshall, who was equalling Graeme Bachop's New Zealand halfback record of 31 Tests. The bench was also given a work-out, Jonah Lomu offering a memorable cameo, beating eight defenders in a trademark 'not of this world' run.

It was by no means a perfect victory. Nevertheless, it was New Zealand's first Tri-Nations win since 1997, and as such represented a continuation of the building of a team both in style and confidence. There was promise of an even brighter future, a win offering many more positives than a loss. The 28–0 result also kept the statisticians happy. It was an all-comers' record-winning margin against South Africa.

Victory also ended what had been a difficult week for coach John Hart on a happy note. On the Thursday before the Test, his brother Graeme had passed away after a long battle with cancer.

South Africa's problems were going to get worse before they got better, and this match proved to be the popular Teichmann's last as a Springbok.

1999

THE SOUTH AFRICAN RESPONSE

TRI-NATIONS IN NEW ZEALAND

by David Williams

A 28–0 DEFEAT by the All Blacks can only be a miserable business but it was not as bad as it looked. Let's start with the records: biggest margin of defeat for the Springboks in 247 Tests against all opposition in 100 years; and the first time South Africa hadn't scored a point in an international match since 1965. Such statistics don't lie, but they don't necessarily mean anything either. The Boks passed up several opportunities to kick for posts in favour of going for tries, and the All Blacks' total would have been 22 in the days when a try counted for only three points.

The worrying issue was not the margin of defeat but the fact that New Zealand scored three tries and South Africa scored none. The All Blacks deserved to win because they played with confidence and a sense of enterprise — although they had to work hard and long to subdue their opposition. So what went wrong for the Boks? Nine, 10 and out — it's as simple as that. Their serious lack of depth at halfback had been identified before the Super 12, and Dunedin in the Tri-Nations was not the ideal time to blood a raw pairing like Gaffie du Toit and Dave von Hoesslin, especially with the flair and experience of Justin Marshall and Andrew Mehrtens against them. Imagine if the All Blacks had fielded novice halfbacks against Henry Honiball and Joost van der Westhuizen.

Du Toit's tactical judgment on the day was the key weakness, compounded by his poor defence. He was also labouring under Nick Mallett's expectations of him. Du Toit and Percy Montgomery often seemed at a loss to know what to do with a hard-won ball beyond kicking it back into the grateful arms of those cool and dangerous veterans Christian Cullen and Jeff Wilson. In retrospect this was an early sign of the tactical poverty that would afflict the Boks in the World Cup a few months later.

Once again comfort was to be had from the performance of the Bok forwards, notably replacement flanker Andre Vos. But a turning point in the match was Du Toit's drop goal attempt at a time when it was looking as if sustained Bok pressure would produce a try. Similarly, the failure of the referee to award Naka Drotske a try, after Gary Teichmann's pass had actually bounced forward off an All Black body, came at a crucial stage when the Boks were trailing by a few points.

That decision by Peter Marshall probably cost Teichmann his place and the captaincy for the World Cup. Teichmann had not looked himself after an injury-ridden season, and, although he played well in Dunedin, the record defeat did nothing to stop his shares sliding in the coach's mind.

A month after the World Cup, Mallett said in an interview with Mike Greenaway of the Johannesburg *Star* that he was convinced Teichmann would have retired at the end of the 1998 season if there had not been the incentive of the World Cup. By the end of the 1999 Super 12, said Mallett, he had felt he had a captain 'who was no longer worth his place in the team, who no longer had the support of his team-mates. The turning point was in Dunedin . . . I believe Gary started losing confidence in himself and in me, and the team in him.'

Even for Mallett, it had not been possible to be so blunt at the time.

1999

HONESTY AND LOST CONFIDENCE

TRI-NATIONS IN SOUTH AFRICA

by David Williams

THIS WAS THE point, between the 1999 Tri-Nations defeat in Dunedin and the return match in Pretoria, at which most people thought Nick Mallett must have lost his marbles. Going into the World Cup, with an important Tri-Nations match against New Zealand looming, he stunned the entire rugby world by dropping his captain. It was not just a question of injury or form: Mallett made it clear Teichmann was no longer part of his planning for the World Cup.

As Dan Retief wrote in a sharp column in the *Sunday Times*, 'Teichmann is not just any rugby player. He is the most-capped Springbok captain in history. Mallett's crass treatment of Teichmann is as deplorable as the manner in which Andre Markgraaff got rid of Francois Pienaar . . . it will be scant consolation to Gary Teichmann to know that he joins a long line of Springbok captains who have been treated disgracefully by rugby's hierarchy.'

Of course, Mallett had not gone mad. He was still the same coach who had guided the Springboks to equalling the All Blacks' record of 17 successive victories. But perhaps he was only now emerging, under the pressures that were inevitable after defeat, as a more complex person. What was not fair was to question his integrity; indeed, he should have been praised for his courage, because not many men would have dared take the step of dropping a captain with Teichmann's record.

My theory about the incident is that Mallett must always have had limited confidence in Teichmann's leadership. But after he inherited the great No. 8 as captain, the team just kept winning. It would have seemed bizarre to have changed the captain during that magnificent sequence of victories.

However, in August 1999, after a remarkably long run without injury, Teichmann appeared fragile. Twice he had to miss internationals with knee troubles, after being crocked for much of the Super 12 campaign. He was taking time to get back to peak fitness and form, even though it was generally accepted he had played well in the recent 28–0 Tri-Nations defeat. I believe Mallett had always felt instinctively that he needed someone more inspirational not only at No. 8, but also, and particularly, as captain. Now the team had lost four games, he felt justified in going for Bobby Skinstad and Joost van der Westhuizen respectively in those roles.

Why did Mallett not wait until the Tri-Nations was over? Because if there was to be a new leader, he must establish himself as soon as possible. If Mallett had really wanted Teichmann, he would have given him more time to prove his fitness and form.

You can see the logic, though you might not agree with it. It was also an approach that carried

1996–1999: ENTER PROFESSIONALISM

high risks. Teichmann was deeply respected by opponents, not least the All Blacks, as well as by his fellow Springboks. Van der Westhuizen and Skinstad would have to be consistently superb to persuade players and supporters alike that Mallett was right. There was also the chance that Skinstad or Van der Westhuizen, or both, could get knocked out by injury before the World Cup.

What about keeping Teichmann in the squad, even if he wasn't captain? Mallett, quite reasonably, must have taken a view similar to that of Kitch Christie in 1995: there could be no room for a former Springbok captain because the effect on the team would be disruptive. The fact that Teichmann had nobly said he would play under another captain did not undermine this reasoning.

If my theory is right, Mallett's first mistake was not to have replaced Teichmann as captain (if not as a player) long before. But the honesty required to explain such a controversial decision would have been beyond even Mallett, with the Springboks on such a winning roll. I may have been complicating matters: former Bok coach Ian McIntosh told me he was convinced Teichmann was dropped simply because Mallett thought he was no longer good enough. McIntosh disagreed strongly with such an assessment, while understanding the coach's line of thinking.

The change must have affected an already shaky team morale. Joost van der Westhuizen led the Boks to a crushing 34–18 defeat at Loftus Versfeld. It was their fourth consecutive defeat and the worst losing sequence since 1974, when the three thrashings by the British Lions had followed the shock 18–9 defeat by England in 1972. It was also the Springboks' worst result against the All Blacks at home, surpassing the 29–18 score at Cape Town three seasons before.

Home critics were now accustomed to looking for reasons for defeat. After all, the side had fielded 36 players in just six Tests. There was no shortage of commitment, but a serious lack of penetration. *The Sunday Times*' Clinton van den Berg neatly summed up the factors in the All Black triumph: 'Joost van der Westhuizen, Andre Venter and Ruben Kruger were lionhearted, but there just wasn't enough firepower on show to really make it count against a team as well drilled as the All Blacks. The back three of Jeff Wilson, Tana Umaga and Christian Cullen were quite splendid and overshadowed the Boks in every department.'

In fact the Bok team still looked very disjointed, on paper and during the game. Montgomery's permanence at fullback, despite appalling form and a loss of confidence, seemed to contradict Mallett's stated policy of rotating players before the World Cup. Deon Kayser was undeniably talented but very new on the wing, while Franco Smith was always going to be somewhere between provincial and national class. Andre Snyman in the other centre spot was hugely reassuring, until he badly damaged his ankle scoring the opening try. The ungainly Rossouw on the other wing was always dangerous on attack but unpredictable.

The loose forwards, Rassie Erasmus, Ruben Kruger and Andre Venter, looked tough and powerful, but Skinstad, still injured, was not yet back to vindicate Mallett's faith in him. The young locks, Albert van den Berg and Selborne Boome, were talented but green. At least the front-row, Cobus Visagie, Naka Drotske and Os du Randt, looked solid enough.

The most obvious symptom of a team psyche that had been distorted by injuries and a run of defeats was Gaffie du Toit's play at flyhalf. He had been singled out by Mallett the year before as a great prospect. Yet now he seemed unconfident in himself and unsure of what tactics to employ. Mallett seemed frustrated, almost angry, that Du Toit was unable to impose himself on the game.

As was customary in the 1990s, South Africa made a storming start. They stole the ball from an early lineout, forced the All Blacks to concede a penalty for offside, and were first on the board with a Du Toit penalty goal. But as was also customary in the 1990s, the All Blacks absorbed the pressure then started coolly applying it in return. Penalties started going the way of the All Blacks and the Springboks lost their early fluency.

Even the Boks' first try came from an error. Du Toit's attempted drop goal hit Tana Umaga, glancing off him perfectly for Snyman to scoop up at pace and sprint for the corner. Snyman's replacement was Robbie Fleck, who seemed to be fussily dangerous on attack without ever quite getting through, while his defence gave everyone heart failure. His first involvement in the game was to watch Cullen run past him.

There were some crumbs of comfort. Van den Berg looked superb in the lineout, and the captaincy seemed to sit easily on Van der Westhuizen. The forwards generally made sure the All Blacks had to work for their victory. But it was almost as if South Africans had lost interest in this game and were looking ahead to the World Cup. Then we would have Henry Honiball back, and Skinstad and Pieter Muller and Brendan Venter. Kayser had looked promising, and there was the lightning pace of Breyten Paulse to fall back on. We would just have to write off the All Black defeats.

The corner seemed to have been turned the following week against Australia. Even though the difference between victory and defeat was the few centimetres by which Matthew Burke missed a late penalty attempt for Australia, the 10–9 win was a win (with the only try going to the Boks) and nobody could say it was not deserved. The forwards were again excellent, and, although the backs were frantic in defence rather than composed, they did the job. Australia's attackers were simply pressured out of the match.

Back at centre, Brendan Venter had a creative effect that endured after he had to leave the field. Jannie de Beer was solid at flyhalf in place of Du Toit, but obviously Henry Honiball was still missed. People continued to wonder whether the squad would have been strengthened by Joel Stransky.

Interestingly, Venter went against the current orthodoxy about players getting too much competitive rugby. Interviewed in the *Daily Telegraph*, he said: 'Tiredness and fatigue is a mental thing. The body is capable of much, much more than most people think. I love rugby. I can't wait to play. Stay fresh mentally, work hard at something else, and rugby is a pleasure. I'd play all the year around given the choice.' This was a startling declaration, because it reminded one of how stale the Boks were looking after the glories of 1998.

Against Australia, in their last big game before the World Cup, the Springboks at last looked fresh, as if they'd resolved to enjoy themselves. Perhaps the corner had been turned in more ways than one. But after Mallett's controversial selections in 1999, there was only one way he would end up being rated one of the great Springbok coaches: he had to bring back the William Webb Ellis Cup. Even reaching the final, only to lose, would be regarded as failure. By firing Teichmann he had upped the stakes tremendously.

It was a measure of Mallett's strength that he understood this perfectly and welcomed the challenge. Not a man to pretend he was omniscient, he was also easily puzzled by the effects of his mistakes. He might be wrong sometimes, but he was not weak.

1999

THE NEW ZEALAND RESPONSE

TRI-NATIONS IN SOUTH AFRICA

by Grant Harding

VICTORY IN THE Pretoria Test won the All Blacks the Tri-Nations, although this was not confirmed until South Africa beat Australia a week later. For the first time since 1997 a Test had been won overseas, and to have achieved that at Loftus Versfeld had to be satisfying.

As regards the World Cup matches ahead, however, an injury to Daryl Gibson was the most significant moment in the game. When he left the field in the first half, coach John Hart took the opportunity to work an experiment he'd talked about since the pre-season had begun. In to centre went Christian Cullen, and with his first touch of the ball he skipped away from Robbie Fleck, after halfback Justin Marshall, having completed a neat double-round with Andrew Mehrtens, threw an inch-perfect pass.

The second outcome of Gibson's injury was significant game time for Jonah Lomu, and with 20 minutes remaining he stormed up the left wing. Anton Oliver carried play on, before Taine Randell, out in the backs, threw a perfect wide ball for Cullen to score an all-comers' record sixth try against South Africa. Cullen wasn't at centre against Australia three weeks later, nor was Lomu in the starting line-up, but the seeds of these players' eventual positionings in the World Cup had been sewn.

A true positive was the goalkicking of Mehrtens. His seven penalty goals were an all-comers' record against South Africa, and he became the first player to score 100 points for his country against the Springboks. Other milestones included Robin Brooke's all-comers' record of a 10th victory over the Springboks, and Jeff Wilson's first drop goal at Test level.

Incredibly, South Africa had made eight changes to their starting line-up since the Dunedin Test, while New Zealand had made just one.

1999 World Cup

Honour from Defeat: The World Cup Play-off

by David Williams

JUST AS NEW ZEALANDERS celebrated when England ended the Springboks' unbeaten run in December 1998, so South Africans were enormously cheered by what the French did to the All Blacks at Twickenham in October 1999. Suddenly our 27–21 defeat by Australia in the other World Cup semi-final the previous day did not seem so bad. If we couldn't be in the final, there was great comfort in knowing that the old enemy had also lost out.

The disappointment was actually greater for the All Blacks. They had made the fatal error of assuming their passage to the final was automatic. Going into the semi-final, they were already thinking about playing Australia and had clearly lost any respect they might have had for the French. When defeat came, it was all the more bitter, arrogance having clearly infected the All Blacks' preparations, however hard their coach and captain must have worked to keep the team in quarantine from it.

Neither side wanted to play for third place, but the All Blacks looked like broken men before they went onto the field on the Thursday before the final. What must have hurt most was the memory of how they had panicked in the semi-final when the French were ahead 36–24 with about 20 minutes to go. All New Zealand needed to do was keep control of the forward game, take the penalty goals that came its way, stretch play wide after sustained pressure, and give the ball to Jonah Lomu. Instead, the All Blacks tried to run every ball in a frantic effort to score tries. Keeping their heads would have unnerved the French, who were all bluff and brio; instead, the New Zealanders threw even their drinking water overboard because the storm seemed so fierce.

The Springboks, by contrast, felt they had lost with honour to Australia, so were better able to dredge up the necessary passion for an otherwise meaningless playoff. And that third-place match in turn demonstrated that the French win over the All Blacks had been no fluke. It became clear that the two best teams at the World Cup had met in the Saturday semi-final. The writing had been on the wall for New Zealand when Scotland did so well against them in the second half of their quarterfinal — and when it was realised the Boks had performed far more impressively than the All Blacks against both Scotland and England.

New Zealand referees also seemed to be out of form. In the decisive Pool C game, Paddy O'Brien gave an appalling performance of whimsical inconsistency to rob Fiji of a victory over France.

O'Brien's refereeing display relates indirectly to a key reason for New Zealand's collapse at the 1999 World Cup. For too long the All Blacks have got away with bending the existing laws and making up their own, with the connivance of their referees. It was wonderful in the semi-final and the third-place play-off to see Josh Kronfeld (and he was only the most obvious culprit) finally getting punished for cynically lingering in offside positions. In fact, the All Black exit was a victory for the rule of law in rugby. If they had won the cup, their intimidatory manipulation of the laws and referees would have been much harder to confront. It is time for the All Blacks to rediscover the spirit of the game and play to it. They are too good to continue to rely on Fitzpatrick-style trickery.

Not that Springbok supporters were feeling great. To fill third place was a consolation, but no more. Coach Nick Mallett had set the stakes very high when he dropped Gary Teichmann before the tournament, and winning the trophy was actually the only way he could have vindicated that decision. An even greater error was the way he talked up three individuals in advance as crucial to the Boks' chances: Bobby Skinstad, Henry Honiball and Brendan Venter. While the first two battled to get over serious injuries and Venter was suspended after being sent off against Uruguay, the logic of Mallett's own words suggested South Africa was now an absolute no-hoper.

It was greatly to the credit of the side, and in particular Jannie de Beer, that they shrugged off their coach's rash talk to crush a tactically inept and arrogant England. But the great irony of the third-place play-off was that the Boks fielded a much stronger attacking force than the one that had taken Australia to extra-time. Mallett had had the guts to drop Teichmann before the World Cup; he should have shown similar courage and dropped the quarter-final hero, De Beer. He should have inserted the now-fit Honiball for the Australia semi-final, in accordance with the obvious principle that De Beer could hardly make lightning strike twice.

Mallett was always going to battle without his two first-choice centres, Venter and Andre Snyman (left at home injured). But there is no doubt Honiball sharpened up the Bok backs against New Zealand, Breyten Paulse added desperately needed flair and scored what turned out to be a crucial try, and Andre Vos at No. 8 was far more forceful and visible than poor Skinstad had been against the Wallabies.

Before the quarter-finals I wrote: 'The All Blacks and England are playing like machines, we are not. That may just be their undoing, and our salvation. They have shown signs of peaking too soon.' And so it proved, although we could not withstand the confident organisation of Australia, which was always a step ahead of us. Both the English and the New Zealanders believed their own press, with fatal results. South Africa, mercifully, was not handicapped by arrogance, but we picked the wrong men at crucial times and lacked the confidence to run at our opponents.

There is no doubt the Springboks will hold the moral high ground when the 2000 Tri-Nations takes the ancient rivalry into a new century. And we're only one Test match behind.

1999

THE BOYS VERSUS THE BOYS

THE WORLD CUP PLAY-OFF

by Grant Harding

NOVEMBER 1, 1999 will be remembered forever in New Zealand as 'Black Monday'. It was the day an overhyped, possibly overconfident All Black team crashed out of the Rugby World Cup to France, an opponent it was expected to beat comfortably. Denied the opportunity of seeing their heros take on Australia in the final, a public made arrogant by ridiculously positive media and marketing messages went dog.

Out of the closet came every Hart-hater to kick the All Black coach when he was at his lowest ebb. The All Blacks were too corporatised, weren't having any fun, were overpaid, were out of touch with the fans, should have played in the NPC, shouldn't have gone to France mid-tournament or were just plain bloody useless. The vitriolic outbursts continued for days. Much of the furore was without basis, and it was embarrassing to think New Zealanders expected to win the World Cup as of right. Few had noticed the French team beaten by the All Blacks at Athletic Park in June was seven positions different from that which took to the field at Twickenham. The new line-up saw the return of hard men Richard Dourthe and Abdelatif Benazzi.

Nevertheless, at Twickenham that day I witnessed the unwitnessable — an All Black team capitulating. But the distance I had to fall was shorter than most, because at no time had I believed the All Blacks were the hot favourites just about everyone had installed them as.

Just before the World Cup I wrote in *Rugby News World Cup Preview 99*: 'The emotional scars [of 1998, when five Tests were lost] had only just healed, when a record loss to Australia in Sydney in late August once again created doubt about Hart's ability to lead the All Blacks to a second Webb Ellis Cup victory.

'Many were prepared to write the performance off as a "shocker", and look immediately ahead to the World Cup. But the performance did beg the question: What did the Tri-Nations prove? Did it prove that we now have a tight five capable of consistently providing front-foot ball for the backline? Did it prove that we've got the best possible combination in our loose forward trio? In the most pressurised situation can Andrew Mehrtens be relied upon to get us out of trouble? Has our midfield got game-breaking potential? Is Jeff Wilson the best option at fullback?'

Well, at Twickenham *les coqs* came home to roost in a 43–31 defeat, France's tally the most points ever conceded by the All Blacks in a single game.

Selection blunders and tactical naivety always threatened to expose the All Blacks at this tournament. It was just that after they had beaten England in pool play, the whole of New Zealand expected them at least to reach the final.

A dejected All Black team say goodbye to their fans after finishing fourth at the 1999 Rugby World Cup.

Ultimately Hart paid for being too dogmatic. Christian Cullen should have played fullback. Under the current laws, an attacking gem like Cullen, who can bring the ball up from the back with side-stepping runs, who has a physical approach to entering the line, who has the ability to beat a cover defender, and who plays a strong tackling game, had to be the best option for that position. Instead, however, Hart chose to use him at centre for minuscule reward. Meanwhile, a brilliant winger became a gesticulating fool at fullback. The signs were clear pre-tournament. Wilson performed abysmally in Sydney, and had rarely been sighted in several other matches. Against France he failed to convert a one-on-one opportunity and was generally found wanting in most aspects of the fullback game. Inevitably Cullen ended the last 40 minutes of the tournament at the back.

Then there was poor Taine Randell. In May I strongly criticised the decision to move Randell back to No. 8 on Television New Zealand's programme *Tight Five*. Again, the current rules made it imperative that a No. 8 provide go-forward, and a power No. 8, if not plan A, had to be plan B.

Once again Hart ignored this call, similarly uttered by thousands of others over two seasons, to his peril. Spinning the ball to the wings is admirable, but without go-forward in the modern game it is nothing more than tactical naivety. In the end the All Black backline was a shambles as it was knocked to pieces by aggressive defence.

The Otago Highlanders' performance against the Stormers in the 1999 Rugby Super 12 semi-final should have been the All Blacks' blueprint for success. That was a performance which showed how New Zealand could have won the World Cup. First-five Tony Brown was masterful in his flat-line running, with the option of going inside to Isitolo Maka (No. 8), Josh Kronfeld or Taine Randell (no. 6), or outside to his centres. When the insertion was made, hard-running tight forwards like Kees Meeuws or Anton Oliver could take it further, and, if a gap appeared, swift movement of the ball created mayhem in the Stormers' defence. It was a masterful performance, and how the All Black selectors missed its point I'll never understand. It was the rugby for its time, it was the rugby that Australia used — without the same flair — to win the World Cup.

New Zealand has brilliant players. They simply weren't organised properly.

There were any number of other discussion points: the dumping of the experienced Justin Marshall for the semi-final; the lack of penetration in midfield; the continued tolerance of Oliver's disgraceful lineout throwing; the humbling of the tight five against France (perhaps there was a case for change after the second-half debacle against Scotland); and the inability to create a true substitute bench and use it.

Leadership was also lacking, never more so than when the All Blacks led 24–10 early in the second half against France. But for two brilliant Lomu tries the All Blacks' performance had been of low quality. Yet it appeared nobody recognised that fact, or saw the potential in playing for position, creating pressure and forcing the French to play catch-up. Instead, mistakes led to the French going on a scoring frenzy of 33 unanswered points.

At the final whistle even French supporters were in shock. Only the South Africans were in total party mode. Now the real World Cup final would be played, many of them commented. But didn't they know it was the boys versus the boys on Thursday? The men were playing Saturday.

So the great rivals came to their 54th clash — the first on foreign soil and a Thursday — at the magnificent Millennium Stadium in Cardiff. After 80 minutes of shocking rugby, South Africa emerged triumphant, 22–18, to earn third place in the World Cup. Springbok prop Os du Randt remarked afterwards that the pleasure of this achievement was like kissing your sister.

How rich it is for my South African colleague to suggest the All Black exit was a 'victory for the rule of law in rugby' in light of the events on November 4, when the Springboks gave up seven kickable penalty-goal opportunities. Their negative tactics were a blight on the game, and had the All Blacks' overall effort matched the passion of front-rowers Kees Meeuws and Mark Hammett, or had any semblance of handling skill or tactical nous been displayed by New Zealand, the spoiling Boks would have got their proverbial bums kicked. As for the contention

DEFINING MOMENT

A Match Too Many
WORLD CUP 3RD/4TH PLACE PLAYOFF, CARDIFF, 4 NOVEMBER, 1999

The defining moment of the third- and fourth-place play-off came when Jim Fleming blew his whistle for the final time at Twickenham the previous Sunday to signal a victory to France. New Zealand, who had expected to progress to the final, was always going to battle to get up for a meaningless — in the context of the World Cup — match four days later. Somehow the contest meant more to the Springboks.

that the two best teams played in the Saturday semi-final, this is the statement of a drowned man clutching at a straw that has long since floated out of reach.

What rugby-minded people should be concerning themselves with is the state of the game. Before the tournament I wrote in *Rugby News World Cup Preview 99*: 'Australia have the talent to cut any side to pieces, but they have adapted a style based on the laws. Low risk rugby backed by astonishing defence. It could be that they're selling themselves short when they have gifted backs. Perhaps not, given the preponderance of penalties in the modern game.' Remember, the Wallabies scored no tries against the drop goal-obsessed, yawn-inducing Springboks in their bleak semi-final, in which the only excitement came from the closeness of the score. And, in the final, tries only became an option for the Wallabies once the match had been won.

Is that the rugby you want to watch? One can only hope that, by the time this book has been published, the lawmakers will have returned rugby to the good old days, when forwards went to rucks (to use their feet) and mauls (to use their hands), and backs used the clean possession won to weave their magic. Played that way, the World Cup in 2003 will be a spectacular, rather than the huge bore it was in 1999. Played that way the quickest, fittest, most aggressive — in a clean sense — and skilful team will win.

Had the World Cup been like that in 1999, it could still have been Australia who came out on top, for the Wallabies are a superbly coached and gifted group of sportsmen. All power to them. But that is not the issue. The issue is the good of the game. Laws need to be made to nurture and protect what should essentially be a running-and-passing game, with some kicking in between. If they have been by the time the new season gets under way, New Zealand will have the moral high ground over the old foe in 2000, because as a country it has, in modern times, attempted to play a brand of rugby far more creative and pleasing to the eye than anything South Africa has offered.

The All Blacks may have finished fourth in the World Cup, but they played in arguably the two best games of the tournament — against England on October 9, and against France in the semi-final. And in Jonah Lomu they had an unrivalled try-scoring machine, his eight touchdowns being a World Cup record. Replays of his efforts against England and France will cheer New Zealanders as the All Blacks regroup to remain the side with more wins than any other in the world of rugby. The World Cup might not be their baby, but there is no team in the international game that stands above the All Blacks in its win-loss record.

1921
FIRST TEST
NEW ZEALAND 13, SOUTH AFRICA 5

At Carisbrook, Dunedin, New Zealand 13 August 1921

For New Zealand: Tries by E. A. Belliss, J. Steel and P. W. Storey; 2 conversions by M. F. Nicholls.

For South Africa: Try by A. J. van Heerden; conversion by P. G. Morkel.

NEW ZEALAND: C. N. Kingstone, P. W. Storey, G. G. Aitken (capt), M. F. Nicholls, J. Steel, C. E. O. Badeley, H. E. Nicholls, J. G. Donald, J. Richardson, A. White, E. A. Belliss, R. Fogarty, W. D. Duncan, J. E. Moffitt, E. Hughes.

SOUTH AFRICA: P. G. Morkel, H. W. Morkel, W. A. Clarkson, C. du P. Meyer, A. J. van Heerden, J. P. Michau, W. H. Townsend, W. H. Morkel (capt), H. Scholtz, H. J. Morkel, J. M. Michau, A. P. Walker, P. J. Mostert, T. L. Kruger, F. W. Mellish.

Referee: E. McKenzie

Crowd: 25,000

1921
SECOND TEST
SOUTH AFRICA 9, NEW ZEALAND 5

At Eden Park, Auckland, New Zealand 27 August 1921

For South Africa: Try by W. D. Sendin; conversion and drop goal by P. G. Morkel.

For New Zealand: Try by A. L. McLean; conversion by M. F. Nicholls.

SOUTH AFRICA: P. G. Morkel, W. C. Zeller, W. A. Clarkson, W. D. Sendin, H. W. Morkel, C. du P. Meyer, J. P. Michau, W. H. Morkel (capt), H. Scholtz, J. A. Morkel, G. W. van Rooyen, M. Ellis, P. J. Mostert, T. L. Kruger, N. J. du Plessis.

NEW ZEALAND: C. N. Kingstone, P. W. Storey, G. G. Aitken (capt) M. F. Nicholls, J. Steel, C. E. O. Badeley, E. J. Roberts, J. G. Donald, J. Richardson, A. H. West, E. A. Belliss, A. L. McLean, W. D. Duncan, J. E. Moffitt, E. Hughes.

Referee: A. E. Neilson

Crowd: 40,000

1921
THIRD TEST
DRAW 0–0

At Athletic Park, Wellington, New Zealand 17 September 1921

NEW ZEALAND: C. N. Kingstone, S. K. Siddells, M. F. Nicholls, K. D. Ifwersen, J. Steel, W. R. Fea, E. J. Roberts (capt), E. A. Belliss, J. Richardson, A. H. West, C. J. C. Fletcher, A. L. McLean, W. D. Duncan, J. E. Moffitt, R. Fogarty.

SOUTH AFRICA: P. G. Morkel, W. C. Zeller, S. S. Strauss, C. du P. Meyer, A. J. van Heerden, J. S. de Kock, J. P. Michau, W. H. Morkel (capt), A. P. Walker, J. A. Morkel, G. W. van Rooyen, M. Ellis, N. J. du Plessis, P. J. Mostert, F. W. Mellish.

Referee: A. E. Neilson

Crowd: 18,000

1928
FIRST TEST
SOUTH AFRICA 17, NEW ZEALAND 0

At Kingsmead, Durban, South Africa 30 June 1928

For South Africa: Try by J. T. Slater; 2 penalty goals and 2 drop goals by B. L. Osler.

SOUTH AFRICA: J. C. Tindall, J. T. Slater, S. G. Osler, B. A. A. Duffy, J. P. Prinsloo, B. L. Osler, P. du P. de Villiers, G. M. Daneel, N. F. Pretorius, H. J. Potgieter, P. J. Nel, N. J. V. van Druten, S. P. van Wyk, T. L. Kruger, P. J. Mostert (capt).

NEW ZEALAND: D. F. Linsday, B. A. Grenside, S. R. Carleton, W. A. Strang, A. C. C. Robilliard, L. M. Johnson, W. C. Dalley, R. T. Stewart, W. E. Hazlett, I. H. Finalyson, M. J. Brownlie (capt), G. T. Alley, J. P. Swain, S. Hadley, G. Scrimshaw.

Referee: V. H. Neser

Crowd: 10,000

1928
SECOND TEST
NEW ZEALAND 7, SOUTH AFRICA 6

At Ellis Park, Johannesburg, South Africa 21 July 1928

For New Zealand: Drop goal by W. A. Strang; penalty goal by D. F. Lindsay.

For South Africa: Goal from a mark by P. J. Mostert; penalty goal by B. L. Osler.

NEW ZEALAND: D. F. Lindsay, B. A. Grenside,
S. R. Carleton, W. A. Strang, A. C. C. Robilliard,
L. M. Johnson, W. C. Dalley, R. T. Stewart, W. E.
Hazlett, I. H. Finlayson, M. J. Brownlie (capt), G. T.
Alley, J. P. Swain, S. Hadley, R. G. McWilliams.
SOUTH AFRICA: J. C. Tindall, G. H. Brand,
J. A. R. Dobie, J. C. van der Westhuizen,
N. S. Tod, B. L. Osler, D. Devine, G. M. Daneel,
N. F. Pretorius, H. J. Potgieter, P. J. Nel,
N. J. V. van Druten, S. P. van Wyk, T. L. Kruger,
P. J. Mostert (capt).
Referee: V. H. Neser
Crowd: 38,000

1928
THIRD TEST
SOUTH AFRICA 11, NEW ZEALAND 6
At Crusader Ground, Port Elizabeth, South Africa
18 August 1928
For South Africa: Tries by P. J. Nel, H. P. K. de
Jongh and G. M. Daneel; conversion by
B. L. Osler.
For New Zealand: Tries by R. T. Stewart and B. A.
Grenside.
SOUTH AFRICA: J. C. Tindall, G. H. Brand, W. P.
Rousseau, J. C. van der Westhuizen, H. P. K. de
Jongh, B. L. Osler, P. du P. de Villiers, G. M.
Daneel, N. F. Pretorius, M. M. Louw, P. J. Nel,
N. J. V. van Druten, A. F. du Toit, P. J. Mostert
(capt), J. F. Oliver.
NEW ZEALAND: D. F. Lindsay, B. A. Grenside,
S. R. Carleton, L. M. Johnson, A. C. C. Robilliard,
H. T. Lilburne, W. C. Dalley, R. T. Stewart, W. E.
Hazlett, I. H. Finlayson, M. J. Brownlie (capt),
G. T. Alley, J. P. Swain, S. Hadley, R. G. McWilliams.
Referee: V. H. Neser
Crowd: 18,500

1928
FOURTH TEST
NEW ZEALAND 13, SOUTH AFRICA 5
At Newlands, Cape Town, South Africa 1 September
1928
For New Zealand: Try by J. P. Swain; 2 penalty goals
and 1 drop goal by M. F. Nicholls.
For South Africa: Try by J. C. van der Westhuizen;
conversion by B. L. Osler.
NEW ZEALAND: H. T. Lilburne, B. A. Grenside,
F. W. Lucas, M. F. Nicholls, A. C. C. Robilliard,
L. M. Johnson, W. C. Dalley, R. T. Stewart, W. E.
Hazlett, I. H. Finlayson, M. J. Brownlie (capt), I. H.
Harvey, J. P. Swain, S. Hadley, R. G. McWilliams.

SOUTH AFRICA: J. C. Tindall, J. A. van Niekerk,
W. P. Rousseau, J. C. van der Westhuizen, P. K.
Morkel, B. L. Osler, P. du P. de Villiers, G. M.
Daneel, N. F. Pretorius, A. F. du Toit, P. J. Nel,
N. J. V. van Druten, M. M. Louw, P. J. Mostert
(capt), J. F. Oliver.
Referee: V. H. Neser
Crowd: 23,000

1937
FIRST TEST
NEW ZEALAND 13, SOUTH AFRICA 7
At Athletic Park, Wellington, New Zealand 14
August 1937
For New Zealand: Try by J. Dick; 2 penalty goals
and 1 drop goal by D. Trevathan.
For South Africa: Try by D. O. Williams; drop goal
by J. White.
NEW ZEALAND: J. M. Taylor, D. G. Cobden, J. L.
Sullivan, J. A. Hooper, J. Dick, D. Trevathan, H. J.
Simon, A. A. Parkhill, R. H. Ward, R. R. King
(capt), S. T. Reid, R. McC. McKenzie, D. Dalton,
A. Lambourn, E. S. Jackson.
SOUTH AFRICA: F. G. Turner, P. J. Lyster, J. White,
L. Babrow, D. O. Williams, D. H. Craven (capt),
P. du P. de Villiers, G. L. van Reenen, W. E.
Bastard, W. F. Bergh, M. A. van den Berg, L. C.
Strachan, C. B. Jennings, J. W. Lotz, S. C. Louw.
Referee: L. E. Macassey
Crowd: 40,000

1937
SECOND TEST
SOUTH AFRICA 13, NEW ZEALAND 6
At Lancaster Park Oval, Christchurch, New Zealand
4 September 1937
For South Africa: Tries by F. G. Turner and
W. E. Bastard; 2 conversions and 1 penalty goal
by G. H. Brand.
For New Zealand: Tries by J. L. Sullivan (2).
SOUTH AFRICA: G. H. Brand, F. G. Turner,
J. White, L. Babrow, D. O. Williams, T. A. Harris,
D. H. Craven, W. F. Bergh, W. E. Bastard, P. J. Nel
(capt), M. A. van den Berg, L. C. Strachan,
M. M. Louw, J. W. Lotz, S. C. Louw.
NEW ZEALAND: J. M. Taylor, W. J. Phillips,
J. L. Sullivan, J. A. Hooper, J. Dick, D. Trevathan,
H. J. Simon, A. A. Parkhill, J. G. Rankin,
R. R. King (capt), S. T. Reid, R. McC. McKenzie,
D. Dalton, A. Lambourn, E. S. Jackson.
Referee: J. S. King
Crowd: 45,000

1937
THIRD TEST
SOUTH AFRICA 17, NEW ZEALAND 6

At Eden Park, Auckland, New Zealand 25
  September 1937

For South Africa: Tries by L. Babrow (2), F. G.
  Turner, D. O. Williams and W. F. Bergh; 1
  conversion by G. H. Brand.

For New Zealand: 2 penalty goals by D. Trevathan.

SOUTH AFRICA: G. H. Brand, F. G. Turner, G. P.
  Lochner, L. Babrow, D. O. Williams, T. A. Harris,
  D. H. Craven, W. F. Bergh, W. E. Bastard, P. J. Nel
  (capt), M. A. van den Berg, L. C. Strachan, M. M.
  Louw, J. W. Lotz, S. C. Louw.

NEW ZEALAND: J. M. Taylor, T. H. C. Caughey,
  N. A. Mitchell, J. A. Hooper, J. L. Sullivan, D.
  Trevathan, H. J. Simon, A. A. Parkhill, R. H.
  Ward, R. R. King (capt), S. T. Reid, R. McC.
  McKenzie, D. Dalton, A. Lambourn, E. S. Jackson.

Referee: J. S. King

Crowd: 58,000

1949
FIRST TEST
SOUTH AFRICA 15, NEW ZEALAND 11

At Newlands, Cape Town, South Africa 16 July 1949

For South Africa: 5 penalty goals by A. O. Geffin.

For New Zealand: Try by P. Henderson; 1
  conversion and 1 penalty goal by R. W. H. Scott;
  drop goal by J. C. Kearney.

SOUTH AFRICA: J. H. van der Schyff, C. Moss,
  F. P. Duvenage, M. T. Lategan, F. P. Marais, J. D.
  Brewis, J. J. Wahl, H. S. V. Muller, L. J. Strydom,
  F. du Plessis (capt), H. V. Koch, B. S. van der
  Merwe, A. O. Geffin, R. P. Jordaan, C. J. van
  Jaarsveld.

NEW ZEALAND: R. W. H. Scott, P. Henderson,
  R. R. Elvidge, F. R. Allen (capt), E. G. Boggs,
  J. C. Kearney, L. T. Savage, N. H. Thornton, J. R.
  McNab, L. R. Harvey, C. Willocks, L. A. Grant,
  J. G. Simpson, E. H. Catley, K. L. Skinner.

Referee: E. W. Hofmeyr

Crowd: 42,000

1949
SECOND TEST
SOUTH AFRICA 12, NEW ZEALAND 6

At Ellis Park, Johannesburg, South Africa 13 August
  1949

For South Africa: Tries by M. T. Lategan and J. D.
  Brewis; 1 drop goal by J. D. Brewis; 1 penalty goal
  by A. O. Geffin.

For New Zealand: 1 penalty goal by R. W. H. Scott;
  1 drop goal by J. C. Kearney.

SOUTH AFRICA: J. H. van der Schyff, C. Moss,
  R. A. M. van Schoor, M. T. Lategan, F. P. Marais, J. D.
  Brewis, P. A. du Toit, H. S. V. Muller, L. J. Strydom,
  F. du Plessis (capt), H. V. Koch, J. A. du Rand,
  A. O. Geffin, R. P. Jordaan, A. C. Koch.

NEW ZEALAND: R. W. H. Scott, P. Henderson,
  R. R. Elvidge, F. R. Allen (capt), W. A. Meates,
  J. C. Kearney, L. T. Savage, P. Johnstone, J. R.
  McNab, L. R. Harvey, H. F. Frazer, L. A. Grant,
  K. L. Skinner, E. H. Catley, J. G. Simpson.

Referee: R. D. Burmeister

Crowd: 71,000

1949
THIRD TEST
SOUTH AFRICA 9, NEW ZEALAND 3

At Kingsmead, Durban, South Africa 3 September
  1949

For South Africa: 3 penalty goals by A. O. Geffin.

For New Zealand: Try by M. P. Goddard.

SOUTH AFRICA: J. H. van der Schyff, C. Moss,
  R. A. M. van Schoor, M. T. Lategan, F. P. Duvenage,
  J. D. Brewis, P. A. du Toit, H. S. V. Muller, H. V.
  Koch, F. du Plessis (capt), P. J. Geel, J. A. du
  Rand, A. O. Geffin, R. P. Jordaan, A. C. Koch.

NEW ZEALAND: R. W. H. Scott, W. A. Meates,
  M. P. Goddard, R. R. Elvidge (capt), P. Henderson,
  J. C. Kearney, N. W. Black, M. J. McHugh, J. R.
  McNab, L. R. Harvey, C. Willocks, P. J. B. Crowley,
  K. L. Skinner, E. H. Catley, J. G. Simpson.

Referee: E. W. Hofmeyr

Crowd: 30,000

1949
FOURTH TEST
SOUTH AFRICA 11, NEW ZEALAND 8

At Crusader Ground, Port Elizabeth, South Africa
  17 September 1949

For South Africa: Try by P. A. du Toit; drop goal by
  J. D Brewis; 1 conversion and 1 penalty goal by
  A. O. Geffin.

For New Zealand: Tries by R. R. Elvidge and P.
  Johnstone; 1 conversion by R. W. H. Scott.

SOUTH AFRICA: J. H. van der Schyff, E. M.
  Geraghty, R. A. M. van Schoor, M. T. Lategan, C.
  Moss, J. D. Brewis, P. A. du Toit, H. S. V. Muller,
  B. J. Kenyon (capt), W. H. M. Barnard, H. V. Koch,
  P. Malan, A. O. Geffin, R. P. Jordaan, A. C. Koch.

NEW ZEALAND: R. W. H. Scott, P. Henderson,
  M. P. Goddard, R. R. Elvidge (capt), W. A. Meates,

G. W. Delamore, L. T. Savage, D. L. Christian,
P. Johnstone, L. R. Harvey, C. Willocks, P. J. B.
Crowley, K. L. Skinner, E. H. Catley, J. G. Simpson.
Referee: R. D. Burmeister
Crowd: 28,500

1956
FIRST TEST
NEW ZEALAND 10, SOUTH AFRICA 6

At Carisbrook Ground, Dunedin, New Zealand 14
July 1956
For New Zealand: Tries by R. A. Jarden and R. A.
White; 2 conversions by R. A. Jarden.
For South Africa: Try by B. F. Howe; penalty goal by
R. G. Dryburgh.
NEW ZEALAND: P. T. Walsh, R. A. Jarden, R. H.
Brown, W. N. Gray, M. J. Dixon, W. R. Archer,
P. B. Vincent (capt), S. F. Hill, D. N. McIntosh,
R. A. White, R. H. Duff, J. B. Buxton, I. J. Clarke,
R. C. Hemi, M. W. Irwin.
SOUTH AFRICA: R. G. Dryburgh, J. G. H. du
Preez, B. F. Howe, J. J. Nel, P. G. A. Johnstone,
C. A. Ulyate, C. F. Strydom, G. P. Lochner, D. F.
Retief, J. T. Claassen, J. A. du Rand (capt), D. S. P.
Ackermann, H. P. J. Bekker, A. J. van der Merwe,
H. N. Walker.
Referee: F. G. M. Parkinson
Crowd: 39,300

1956
SECOND TEST
SOUTH AFRICA 8, NEW ZEALAND 3

At Athletic Park, Wellington, New Zealand 4 August
1956
For South Africa: Tries by J. A. du Rand and D. F.
Retief; 1 conversion by S. S. Viviers.
For New Zealand: Try by R. H. Brown.
SOUTH AFRICA: S. S. Viviers (capt), P. G. A.
Johnstone, A. I. Kirkpatrick, J. J. Nel, T. P. D.
Briers, C. A. Ulyate, T. A. Gentles, J. A. J. Pickard,
D. F. Retief, J. T. Claassen, J. A. du Rand, G. P.
Lochner, H. P. J. Bekker, A. J. van der Merwe,
A. C. Koch.
NEW ZEALAND: P. T. Walsh, R. A. Jarden, R. H.
Brown, W. N. Gray, M. J. Dixon, S. G. Bremner,
P. B. Vincent (capt), I. N. MacEwan, D. N.
McIntosh, R. A. White, R. H. Duff, W. H. Clark,
F. S. McAtamney, D. Young, I. J. Clarke.
Referee: F. G. M. Parkinson
Crowd: 47,500

1956
THIRD TEST
NEW ZEALAND 17, SOUTH AFRICA 10

At Lancaster Park Oval, Christchurch, New Zealand
18 August 1956
For New Zealand: Tries by R. A. Jarden, M. J.
Dixon and R. A. White; 1 conversion and 2
penalty goals by D. B. Clarke.
For South Africa: Tries by W. Rosenberg and G. P.
Lochner; 2 conversions by S. S. Viviers.
NEW ZEALAND: D. B. Clarke, R. A. Jarden, R. H.
Brown, W. N. Gray, M. J. Dixon, W. R. Archer,
A. R. Reid, P. F. H-Jones, S. F. Hill, R. A. White,
R. H. Duff (capt), W. H. Clark, K. L. Skinner,
R. C. Hemi, I. J. Clarke.
SOUTH AFRICA: S. S. Viviers (capt), K. T. van
Vollenhoven, W. Rosenberg, J. J. Nel, T. P. D.
Briers, C. A. Ulyate, T. A. Gentles, D. F. Retief,
G. P. Lochner, J. T. Claassen, J. A. du Rand,
D. S. P. Ackermann, H. P. J. Bekker, A. J. van der
Merwe, A. C. Koch.
Referee: W. H. Fright
Crowd: 51,000

1956
FOURTH TEST
NEW ZEALAND 11, SOUTH AFRICA 5

At Eden Park, Auckland, New Zealand 1 September
1956
For New Zealand: Try by P. F. H-Jones; 1 conversion
and 2 penalty goals by D. B. Clarke.
For South Africa: Try by R. G. Dryburgh; conversion
by S. S. Viviers.
NEW ZEALAND: D. B. Clarke, R. A. Jarden, P. T.
Walsh, W. N. Gray, M. J. Dixon, R. H. Brown,
A. R. Reid, P. F. H-Jones, S. F. Hill, R. A. White,
R. H. Duff (capt), W. H. Clark, K. L. Skinner,
R. C. Hemi, I. J. Clarke.
SOUTH AFRICA: S. S. Viviers (capt), R. G.
Dryburgh, P. G. A. Johnstone, J. J. Nel, T. P. D.
Briers, B. F. Howe, C. F. Strydom, G. P. Lochner,
D. F. Retief, J. T. Claassen, J. A. du Rand, J. J. Starke,
H. P. J. Bekker, A. J. van der Merwe, H. N. Walker.
Referee: W. H. Fright
Crowd: 61,300

1960
FIRST TEST
SOUTH AFRICA 13, NEW ZEALAND 0

At Ellis Park, Johannesburg, South Africa 25 June
1960

For South Africa: Tries by H. J. van Zyl (2); 1 conversion by R. G. Dryburgh; 1 conversion and 1 penalty goal by R. J. Lockyear.

SOUTH AFRICA: R. G. Dryburgh (capt), H. J. van Zyl, A. I. Kirkpatrick, J. L. Gainsford, J. G. M. Antelme, K. Oxlee, R. J. Lockyear, J. A. Nel, H. J. M. Pelser, J. T. Claassen, A. S. Malan, G. H. van Zyl, P. S. du Toit, G. F. Malan, A. C. Koch.

NEW ZEALAND: D. B. Clarke, R. W. Caulton, T. P. A. O'Sullivan, T. R. Lineen, J. R. Watt, A. H. Clarke, K. C. Briscoe, R. J. Conway, P. F. H-Jones, I. N. MacEwan, C. E. Meads, K. R. Tremain, M. W. Irwin, D. Young, W. J. Whineray (capt).

Referee: E. A. Strasheim

Crowd: 75,000

1960
SECOND TEST
NEW ZEALAND 11, SOUTH AFRICA 3

At Newlands, Cape Town, South Africa 23 July 1960

For New Zealand: Try by C. E. Meads; 1 conversion, 1 penalty goal and 1 drop goal by D. B. Clarke.

For South Africa: Try by K. Oxlee.

NEW ZEALAND: D. B. Clarke, R. F. McMullen, K. F. Laidlaw, T. R. Lineen, J. R. Watt, S. R. Nesbit, K. C. Briscoe, C. E. Meads, D. J. Graham, I. N. MacEwan, R. H. Horsley, K. R. Tremain, I. J. Clarke, D. Young, W. J. Whineray (capt).

SOUTH AFRICA: R. G. Dryburgh (capt), H. J. van Zyl, A. I. Kirkpatrick, J. L. Gainsford, J. G. M. Antelme, K. Oxlee, R. J. Lockyear, J. A. Nel, H. J. M. Pelser, J. T. Claassen, A. S. Malan, G. H. van Zyl, P. S. du Toit, A. J. van der Merwe, A. C. Koch.

Referee: M. J. Slabber

Crowd: 46,000

1960
THIRD TEST
DRAW 11–11

At Free State Stadium, Bloemfontein, South Africa 13 August 1960

For South Africa: Try by K. Oxlee; 1 conversion and 2 penalty goals by R. J. Lockyear.

For New Zealand: Try by R. F. McMullen; 1 conversion and 2 penalty goals by D. B. Clarke.

SOUTH AFRICA: L. G. Wilson, H. J. van Zyl, A. I. Kirkpatrick, J. L. Gainsford, J. G. M. Antelme, K. Oxlee, R. J. Lockyear, D. J. Hopwood, H. J. M. Pelser, J. T. Claassen, A. S. Malan (capt), G. H. van Zyl, P. S. du Toit, G. F. Malan, S. P. Kuhn.

NEW ZEALAND: D. B. Clarke, R. F. McMullen,

K. F. Laidlaw, T. R. Lineen, J. R. Watt, S. R. Nesbit, K. C. Briscoe, R. J. Conway, D. J. Graham, R. H. Horsley, C. E. Meads, K. R. Tremain, I. N. MacEwan, D. Young, W. J. Whineray (capt).

Referee: R. D. Burmeister

Crowd: 56,000

1960
FOURTH TEST
SOUTH AFRICA 8, NEW ZEALAND 3

At Boet Erasmus Stadium, Port Elizabeth, South Africa 27 August 1960

For South Africa: Try by H. J. M. Pelser; 1 conversion and 1 penalty goal by R. J. Lockyear.

For New Zealand: 1 penalty goal by D. B. Clarke.

SOUTH AFRICA: L. G. Wilson, H. J. van Zyl, A. I. Kirkpatrick, J. L. Gainsford, J. G. M. Antelme, K. Oxlee, R. J. Lockyear, D. J. Hopwood, H. J. M. Pelser, H. S. van der Merwe, A. S. Malan (capt), G. H. van Zyl, P. S. du Toit, G. F. Malan, S. P. Kuhn.

NEW ZEALAND: D. B. Clarke, R. W. Caulton, R. F. McMullen, K. F. Laidlaw, J. R. Watt, W. A. Davies, K. C. Briscoe, R. J. Conway, C. E. Meads, I. N. MacEwan, R. H. Horsley, K. R. Tremain, I. J. Clarke, D. Young, W. J. Whineray (capt).

Referee: R. D. Burmeister

Crowd: 60,000

1965
FIRST TEST
NEW ZEALAND 6, SOUTH AFRICA 3

At Athletic Park, Wellington, New Zealand 31 July 1965

For New Zealand: Tries by W. M. Birtwistle and K. R. Tremain.

For South Africa: Drop goal by K. Oxlee.

NEW ZEALAND: M. Williment, I. S. T. Smith, R. E. Rangi, J. L. Collins, W. M. Birtwistle, P. H. Murdoch, C. R. Laidlaw, B. J. Lochore, R. J. Conway, S. T. Meads, C. E. Meads, K. R. Tremain, K. F. Gray, B. E. McLeod, W. J. Whineray (capt).

SOUTH AFRICA: L. G. Wilson, G. S. Brynard, F. du T. Roux, J. L. Gainsford, J. P. Engelbrecht, K. Oxlee, D. J. de Villiers (capt), J. A. Nel, J. H. Ellis, J. P. Naudé, F. C. H. du Preez, J. Schoeman, A. W. MacDonald, G. F. Malan, C. G. P. van Zyl.

Referee: J. P. Murphy

Crowd: 46,200

1965
SECOND TEST
NEW ZEALAND 13, SOUTH AFRICA 0
At Carisbrook Ground, Dunedin, New Zealand 21 August 1965

For New Zealand: Tries by R. E. Rangi, B. E. McLeod and K. R. Tremain; 2 conversions by M. Williment.

NEW ZEALAND: M. Williment, I. S. T. Smith, R. E. Rangi, R. C. Moreton, W. M. Birtwistle, P. H. Murdoch, C. R. Laidlaw, B. J. Lochore, R. J. Conway, S. T. Meads, C. E. Meads, K. R. Tremain, K. F. Gray, B. E. McLeod, W. J. Whineray (capt).

SOUTH AFRICA: L. G. Wilson, G. S. Brynard, F. du T. Roux, J. L. Gainsford, J. P. Engelbrecht, K. Oxlee, C. M. Smith (capt), J. A. Nel, J. H. Ellis, C. P. Goosen, F. C. H. du Preez, J. Schoeman, A. W. MacDonald, G. F. Malan, C. G. P. van Zyl.

Referee: J. P. Murphy

Crowd: 35,000

1965
THIRD TEST
SOUTH AFRICA 19, NEW ZEALAND 16
At Lancaster Park Oval, Christchurch, New Zealand 4 September 1965

For South Africa: Tries by G. S. Brynard (2) and J. L. Gainsford (2); 2 conversions and 1 penalty goal by J. P. Naudé.

For New Zealand: Tries by R. E. Rangi, R. C. Moreton and K. R. Tremain; 2 conversions and 1 penalty goal by M. Williment.

SOUTH AFRICA: L. G. Wilson, G. S. Brynard, F. du T. Roux, J. L. Gainsford, J. P. Engelbrecht, J. H. Barnard, D. J. de Villiers (capt), D. J. Hopwood, J. H. Ellis, J. P. Naudé, F. C. H. du Preez, J. A. Nel, A. W. MacDonald, D. C. Walton, C. G. P. van Zyl.

NEW ZEALAND: M. Williment, M. J. Dick, R. E. Rangi, R. C. Moreton, W. M. Birtwistle, P. H. Murdoch, C. R. Laidlaw, B. J. Lochore, R. J. Conway, S. T. Meads, C. E. Meads, K. R. Tremain, K. F. Gray, B. E. McLeod, W. J. Whineray (capt).

Referees: J. P. Murphy injured, replaced by A. R. Taylor

Crowd: 53,500

1965
FOURTH TEST
NEW ZEALAND 20, SOUTH AFRICA 3
At Eden Park, Auckland, New Zealand 18 September 1965

For New Zealand: Tries by I. S. T. Smith (2), W. M. Birtwistle, K. F. Gray and R. J. Conway; 1 conversion by W. F. McCormick; drop goal by M. A. Herewini.

For South Africa: 1 penalty goal by J. P. Naudé.

NEW ZEALAND: W. F. McCormick, I. S. T. Smith, R. E. Rangi, J. L. Collins, W. M. Birtwistle, M. A. Herewini, C. R. Laidlaw, B. J. Lochore, R. J. Conway, S. T. Meads, C. E. Meads, K. R. Tremain, K. F. Gray, B. E. McLeod, W. J. Whineray (capt).

SOUTH AFRICA: L. G. Wilson, G. S. Brynard, F. du T. Roux, J. L. Gainsford, J. P. Engelbrecht, J. H. Barnard, D. J. de Villiers (capt), D. J. Hopwood, J. H. Ellis, J. P. Naudé, F. C. H. du Preez, J. A. Nel, A. W. MacDonald, D. C. Walton, C. G. P. van Zyl.

Referee: D. H. Millar

Crowd: 56,500

1970
FIRST TEST
SOUTH AFRICA 17, NEW ZEALAND 6
At Loftus Versfeld, Pretoria, South Africa 25 July 1970

For South Africa: Tries by S. H. Nomis and D. J. de Villiers; 1 conversion and 2 penalty goals by I. D. McCallum; drop goal by P. J. Visagie.

For New Zealand: Try by B. G. Williams; penalty goal by W. F. McCormick.

SOUTH AFRICA: I. D. McCallum, G. H. Muller, J. S. Jansen, F. du T. Roux, S. H. Nomis, P. J. Visagie, D. J. de Villiers (capt), A. J. Bates, J. H. Ellis, J. J. Spies, F. C. H. du Preez, P. J. F. Greyling, J. F. K. Marais, J. F. B. van Wyk, J. B. Neethling.

NEW ZEALAND: W. F. McCormick, B. G. Williams, G. S. Thorne, I. R. MacRae, M. J. Dick, W. D. Cottrell, C. R. Laidlaw (replaced by S. M. Going), B. J. Lochore (capt), T. N. Lister, S. C. Strahan, A. E. Smith, I. A. Kirkpatrick, B. L. Muller, B. E. McLeod, A. E. Hopkinson.

Referee: P. Robbertse

Crowd: 55,000

1970
SECOND TEST
NEW ZEALAND 9, SOUTH AFRICA 8
At Newlands, Cape Town, South Africa 8 August 1970

For New Zealand: Tries by C. R. Laidlaw and I. A. Kirkpatrick; penalty goal by W. F. McCormick.

For South Africa: Try by J. S. Jansen; 1 conversion and 1 penalty goal by I. D. McCallum.

NEW ZEALAND: W. F. McCormick, G. S. Thorne,
W. L. Davis, I. R. MacRae, B. G. Williams,
E. W. Kirton, C. R. Laidlaw, B. J. Lochore (capt),
A. J. Wyllie, S. C. Strahan, A. R. Sutherland,
I. A. Kirkpatrick, B. L. Muller, B. E. McLeod,
A. E. Hopkinson.
SOUTH AFRICA: I. D. McCallum, G. H. Muller,
J. S. Jansen, F. du T. Roux, S. H. Nomis, P. J. Visagie,
D. J. de Villiers (capt), A. J. Bates, J. H. Ellis,
J. J. Spies, F. C. H. du Preez, P. J. F. Greyling,
J. F. K. Marais, J. F. B. van Wyk, J. B. Neethling.
Referee: W. C. Malan
Crowd: 52,000

1970
THIRD TEST
SOUTH AFRICA 14, NEW ZEALAND 3
At Boet Erasmus Stadium, Port Elizabeth, South
Africa 29 August 1970
For South Africa: Tries by G. H. Muller (2); 1
conversion and 2 penalty goals by I. D. McCallum.
For New Zealand: 1 penalty goal by B. G. Williams.
SOUTH AFRICA: I. D. McCallum, G. H. Muller,
J. S. Jansen, F. du T. Roux, S. H. Nomis, P. J.
Visagie, D. J. de Villiers (capt), J. A. Nel, J. H. Ellis,
J. J. Spies, F. C. H. du Preez, P. J. F. Greyling,
J. F. K. Marais, J. F. B. van Wyk, J. L. Myburgh.
NEW ZEALAND: W. F. McCormick, H. P. Milner,
B. G. Williams, I. R. MacRae, G. S. Thorne, E. W.
Kirton, C. R. Laidlaw, B. J. Lochore (capt), A. J.
Wyllie, S. C. Strahan, C. E. Meads, I. A. Kirkpatrick,
N. W. Thimbleby, R. A. Urlich, A. E. Hopkinson.
Referee: P. Robbertse
Crowd: 55,000

1970
FOURTH TEST
SOUTH AFRICA 20, NEW ZEALAND 17
At Ellis Park, Johannesburg, South Africa 12
September 1970
For South Africa: Tries by G. H. Muller and P. J.
Visagie; 1 conversion and 4 penalty goals by I. D.
McCallum.
For New Zealand: Try by B. G. Williams; 1
conversion and 4 penalty goals by G. F. Kember.
SOUTH AFRICA: I. D. McCallum, G. H. Muller,
J. S. Jansen, F. du T. Roux, S. H. Nomis, P. J.
Visagie, D. J. de Villiers (capt), J. A. Nel, J. H.
Ellis, J. J. Spies, F. C. H. du Preez, P. J. F. Greyling,
J. F. K. Marais, J. F. B. van Wyk, J. L. Myburgh.
NEW ZEALAND: G. F. Kember, B. G. Williams,

G. S. Thorne, I. R. MacRae, M. J. Dick,
B. D. M. Furlong, S. M. Going, B. J. Lochore
(capt), T. N. Lister, A. R. Sutherland, C. E. Meads,
I. A. Kirkpatrick, B. L. Muller, R. A. Urlich,
K. Murdoch.
Referee: T. H. Woolley
Crowd: 65,000

1976
FIRST TEST
SOUTH AFRICA 16, NEW ZEALAND 7
At King's Park, Durban, South Africa 24 July 1976
For South Africa: Tries by J. S. Germishuys and
E. F. W. Krantz; drop goal by I. W. Robertson;
conversion and penalty goal by G. R. Bosch.
For New Zealand: Try by J. L. Jaffray; penalty goal
by B. G. Williams.
SOUTH AFRICA: I. W. Robertson, J. S. Germishuys,
P. J. M. Whipp, J. J. Oosthuizen, E. F. W. Krantz,
G. R. Bosch (replaced by W. J. de W. Ras), P. C. R.
Bayvel, M. du Plessis (capt), J. H. Ellis, J. G.
Williams, J. L. van Heerden, J. H. H. Coetzee,
D. S. van den Berg, R. J. Cockrell, J. C. J. Stander.
NEW ZEALAND: D. J. Robertson, G. B. Batty, B. J.
Robertson, J. L. Jaffray, B. G. Williams, O. D. Bruce,
S. M. Going, A. R. Leslie (capt), K. W. Stewart,
P. J. Whiting, H. H. Macdonald, I. A. Kirkpatrick,
K. K. Lambert, R. W. Norton, K. J. Tanner.
Referee: I. W. Gourlay
Crowd: 46,000

1976
SECOND TEST
NEW ZEALAND 15, SOUTH AFRICA 9
At Free State Stadium, Bloemfontein, South Africa
14 August 1976
For New Zealand: Try by J. E. Morgan; drop goal by
O. D. Bruce; conversion and 2 penalty goals by
S. M. Going.
For South Africa: 3 penalty goals by G. R. Bosch.
NEW ZEALAND: C. L. Fawcett, G. B. Batty
(replaced by W. M. Osborne), B. J. Robertson,
J. E. Morgan, B. G. Williams, O. D. Bruce, S. M.
Going, A. R. Leslie (capt), K. A. Eveleigh, P. J.
Whiting, H. H. Macdonald, I. A. Kirkpatrick,
W. K. Bush, R. W. Norton, B. R. Johnstone.
SOUTH AFRICA: D. S. L. Snyman, J. S. Germishuys,
I. W. Robertson, J. J. Oosthuizen, C. F. Pope,
G. R. Bosch, P. C. R. Bayvel, M. du Plessis (capt),
M. T. S. Stofberg, J. G. Williams (replaced by
K. B. H. de Klerk), J. L. van Heerden, J. H. H.

Coetzee, D. S. van den Berg, R. J. Cockrell,
J. C. J. Stander.

Referee: G. P. Bezuidenhout

Crowd: 73,000

1976
THIRD TEST
SOUTH AFRICA 15, NEW ZEALAND 10

At Newlands, Cape Town, South Africa 4 September
1976

For South Africa: Try by J. J. Oosthuizen; drop goal
by D. S. L. Snyman; conversion and 2 penalty
goals by G. R. Bosch.

For New Zealand: Try by B. J. Robertson; 2 penalty
goals by B. G. Williams.

SOUTH AFRICA: D. S. L. Snyman, J. S. Germishuys,
P. J. M. Whipp, J. J. Oosthuizen, C. F. Pope,
G. R. Bosch, P. C. R. Bayvel, M. du Plessis (capt),
M. T. S. Stofberg, K. B. H. de Klerk, J. L. van
Heerden, J. H. H. Coetzee, J. H. P. Strauss,
J. F. B. van Wyk, J. C. J. Stander.

NEW ZEALAND: C. L. Fawcett, G. B. Batty,
B. J. Robertson, J. E. Morgan, B. G. Williams,
D. J. Robertson, S. M. Going, A. R. Leslie (capt),
K. W. Stewart, P. J. Whiting, H. H. Macdonald,
I. A. Kirkpatrick, K. K. Lambert, R. W. Norton,
P. C. Harris.

Referee: G. P. Bezuidenhout

Crowd: 38,000

1976
FOURTH TEST
SOUTH AFRICA 15, NEW ZEALAND 14

At Ellis Park, Johannesburg, South Africa 18
September 1976

For South Africa: Try by J. L. Kritzinger; conversion,
drop goal and 2 penalty goals by G. R. Bosch.

For New Zealand: Tries by S. M. Going and I. A.
Kirkpatrick; penalty goal by B. G. Williams; drop
goal by O. D. Bruce.

SOUTH AFRICA: I. W. Robertson, J. S.
Germishuys, P. J. M. Whipp, J. J. Oosthuizen,
C. F. Pope, G. R. Bosch, P. C. R. Bayvel, M. du
Plessis (capt), J. L. Kritzinger, K. B. H. de Klerk,
J. L. van Heerden, J. H. H. Coetzee, J. H. P.
Strauss, J. F. B. van Wyk, J. C. J. Stander.

NEW ZEALAND: D. J. Robertson, G. B. Batty
(replaced by T. W. Mitchell), B. J. Robertson,
J. E. Morgan (replaced by W. M. Osborne), B. G.
Williams, O. D. Bruce, S. M. Going, A. R. Leslie
(capt), K. A. Eveleigh, P. J. Whiting, F. J. Oliver,

I. A. Kirkpatrick, W. K. Bush, R. W. Norton, K. K.
Lambert.

Referee: G. P. Bezuidenhout

Crowd: 74,000

1981
FIRST TEST
NEW ZEALAND 14, SOUTH AFRICA 9

At Lancaster Park Oval, Christchurch, New Zealand
15 August 1981

For New Zealand: Tries by S. S. Wilson, D. L.
Rollerson and M. W. Shaw; conversion by D. L.
Rollerson.

For South Africa: Try by H. J. Bekker; conversion
and drop goal by H. E. Botha.

NEW ZEALAND: A. R. Hewson (replaced by B. J.
McKechnie), B. G. Fraser, S. S. Wilson (replaced
by L. M. Cameron), A. C. R. Jefferd, F. A.
Woodman, D. L. Rollerson, D. S. Loveridge,
M. G. Mexted, K. W. Stewart, A. M. Haden,
G. Higginson, M. W. Shaw, G. A. Knight,
A. G. Dalton (capt), J. C. Ashworth.

SOUTH AFRICA: Z. M. J. Pienaar, D. S. Botha,
D. M. Gerber, W. du Plessis, R. H. Mordt,
H. E. Botha, D. J. Serfontein, R. J. Louw, M. T. S.
Stofberg (capt), L. C. Moolman, H. J. Bekker,
E. Jansen, P. G. du Toit, R. J. Cockrell, H. J. van
Aswegen.

Referee: L. M. Prideaux (England)

Crowd: 41,000

1981
SECOND TEST
SOUTH AFRICA 24, NEW ZEALAND 12

At Athletic Park, Wellington, New Zealand 29
August 1981

For South Africa: Try by J. S. Germishuys;
conversion, drop goal and 5 penalty goals by
H. E. Botha.

For New Zealand: 4 penalty goals by A. R. Hewson.

SOUTH AFRICA: Z. M. J. Pienaar, J. S. Germishuys,
D. M. Gerber, W. du Plessis (replaced by J. J.
Beck), R. H. Mordt, H. E. Botha, D. J. Serfontein,
W. Claassen, (capt), M. T. S. Stofberg, L. C.
Moolman, J. de V. Visser, S. B. Geldenhuys,
P. R. van der Merwe, W. J. H. Kahts (replaced by
R. J. Cockrell), O. W. Oosthuizen.

NEW ZEALAND: A. R. Hewson, B. G. Fraser,
S. S. Wilson, L. M. Cameron, F. A. Woodman,
D. L. Rollerson, D. S. Loveridge, M. G. Mexted,
K. W. Stewart, A. M. Haden, F. J. Oliver, M. W.

Shaw, G. A. J. Burgess, A. G. Dalton (capt), J. C.
Ashworth.
Referee: C. Norling (Wales)
Crowd: 32,000

1981
THIRD TEST
NEW ZEALAND 25, SOUTH AFRICA 22
At Eden Park, Auckland, New Zealand 12
  September 1981
For New Zealand: Tries by S. S. Wilson and
  G. A. Knight; 3 penalty goals by A. R. Hewson;
  conversion, penalty goal and drop goal by
  D. L. Rollerson.
For South Africa: Tries by R. H. Mordt (3); 2
  conversions and 2 penalty goals by H. E. Botha.
NEW ZEALAND: A. R. Hewson, B. G. Fraser,
  S. T. Pokere, L. M. Cameron, S. S. Wilson,
  D. L. Rollerson, D. S. Loveridge (replaced by
  M. W. Donaldson), M. G. Mexted, F. N. K.
  Shelford, A. M. Haden, G. W. Whetton, G. H. Old,
  G. A. Knight, A. G. Dalton (capt), J. C. Ashworth.
SOUTH AFRICA: Z. M. J. Pienaar (replaced by
  J. W. Heunis), J. S. Germishuys, D. M. Gerber,
  W. du Plessis (replaced by J. J. Beck), R. H.
  Mordt, H. E. Botha, D. J. Serfontein, W. Claassen
  (capt), S. B. Geldenhuys, L. C. Moolman,
  H. J. Bekker, R. J. Louw, P. R. van der Merwe,
  R. J. Cockrell, O. W. Oosthuizen.
Referee: C. Norling (Wales)
Crowd: 49,000

1992
TEST
NEW ZEALAND 27, SOUTH AFRICA 24
At Ellis Park, Johannesburg, South Africa 15 August
  1992
For New Zealand: Tries by Z. V. Brooke, J. J. Kirwan
  and J. K. R. Timu; 3 conversions and 2 penalty
  goals by G. J. Fox.
For South Africa: Tries by D. M. Gerber (2) and
  P. G. Muller; 3 conversions and 1 penalty goal by
  H. E. Botha.
NEW ZEALAND: J. K. R. Timu, J. J. Kirwan, F. E.
  Bunce, W. K. Little, V. L. Tuigamala (replaced by
  M. J. A. Cooper), G. J. Fox, A. D. Strachan
  (replaced by J. P. Preston), Z. V. Brooke, M. N.
  Jones, R. M. Brooke, I. D. Jones, J. W. Joseph,
  O. M. Brown, S. B. T. Fitzpatrick (capt), R. W. Loe.
SOUTH AFRICA: J. T. J. van Rensburg, P. Hendriks,
  P. G. Muller, D. M. Gerber, J. Small (replaced by

H. Fuls), H. E. Botha (capt), R. J. du Preez, J. C.
  Breedt, I. Macdonald, A. W. Malan, A. Geldenhuys,
  W. J. Bartmann, P. H. Rodgers (replaced by J. J.
  Styger), U. L. Schmidt, L. J. J. Muller.
Referee: A. R. MacNeill (Australia)
Crowd: 72,000

1994
FIRST TEST
NEW ZEALAND 22, SOUTH AFRICA 14
At Carisbrook, Dunedin, New Zealand 9 July 1994
For New Zealand: Try by J. J. Kirwan; 1 conversion
  and 5 penalty goals by S. P. Howarth.
For South Africa: Try by R. A. W. Straeuli; 3 penalty
  goals by A. J. Joubert.
NEW ZEALAND: S. P. Howarth, J. J. Kirwan,
  F. E. Bunce, A. Ieremia, J. K. R. Timu, S. J. Bachop,
  G. T. M. Bachop, Z. V. Brooke, M. R. Brewer,
  M. S. B. Cooksley, I. D. Jones (replaced by
  A. R. B. Pene; Pene replaced by C. W. Dowd),
  B. P. Larsen, O. M. Brown, S. B. T. Fitzpatrick
  (capt), R. W. Loe.
SOUTH AFRICA: A. J. Joubert, C. M. Williams,
  B. J. Venter, P. G. Muller, J. T. Small, H. P. le
  Roux, J. P. Roux, A. H. Richter, C. P. Strauss
  (capt), M. G. Andrews, S. Atherton, R. A. W.
  Straeuli, I. S. de V. Swart (replaced by G. R.
  Kebble), J. Allan, J. H. S. le Roux.
Referee: B. W. Stirling (Ireland)
Crowd: 41,000

1994
SECOND TEST
NEW ZEALAND 13, SOUTH AFRICA 9
At Athletic Park, Wellington, New Zealand 23 July
  1994
For New Zealand: Tries by J. K. R. Timu and Z .V.
  Brooke; penalty goal by S. P. Howarth.
For South Africa: 3 penalty goals by J. T. J. van
  Rensburg.
NEW ZEALAND: S. P. Howarth, J. J. Kirwan,
  F. E. Bunce (replaced by W. K. Little), A. Ieremia,
  J. K. R. Timu, S. J. Bachop, G. T. M. Bachop, Z. V.
  Brooke (substituted temporarily by J. W. Joseph),
  M. R. Brewer, M. S. B. Cooksley, R. M. Brooke,
  B. P. Larsen, O. M. Brown, S. B. T. Fitzpatrick
  (capt), R. W. Loe.
SOUTH AFRICA: J. T. J. van Rensburg (replaced by
  A. J. Joubert), C. M. Williams, B. J. Venter,
  J. C. Mulder, J. T. Small, H. P. le Roux, J. P. Roux,
  A. H. Richter, C. P. Strauss, M. G. Andrews,

S. Atherton, J. F. Pienaar (capt), G. R. Kebble,
J. Allan, J. H. S. le Roux.
Referee: B. W. Stirling (Ireland)
Crowd: 38,600

1994
THIRD TEST
DRAW 18–18

At Eden Park, Auckland, New Zealand 6 August
  1994
For New Zealand: 6 penalty goals by S. P. Howarth.
For South Africa: Tries by G. K. Johnson and B. J.
  Venter; 1 conversion and 2 penalty goals by G. K.
  Johnson.
NEW ZEALAND: S. P. Howarth, J. J. Kirwan, F. E.
  Bunce, A. Ieremia, J. K. R. Timu, S. J. Bachop,
  G. T. M. Bachop, Z. V. Brooke, M. R. Brewer, I. D.
  Jones, R. M. Brooke, B. P. Larsen (replaced by
  M. N. Jones), O. M. Brown, S. B. T. Fitzpatrick
  (capt), R. W. Loe.
SOUTH AFRICA: A. J. Joubert, C. M. Williams,
  B. J. Venter, J. C. Mulder, G. K. Johnson
  (substituted temporarily by J. T. Small), H. P. le
  Roux, J. P. Roux, A. H. Richter, J. F. Pienaar
  (capt), M. G. Andrews, S. Atherton, F. J. van
  Heerden, I. S. de V. Swart, J. Allan, K. S. Andrews.
Referee: R. Yeman (Wales)
Crowd: 50,100

1995
WORLD CUP FINAL
SOUTH AFRICA 15, NEW ZEALAND 12

At Ellis Park, Johannesburg, South Africa 24 June
  1995
For South Africa: 3 penalty goals and 2 drop goals
  by J. T. Stransky.
For New Zealand: 3 penalty goals and 1 drop goal
  by A. P. Mehrtens.
SOUTH AFRICA: A. J. Joubert, C. M. Williams,
  H. P. le Roux, J. C. Mulder, J. T. Small (replaced
  by B. Venter), J. T. Stransky, J. H. van der
  Westhuizen, M. G. Andrews (replaced by R. A. W.
  Straeuli), J. F. Pienaar (capt), J. J. Wiese, J. J.
  Strydom, R. J. Kruger, J. P. du Randt, C. le C.
  Rossouw, I. S. de V. Swart (replaced by G. L. Pagel).
NEW ZEALAND: G. M. Osborne, J. W. Wilson
  (replaced by M. C. G. Ellis), F. E. Bunce, W. K.
  Little, J. T. Lomu, A. P. Mehrtens, G. T. M. Bachop
  (bloodbin substitution by A. D. Strachan), Z. V.
  Brooke, J. A. Kronfeld, R. M. Brooke, I. D. Jones,
  M. R. Brewer (replaced by J. W. Joseph), O. M.

Brown, S. B. T. Fitzpatrick (capt), C. W. Dowd
  (replaced by R. W. Loe).
Referee: E. F. Morrison (England)
Crowd: 62,000

1996
TRI-NATIONS
NEW ZEALAND 15, SOUTH AFRICA 11

At Lancaster Park, Christchurch, New Zealand 20
  July 1996
For New Zealand: 5 penalty goals by A. P. Mehrtens.
For South Africa: Try by A. J. Joubert; 2 penalty
  goals by J. T. Stransky.
NEW ZEALAND: C. M. Cullen, J. W. Wilson
  (replaced by E. J. Rush), F. E. Bunce, W. K. Little,
  J. T. Lomu, A. P. Mehrtens, J. W. Marshall, Z. V.
  Brooke, J. A. Kronfeld, R. M. Brooke, I. D. Jones,
  M. N. Jones, O. M. Brown, S. B. T. Fitzpatrick
  (capt), C. W. Dowd.
SOUTH AFRICA: A. J. Joubert (replaced by J. S.
  Swart), P. Hendriks, B. J. Venter, J. C. Mulder, J. T.
  Small, J. T. Stransky, J. P. Roux, G. H. Teichmann,
  J. F. Pienaar (capt), J. N. Ackermann, M. G.
  Andrews, R. J. Kruger, J. P. du Randt, J. Allan,
  M. H. Hurter.
Referee: R. J. Megson (Scotland)
Crowd: 38,000

1996
TRI-NATIONS
NEW ZEALAND 29, SOUTH AFRICA 18

At Norwich Park Newlands, Cape Town, South
  Africa 10 August 1996
For New Zealand: Tries by G. M. Osborne and
  C. W. Dowd; 2 conversions and 5 penalty goals by
  A. P. Mehrtens.
For South Africa: Tries by J. C. Mulder and J. P. du
  Randt; 1 conversion and 2 penalty goals by J. T.
  Stransky.
NEW ZEALAND: C. M. Cullen, J. W. Wilson,
  F. E. Bunce, W. K. Little (replaced by A. Ieremia),
  G. M. Osborne, A. P. Mehrtens, J. W. Marshall,
  Z. V. Brooke, J. A. Kronfeld (replaced by A. F.
  Blowers), R. M. Brooke, I. D. Jones, M. N. Jones,
  O. M. Brown, S. B. T. Fitzpatrick (capt),
  C. W. Dowd.
SOUTH AFRICA: J. T. Small, P. Hendriks, H. P. le
  Roux, J. C. Mulder, J. S. Swart, J. T. Stransky,
  J. H. van der Westhuizen, G. H. Teichmann,
  J. F. Pienaar (capt) (replaced by J. J. Strydom),
  S. Atherton, M. G. Andrews, R. J. Kruger, J. P. du

Randt (replaced by D. F. Theron), J. Allan,
M. H. Hurter.

Referee: D. T. M. McHugh (Ireland)

Crowd: 51,000

1996
FIRST TEST
NEW ZEALAND 23, SOUTH AFRICA 19

At The Stadium Kings Park, Durban, South Africa
17 August 1996

For New Zealand: Tries by J. W. Wilson, C. M.
Cullen and Z. V. Brooke; 1 conversion and 2
penalty goals by S. D. Culhane.

For South Africa: Try by D. van Schalkwyk; 1
conversion and 4 penalty goals by J. T. Stransky.

NEW ZEALAND: C. M. Cullen, J. W. Wilson, F. E.
Bunce, W. K. Little, G. M. Osborne, S. D. Culhane,
J. W. Marshall, Z. V. Brooke, J. A. Kronfeld, R. M.
Brooke, I. D. Jones, M. N. Jones, O. M. Brown,
S. B. T. Fitzpatrick (capt), C. W. Dowd.

SOUTH AFRICA: A. J. Joubert, P. Hendriks,
D. van Schalkwyk, A. H. Snyman, J. S. Swart, J. T.
Stransky (temporary substitution by N. V. Cilliers),
J. P. Roux (replaced by J. H. van der Westhuizen),
G. H. Teichmann (capt), R. J. Kruger, J. J. Strydom
(replaced by J. J. Wiese), M. G. Andrews, A. G.
Venter, J. P. du Randt, H. Tromp, M. H. Hurter.

Referee: P. Thomas (France)

Crowd: 52,000

1996
SECOND TEST
NEW ZEALAND 33, SOUTH AFRICA 26

At Loftus Versfeld Stadium, Pretoria, South Africa
24 August 1996

For New Zealand: Tries by J. W. Wilson (2) and
Z. V. Brooke; 3 conversions and a penalty goal by
S. D. Culhane; 2 penalty goals by J. P. Preston;
drop goal by Z. V. Brooke.

For South Africa: Tries by J. J. Strydom, R. J.
Kruger and J. H. van der Westhuizen; 1 conversion
and 3 penalty goals by J. T. Stransky.

NEW ZEALAND: C. M. Cullen, J. W. Wilson, F. E.
Bunce, W. K. Little, G. M. Osborne, S. D. Culhane
(replaced by J. P. Preston), J. W. Marshall, Z. V.
Brooke, J. A. Kronfeld (replaced by A. F. Blowers),
R. M. Brooke, I. D. Jones (replaced by B. P. Larsen),
M. N. Jones, O. M. Brown, S. B. T. Fitzpatrick
(capt), C. W. Dowd.

SOUTH AFRICA: A. J. Joubert, P. Hendriks,
D. van Schalkwyk, A. H. Snyman, J. S. Swart,

J. T. Stransky, J. H. van der Westhuizen, G. H.
Teichmann (capt) (temporary substitution and
later replaced by W. Fyvie), R. J. Kruger, J. J.
Strydom (replaced by J. J. Wiese), M. G. Andrews,
A. G. Venter, J. P. du Randt, H. Tromp (replaced
by J. Dalton), M. H. Hurter.

Referee: D. Mene (France)

Crowd: 51,000

1996
THIRD TEST
SOUTH AFRICA 32, NEW ZEALAND 22

At Ellis Park Stadium, Johannesburg, South Africa
31 August 1996

For South Africa: Tries by J. H. van der Westhuizen
(2) and A. J. Joubert; 1 conversion and 2 penalty
goals by H. W. Honiball; 3 penalty goals by A. J.
Joubert.

For New Zealand: Tries by S. B. T. Fitzpatrick,
W. K. Little and J. W. Marshall; 2 conversions and
1 penalty goal by A. P. Mehrtens.

SOUTH AFRICA: A. J. Joubert, P. Hendriks,
D. van Schalkwyk, J. C. Mulder (replaced by J. T.
Stransky), J. S. Swart, H. W. Honiball, J. H. van
der Westhuizen, G. H. Teichmann (capt), R. J.
Kruger, J. J. Wiese, M. G. Andrews (replaced by
F. J. van Heerden), A. G. Venter (replaced by
W. Fyvie), D. F. Theron (replaced by G. L. Pagel),
J. Dalton, M. H. Hurter.

NEW ZEALAND: C. M. Cullen (replaced by A.
Ieremia), J. W. Wilson, F. E. Bunce, W. K. Little,
G. M. Osborne, A. P. Mehrtens, J. W. Marshall,
Z. V. Brooke, J. A. Kronfeld, R. M. Brooke, I. D.
Jones (replaced by G. L. Taylor), M. N. Jones,
O. M. Brown, S. B. T. Fitzpatrick (capt), C. W.
Dowd.

Referee: W. D. Bevan (Wales)

Crowd: 63,000

1997
TRI-NATIONS
NEW ZEALAND 35, SOUTH AFRICA 32

At Ellis Park Stadium, Johannesburg, South Africa
19 July 1997

For New Zealand: Tries by F. E. Bunce (2), J. W.
Wilson and C. J. Spencer; 3 conversions and 3
penalty goals by C. J. Spencer.

For South Africa: Tries by A. E. Drotské and R. G.
Bennett; 2 conversions, 4 penalty goals and 2
dropped goals by J. H. de Beer.

NEW ZEALAND: C. M. Cullen, J. W. Wilson, F. E.

Bunce, L. Stensness, T. J. F. Umaga (replaced by A. Ieremia), C. J. Spencer, J. W. Marshall, Z. V. Brooke, J. A. Kronfeld, R. M. Brooke, I. D. Jones, T. C. Randell, O. M. Brown, S. B. T. Fitzpatrick (capt) (replaced by N. J. Hewitt), C. W. Dowd.

SOUTH AFRICA: R. G. Bennett (replaced by J. T. Small), P. W. G. Rossouw, D. van Schalkwyk, P. C. Montgomery (replaced by H. W. Honiball), A. H. Snyman, J. H. de Beer, J. H. van der Westhuizen, G. H. Teichmann (capt), R. J. Kruger, K. Otto, M. G. Andrews (replaced by F. J. van Heerden), A. G. Venter, J. P. du Randt (replaced by D. F. Theron), A. E. Drotské, M. H. Hurter.

Referee: P. L. Marshall (Australia)

Crowd: 60,000

1997
TRI-NATIONS
NEW ZEALAND 55, SOUTH AFRICA 35

At Eden Park, Auckland, New Zealand 9 August 1997

For New Zealand: Tries by C. M. Cullen (2), A. Ieremia, C. J. Spencer, J. W. Marshall, T. C. Randell and T. J. F. Umaga; 4 conversions and 4 penalty goals by C. J. Spencer.

For South Africa: Tries by R. J. Kruger, G. H. Teichmann, P. C. Montgomery, J. H. van der Westhuizen and P. W. G. Rossouw; 3 conversions by J. de Beer; 2 conversions by H. W. Honiball.

NEW ZEALAND: C. M. Cullen, J. W. Wilson, F. E. Bunce, A. Ieremia, T. J. F. Umaga, C. J. Spencer (replaced by A. P. Mehrtens), J. W. Marshall, Z. V. Brooke (replaced temporarily by C. C. Riechelmann), J. A. Kronfeld, R. M. Brooke, I. D. Jones, T. C. Randell, O. M. Brown, S. B. T. Fitzpatrick (capt), C. W. Dowd (replaced by M. R. Allen).

SOUTH AFRICA: R. G. Bennett, A. H. Snyman, H. W. Honiball, P. C. Montgomery, J. T. Small, J. H. de Beer (replaced by P. W. G. Rossouw), J. H. van der Westhuizen, G. H. Teichmann (capt), R. J. Kruger (replaced by F. J. van Heerden), K. Otto (replaced by A. E. Drotské), M. G. Andrews, A. G. Venter (sent off 47th minute), J. P. du Randt (replaced by D. F. Theron), J. Dalton, M. H. Hurter.

Referee: W. D. Bevan (Wales)

Crowd: 48,000

1998
TRI-NATIONS
SOUTH AFRICA 13, NEW ZEALAND 3

At Athletic Park, Wellington, New Zealand July 25 1998

For South Africa: Try by P. W. G. Rossouw; conversion and 2 penalty goals by P. C. Montgomery.

For New Zealand: Penalty goal by A. P. Mehrtens.

SOUTH AFRICA: P. C. Montgomery, P. W. G. Rossouw (replaced temporarily by C. M. Williams), P. G. Muller, A. H. Snyman (replaced by P. F. Smith), C. S. Terblanche, H. W. Honiball, J. H. van der Westhuizen, G. H. Teichmann (capt), A. D. Aitken (replaced by R. B. Skinstad), M. G. Andrews, K. Otto, A. G. Venter, R. B. Kempson (replaced by A. H. le Roux), J. Dalton, A. C. Garvey.

NEW ZEALAND: C. M. Cullen, J. W. Wilson, M. A. Mayerhofler (replaced by S. J. McLeod), W. K. Little, J. T. Lomu, C. J. Spencer (replaced by A. P. Mehrtens), J. W. Marshall (replaced by O. F. J. Tonu'u), T. C. Randell (capt), J. A. Kronfeld, R. M. Brooke, I. D. Jones, M. N. Jones (replaced by I. Maka), O. M. Brown, A. D. Oliver, C. W. Dowd.

Referee: E. F. Morrison (England)

Crowd: 39,500

1998
TRI-NATIONS
SOUTH AFRICA 24, NEW ZEALAND 23

At Kings Park, Durban, South Africa 15 August 1998

For South Africa: Tries by C. S. Terblanche, J. H. van der Westhuizen, R. B. Skinstad and J. Dalton; 2 conversions by P. C. Montgomery.

For New Zealand: Tries by J. W. Marshall and T. C. Randell; 2 conversions and 3 penalty goals by A. P. Mehrtens.

SOUTH AFRICA: P. C. Montgomery, P. W. G. Rossouw, P. G. Muller, A. H. Snyman (replaced by P. F. Smith), C. S. Terblanche, H. W. Honiball, J. H. van der Westhuizen, G. H. Teichmann (capt), J. Erasmus (replaced by A. D. Aitken), M. G. Andrews (replaced by K. Otto), K. Otto (replaced by R. B. Skinstad), A. G. Venter, R. B. Kempson, J. Dalton, A. C. Garvey (replaced by A. H. le Roux).

NEW ZEALAND: C. M. Cullen, J. W. Wilson, E. Clarke (replaced by N. R. Berryman), M. A. Mayerhofler, J. T. Lomu, A. P. Mehrtens, J. W. Marshall, I. Maka (replaced by S. M. Robertson), J. A. Kronfeld, R. M. Brooke, R. K. Willis, T. C.

Randell (capt), O. M. Brown, A. D. Oliver, C. H. Hoeft.

Referee: P. L. Marshall (Australia)

Crowd: 52,000

1999
TRI-NATIONS
NEW ZEALAND 28, SOUTH AFRICA 0

At Carisbrook, Dunedin, New Zealand 10 July 1999

For New Zealand: Tries by C. M. Cullen, J. W. Wilson and J. W. Marshall; conversion by T. E. Brown; conversion and 3 penalty goals by A. P. Mehrtens.

NEW ZEALAND: J. W. Wilson, C. M. Cullen, A. Ieremia, D. P. E. Gibson (replaced by B. T. Kelleher), T. J. F. Umaga (replaced by J. T. Lomu), A. P. Mehrtens (replaced by T. E. Brown), J. W. Marshall, T. C. Randell (capt), J. A. Kronfeld, R. M. Brooke (replaced by R. K. Willis), N. M. Maxwell, A. F. Blowers (replaced by D. G. Mika), K. J. Meeuws, A. D. Oliver, C. H. Hoeft.

SOUTH AFRICA: P. C. Montgomery (replaced by A. J. B. van Straaten), P. W. G. Rossouw, J. C. Mulder, P. G. Muller (replaced by R. F. Fleck), B. J. Paulse, G. S. du Toit, D. J. B. von Hoesslin, G. H. Teichmann (capt), C. P. J. Krige (replaced by A. N. Vos), M. G. Andrews (replaced by C. S. Boome), K. Otto, A. G. Venter, J. P. du Randt (replaced by A. H. le Roux), A. E. Drotské, I. J. Visagie (replaced by W. Meyer).

Referee: P. L. Marshall (Australia)

Crowd: 41,500

1999
TRI-NATIONS
NEW ZEALAND 34, SOUTH AFRICA 18

At Minolta Loftus, Pretoria, South Africa 7 August 1999

For New Zealand: Tries by C. M. Cullen (2); 7 penalty goals by A. P. Mehrtens; drop goal by J. W. Wilson.

For South Africa: Tries by A. H. Snyman and J. H. van der Westhuizen; 1 conversion and 2 penalty goals by G. S. du Toit.

NEW ZEALAND: J. W. Wilson, C. M. Cullen, A. Ieremia, D. P. E. Gibson (replaced by J. T. Lomu),

T. J. F. Umaga, A. P. Mehrtens, J. W. Marshall, T. C. Randell (capt), J. A. Kronfeld, R. M. Brooke (replaced by R. K. Willis), N. M. Maxwell, A. F. Blowers (replaced by R. D. Thorne), K. J. Meeuws (replaced by C. W. Dowd), A. D. Oliver (replaced temporarily by M. G. Hammett), G. E. Feek.

SOUTH AFRICA: P. C. Montgomery, P. W. G. Rossouw (replaced by C. S. Terblanche), P. F. Smith, A. H. Snyman (replaced by R. F. Fleck), D. J. Kayser, G. S. du Toit, J. H. van der Westhuizen (capt), J. Erasmus, R. J. Kruger (replaced by A. N. Vos), P. A. van den Berg, C. S. Boome (replaced by M. G. Andrews), A. G. Venter, J. P. du Randt (replaced by A. H. le Roux), A. E. Drotské (replaced by C. le C. Rossouw), I. J. Visagie.

Referee: E. F. Morrison (England)

Crowd: 51,000

1999
WORLD CUP (Playoff for Third/Fourth)
SOUTH AFRICA 22, NEW ZEALAND 18

At Millennium Stadium, Cardiff, Wales 4 November 1999

For South Africa: Try by B. J. Paulse; 1 conversion and 3 penalty goals by H. W. Honiball; and 2 drop goals by P. C. Montgomery.

For New Zealand: 6 penalty goals by A. P. Mehrtens.

SOUTH AFRICA: P. C. Montgomery, B. J. Paulse, R. F. Fleck, P. G. Muller, C. S. Terblanche, H. W. Honiball, J. H. van der Westhuizen (temporarily replaced by W. Swanepoel), A. N. Vos (replaced by R. J. Kruger), A. G. Venter, M. G. Andrews (replaced by P. A. van den Berg), K. Otto, J. Erasmus, I. J. Visagie, A. E. Drotske (replaced by C. le C. Roussouw), J. P. du Randt (replaced by A. H. le Roux).

NEW ZEALAND: J. W. Wilson, T. J. F. Umaga (replaced by P. P. F. Alatini), C. M. Cullen, A. Ieremia, J. T. Lomu, A. P. Mehrtens, J. W. Marshall, T. C. Randell (capt), J. A. Kronfeld, R. K. Willis, N. M. Maxwell, R. D. Thorne (replaced by D. G. Mika), K. J. Meeuws, M. G. Hammett (replaced by A. D. Oliver), C. W. Dowd (replaced by C. H. Hoeft).

Referee: P. L. Marshall (Australia)

Crowd: 60,000

TEST MATCH SCORES

	ALL BLACK	SPRINGBOK
1921	13	5
	5	9
	0	0
1928	0	17
	7	6
	6	11
	13	5
1937	13	7
	6	13
	6	17
1949	11	15
	6	12
	3	9
	8	11
1956	10	6
	3	8
	17	10
	11	5
1960	0	13
	11	3
	11	11
	3	8
1965	6	3
	13	0
	16	19
	20	3
1970	6	17
	9	8
	3	14
	17	20
1976	7	16
	15	9
	10	15
	14	15
1981	14	9
	12	24
	25	22

TEST MATCH SCORES

	ALL BLACK	SPRINGBOK
1992	27	24
1994	22	14
	13	9
	18	18
1995	12	15
1996	15	11
	29	18
	23	19
	33	26
	22	32
1997	35	32
	55	35
1998	3	13
	23	24
1999	28	0
	34	18
	18	22

NEW ZEALAND SOUTH AFRICA TEST MATCHES
WINNING MARGINS

Points	Games
0	3
1	4
2	0
3	8
4	7
5	5
6	5
7	3
8	4
9	1
10+	14

27 games, or half have had a margin of five points or less

SUMMARY OF THE SERIES

	NEW ZEALAND			SOUTH AFRICA		
PLAYED	54			54		
WON	26			25		
DREW	3			3		
Last won at home:	1999			1998		
Last won away:	1999			1999		
TOTAL Points	760			725		
Tries	85			80		
Conversions	43			49		
Penalties	99			84		
Drop Goals	13			19		
Marks	0			1		
TEAM PERFORMANCES						
Highest Score	55	1997		35	1997	
Biggest Winning Margin	28	1999		17	1928	
Most Tries In a Test	7	1997		5	1937 + 1997	
Biggest Winning Sequence	4	games		6	games	
No Points Surrendered	3	games		3	games	
Maiden Try-line	11	games		14	games	
PERFORMANCES IN A GAME						
Most Points	25	C. J. Spencer	1997	22	J. H. de Beer	1997
Most Tries	2	J. L. Sullivan	1937	3	R. H. Mordt	1981
	2	I. S. T. Smith	1965			
	2	J. W. Wilson	1996			
	2	F. E. Bunce	1997			
	2	C. M. Cullen	1997			
	2	C. M. Cullen	1997			
Most Conversions	4	C. J. Spencer	1999	3	H. E. Botha	1992
				3	J. H. de Beer	1997
Most Penalties	7	A. P. Mehrtens	1999	5	A. O. Geffin	1949
				5	H. E. Botha	1981
Most Drop Goals	1	on 13 occasions		2	B. L. Osler	1928
				2	J. T. Stransky	1995
				2	J. H. de Beer	1997
					P. C. Montgomery	1999
CAREER PERFORMANCES						
Most Points	119	A. P. Mehrtens		54	J. T. Stransky	
Most Tries	6	C. M. Cullen		6	J. H. van der Westhuizen	
Most Conversions	7	A. P. Mehrtens		7	H. E. Botha	
	7	C. J. Spencer				
Most Penalties	28	A. P. Mehrtens		14	J. T. Stransky	
Most Drop Goals	2	J. C. Kearney		2	B. L. Osler	
	2	O. D. Bruce		2	J. D. Brewis	
				2	J. T. Stransky	
				2	H. E. Botha	
				2	J. H. de Beer	
				2	P. C. Montgomery	

MOST POINTS IN TEST MATCHES
NEW ZEALAND
119	A. P. Mehrtens
45	C. J. Spencer
38	S. P. Howarth
35	D. B. Clarke
30	C. M. Cullen

SOUTH AFRICA
54	J. T. Stransky
44	H. E. Botha
35	I. D. McCallum
33	G. R. Bosch
32	A. O. Geffin

MOST TRIES IN TEST MATCHES
NEW ZEALAND
6	C. M. Cullen
5	J. W. Wilson
4	J. W. Marshall
3	Z. V. Brooke
3	K. R. Tremain

SOUTH AFRICA
6	J. H. van der Westhuizen
3	G. H. Muller
3	R. H. Mordt

FIFTEEN OR MORE POINTS IN A TEST MATCH
NEW ZEALAND
25	C. J. Spencer at Auckland	1997
21	A. P. Mehrtens at Pretoria	1999
20	C. J. Spencer at Johannesburg	1997
19	A. P. Mehrtens at Cape Town	1996
18	S. P. Howarth at Auckland	1994
18	A. P. Mehrtens at Cardiff	1999
17	S. P. Howarth at Dunedin	1994
15	A. P. Mehrtens at Christchurch	1996

SOUTH AFRICA
22	J. H. de Beer at Johannesburg	1997
20	H. E. Botha at Wellington	1981
15	A. O. Geffin at Cape Town	1949
15	J. T. Stransky at Johannesburg	1995

TWO OR MORE TRIES IN A TEST MATCH
NEW ZEALAND
2	J. L. Sullivan at Christchurch	1937
2	I. S. T. Smith at Auckland	1965
2	J. W. Wilson at Pretoria	1996
2	F. E. Bunce at Johannesburg	1997
2	C. M. Cullen at Auckland	1997
2	C. M. Cullen at Pretoria	1999

SOUTH AFRICA
3	R. H. Mordt at Auckland	1981
2	L. Babrow at Auckland	1937
2	H. J. van Zyl at Johannesburg	1960
2	J. L. Gainsford at Christchurch	1965
2	G. S. Brynard at Christchurch	1965
2	G. H. Muller at Port Elizabeth	1970
2	D. M. Gerber at Johannesburg	1992
2	J. H. van der Westhuizen at Johannesburg	1996

MOST APPEARANCES
TEN OR MORE GAMES FOR NEW ZEALAND
15	R. M. Brooke
14	O. M. Brown
12	Z. V. Brooke
12	F. E. Bunce
12	S. B. T. Fitzpatrick
12	I. D. Jones
13	J. A. Kronfeld
14	J. W. Wilson
12	C. M. Cullen
12	C. W. Dowd
12	J. W. Marshall
10	C. E. Meads
10	A. Ieremia
10	A. P. Mehrtens

TEN OR MORE GAMES FOR SOUTH AFRICA
15	M. G. Andrews
11	J. H. van der Westhuizen
10	G. H. Teichmann
10	J. P. du Randt
10	R. J. Kruger
10	A. G. Venter

MOST VICTORIES
FOR NEW ZEALAND
10	R. M. Brooke
9	O. M. Brown
9	Z. V. Brooke
9	F. E. Bunce
9	S. B. T. Fitzpatrick
8	C. M. Cullen
8	C. W. Dowd
8	I. D. Jones
8	J. A. Kronfeld
8	J. W. Marshall
8	J. W. Wilson

FOR SOUTH AFRICA
5	A. C. Koch
5	J. H. van der Westhuizen
5	M. G. Andrews

HOME TOWN ADVANTAGE ?

Until the advent of neutral referees in 1981, the cry of 'biased refereeing' was the final sound from many tours. How real was this?

RESULTS	PRE NEUTRAL REFEREES	
In New Zealand	All Blacks	won 8 Test matches lost 5
In South Africa	All Blacks	won 5 Test matches lost 14
	POST NEUTRAL REFEREES	
In New Zealand	All Blacks	won 7 Test matches lost 2
In South Africa	All Blacks	won 6 Test matches lost 3

PRE NEUTRAL REFEREES

All Blacks scored 44 tries and kicked 31 penalties
Springboks scored 44 tries and kicked 38 penalties
Okay, so South Africa kicked the more penalties
But over this period
South Africa converted 25 of 44 tries
New Zealand converted 18 of 44 tries
Perhaps South Africa had more reliable goal kickers ?

PER SERIES
IN NEW ZEALAND

	ALL BLACKS					SPRINGBOKS				
YEAR	(21)	(37)	(56)	(65)	TOTAL	(21)	(37)	(56)	(65)	TOTAL
TRIES	3	3	7	13	**26**	2	9	6	4	**21**
PENS	0	4	4	1	**9**	0	1	1	2	**4**

IN SOUTH AFRICA

	ALL BLACKS						SPRINGBOKS					
YEAR	(28)	(49)	(60)	(70)	(76)	TOTAL	(28)	(49)	(60)	(70)	(76)	TOTAL
TRIES	3	4	2	4	5	**18**	4	3	5	7	4	**23**
PENS	3	2	4	7	6	**22**	3	10	4	9	8	**34**

NOTE
- There were just 13 penalty goals kicked in four series in New Zealand
- There were 56 penalty goals kicked in five series in South Africa
- Until neutral referees, South Africa had kicked just four penalty goals in New Zealand
- There were 47 tries scored in 14 Tests on New Zealand's heavy fields
- There were 41 tries scored in 19 Tests on South Africa's hard and fast fields

POST NEUTRAL REFEREES

All Blacks scored 41 tries and kicked 62 penalties
Springboks scored 35 tries and kicked 43 penalties

SUMMARY OF NEW ZEALAND/SOUTH AFRICA TEST MATCHES BY YEAR

YEAR	HOST COUNTRY	TEAM	PLAYED	WON	LOST	DRAWN	TRIES	CONV	PG	DG	MARK	POINTS
1921	New Zealand	NZ	3	1	1	1	4	3				18
		SA	3	1	1	1	2	2		1		14
1928	South Africa	NZ	4	2	2		3		3	2		26
		SA	4	2	2		5	2	3	2	1	39
1937	New Zealand	NZ	3	1	2		3		4	1		25
		SA	3	2	1		8	3	1	1		37
1949	South Africa	NZ	4	0	4		4	2	2	2		28
		SA	4	4	0		3	1	10	2		47
1956	New Zealand	NZ	4	3	1		7	4	4			41
		SA	4	1	3		6	4	1			29
1960	South Africa	NZ	4	1	2	1	2	2	4	1		25
		SA	4	2	1	1	5	4	4			35
1965	New Zealand	NZ	4	3	1		13	5	1	1		55
		SA	4	1	3		4	2	2	1		25
1970	South Africa	NZ	4	1	3		4	1	7			35
		SA	4	3	1		7	4	9	1		59
1976	South Africa	NZ	4	1	3		5	1	6	2		46
		SA	4	3	1		4	3	8	3		55
1981	New Zealand	NZ	3	2	1		5	2	8	1		51
		SA	3	1	2		5	4	7	2		55
1992	South Africa	NZ	1	1			3	3	2			27
		SA	1		1		3	3	1			24
1994	New Zealand	NZ	3	2		1	3	1	12			53
		SA	3		2	1	3	1	8			41
1995	South Africa	NZ	1		1				3	1		12
		SA	1	1					3	2		15
1996	New Zealand	NZ	1	1					5			15
		SA	1		1		1		2			11
	South Africa	NZ	4	3	1		11	8	11	1		107
		SA	4	1	3		9	4	14			95
1997	South Africa	NZ	1	1			4	3	3			35
		SA	1		1		2	2	4	2		32
	New Zealand	NZ	1	1			7	4	4			55
		SA	1		1		5	5				35
1998	New Zealand	NZ	1		1				1			3
		SA	1	1			1	1	2			13
	South Africa	NZ	1		1		2	2	3			23
		SA	1	1			4	2				24
1999	New Zealand	NZ	1	1			3	2	3			28
		SA	1		1							0
	South Africa	NZ	1	1			2		7	1		34
		SA	1		1		2	1	2			18
	England	NZ	1		1				6			18
		SA	1	1			2		2	2		22

INDEX

Grant Harding has worked in the media since 1987, and is currently producer of Sky Television's weekly rugby show, *Reunion*. From 1993–99 he worked for weekly national rugby magazine, *Rugby News* (from 1996 as Managing-Editor). During that time he covered the 1994 Springbok tour to New Zealand, the All Blacks tour to South Africa in 1996, and three other Tests between New Zealand and South Africa. In 1999 he attended the New Zealand-South Africa clash at the Millennium Stadium, while making a documentary on All Black fans for TV3. His rugby resume also includes Television New Zealand series *Mud and Glory* (researcher, 1990–91) and *Tight Five* (associate producer, 1999). This is his second rugby book.

David Williams traces his love for rugby to a blurred memory of the 1960 All Black tour to South Africa. He played hooker for King Edward VII School and Transvaal Schools, in the army, and at university, until concussion ended his playing career. He coached and refereed at his old school and at Clifton College in Bristol, where he took the 1st XV with former England international Peter Knight. He has worked extensively in sports broadcasting on radio and television in South Africa, and worked for 11 years at the Johannesburg *Financial Mail*, specialising in politics, education, the arts and business. He is now Communications Manager at South African Breweries Limited, suppliers of Castle Lager to the Springbok rugby team.

ACKNOWLEDGEMENTS — GRANT HARDING

Thanks to my parents, Gordon and Joyce Harding of Hastings, who encouraged my love of sport from an early age; the late and great Kelvin R. Tremain and the 1966–69 Hawke's Bay Ranfurly Shield holding team who inspired my passion for rugby; Havelock North RFC and Tring RFC (England) where I learned, as a late developer, the joys of playing the game; my brother Paul Harding – the best coach I ever played under and a fellow enthusiast for the game; *Rugby News* (New Zealand) and Jeff Mann for giving me the opportunity to work at the top levels of rugby, and to experience the difficulties the All Blacks face playing in South Africa and the opportunity to see them overcome those difficulties in 1996; everyone who's ever given me a job – long may it continue; the many hard-working writers, photographers and broadcasters whose work has informed me about this great game, and in relation to this book, the rivalry between New Zealand and South Africa; co-author David Williams – not a bad guy for a South African; Geoff Walker and the team at Penguin Books NZ Ltd for their patience and positive attitude; my wife Shelly for helping me juggle four jobs when this book was approaching deadline; and finally, the All Blacks, for being a team who rarely disappoint, and often thrill.

ACKNOWLEDGEMENTS — DAVID WILLIAMS

The following people helped directly in the writing of my part of the book: Grant Harding, who made it possible with his enthusiasm, industry and patience; Geoff Walker, Nicola Strawbridge and Louise Armstrong of Penguin New Zealand; Alison Lowry and Claire Heckrath of Penguin South Africa; Duncan Johnstone, who helped in the conception of the project; the staff of the newspaper reading room at the Johannesburg Public Library; Robin Kempthorne and Mike Lugg of M-Net Supersport; Edward Griffiths of SABC Topsport; the Cape Town publisher Don Nelson; Chris Whales of Sable Publishing; Daan Retief, old friend and Rugby Correspondent of the *Sunday Times*; Rugby men who talked to me, especially Gary Teichmann, Ian McIntosh, Syd Nomis and Wilf Rosenberg; my family, Patricia, Robbie and Morgan, for their enthusiasm and patience. These people helped indirectly through their knowledge, judgment and enthusiasm: Bruce McMurray, Norman McFarland and Nic Myburgh, my school coaches; Ben Brooks and John Hurry, who taught me most about coaching and refereeing; John Robbie; Professor Bob Charlton; and the benevolent spirit of Chris Greyvenstein, which hovered over the project from the beginning.

ILLUSTRATION CREDITS

The authors and publishers wish to thank the following organisations and people who provided photographs and gave permission for their use. The numbers below indicate the page on which each is represented. Abbreviations are as follows: Alexander Turnbull Library – ATL, Auckland Public Library collection – APL, Crown Studios – CS, Fotopacific – FP, New Zealand Herald – NZH, News Media Auckland – NMA Photosport – PS, New Zealand Rugby Museum – RM.

1 PS/Neil Mackenzie
2–3 PS/Joanna Caird
13 & 17 NZH/RM
15 APL
21 RM/Zenith Studio, Dunedin
22 & 30 RM/Blyth Clayton
24 RM/Smith's African Press Photo Service
26 RM
27 APL
29 CS
31 RM/Blyth Clayton
32 & 36 RM/NZH
34 RM
35 (top) RM/ATL – F2325MNZ?
35 & 40 (bottom) RM
37 RM/Green & Hahn, Christchurch
38 Chris Greyvenstein/Don Nelson Publishers
42 & 48 Times Media Ltd, South Africa
44 RM/J.H. Parker collection
46 Joseph Romanos & Rugby Press Ltd
47 Chris Greyvenstein/Don Nelson Publishers
49 RM/CS
51 RM
52 & 55 RM/NZH
54 RM/Photo News, Wellington
57 Evening Post/ATL 1956/Springboks/fr 13
58 NZH
59 RM/NZH
60 NMA
61 CS
63 Don Nelson Publishers
64 NZH
65 & 69 RM
67 RM
68 Joseph Romanos & Rugby Press Ltd
74 & 79 FP/Morrie Hill
76 FP/Morrie Hill
78 FP/Morrie Hill
83 FP/Morrie Hill
83 (inset) NZH
84 Chris Greyvenstein/Don Nelson Publishers
85 & 87 FP/Ray Pigney
89 FP/Ray Pigney
91 FP/Ray Pigney
93 FP/Ray Pigney
94 FP/Ray Pigney

95 FP/Ray Pigney
98 FP/Ross Setford
99 & 104 Ian Mackley, *Evening Post*
101 Peter Bush
102 Don Nelson Publishers
108 Rugby Press Ltd
110 Peter Bush
112 & 114 Mark Hantler/Athol McCredie
117 NMA
119 NZH
123 NMA
125 & 135 Wessel Oosthuizen/South Seas Visuals
127 Rugby Press Ltd
129 FP/Ross Setford
130 Rugby Press Ltd
136 & 159 PS ?
138 FP/Ross Setford
139 FP/Ross Setford
145 FP/Ross Setford
150 PS/Andrew Cornaga
151 PS/Andrew Cornaga
156 PS/Andrew Cornaga
161 FP/Ross Setford
163 PS/Mark Leech
165 FP/Empics
171 & 200 PS
173 PS
174 PS
176 FP/Kenny Rodger
180 PS
182 PS
186 PS/Andrew Cornaga
189 PS/Andrew Cornaga
191 PS/Andrew Cornaga
192 PS/Andrew Cornaga
196 FP/Touchline
197 FP/Ross Setford
199 PS/Andrew Cornaga
203 PS
206 PS/Neil Mackenzie
208 FP/Ross Land
212 PS/Andrew Cornaga
213 PS/Andrew Cornaga
218 PS/Andrew Cornaga
230 PS

The Silver Fern logo is a registered trademark of the NZRFU and has been reproduced with NZRFU's permission.

Every attempt has been made to contact photograph copyright-holders. Please contact the publisher with any queries pertaining to their use.